XHTML

fast&easy ™

web development

Send Us Your Comments

To comment on this book or any other PRIMA TECH title, visit our reader response page on the Web at **www.prima-tech.com/comments**.

How to Order

For information on quantity discounts, contact the publisher: Prima Publishing, P.O. Box 1260BK, Rocklin, CA 95677-1260; (916) 787-7000. On your letterhead, include information concerning the intended use of the books and the number of books you want to purchase.

XHTML

fast&easy™

web development

Brian Proffitt
with
Ann Zupan

A DIVISION OF PRIMA PUBLISHING

A Division of Prima Publishing

Prima Publishing and colophon are registered trademarks of Prima Communications, Inc. PRIMA TECH and Fast & Easy are trademarks of Prima Communications, Inc., Roseville, California 95661.

Publisher: Stacy L. Hiquet
Marketing Manager: Judi Taylor
Associate Marketing Manager: Heather Buzzingham
Managing Editor: Sandy Doell
Acquisitions Editor: Kim Spilker
Project Editor: Lorraine Cooper
Copy Editor: Keith Davenport
Proofreader: Mitzi Foster
Interior Layout: Bill Hartman
Cover Design: Barbara Kordesh
Indexer: Johnna VanHoose Dinse

Microsoft, Windows, and Internet Explorer are trademarks or registered trademarks of Microsoft Corporation. Netscape is a registered trademark of Netscape Communications Corporation.

Important: Prima Publishing cannot provide software support. Please contact the appropriate software manufacturer's technical support line or Web site for assistance.

Prima Publishing and the author have attempted throughout this book to distinguish proprietary trademarks from descriptive terms by following the capitalization style used by the manufacturer.

Information contained in this book has been obtained by Prima Publishing from sources believed to be reliable. However, because of the possibility of human or mechanical error by our sources, Prima Publishing, or others, the Publisher does not guarantee the accuracy, adequacy, or completeness of any information and is not responsible for any errors or omissions or the results obtained from use of such information. Readers should be particularly aware of the fact that the Internet is an ever-changing entity. Some facts may have changed since this book went to press.

ISBN: 0-7615-2785-0
Library of Congress Catalog Card Number: 00-10182
Printed in the United States of America

00 01 02 03 04 DD 10 9 8 7 6 5 4 3 2

*For my aunts, uncles, and cousins, who showed
an only child he would never be alone*

—Brian Proffitt

*To Mark, who listens and supports; to Meredith,
for sticking it out for 30 years of friendship;
and to Mary Ann, for being the most supportive
mother there is, I dedicate this book*

—Ann Zupan

Acknowledgments

So I just get off a stint of writing books about Linux when my acquisitions editor says to me, "Hey, how about a book on HTML?" *Sure*, I think, *how hard can this be?* I had learned SGML for one of my "real" jobs, and HTML was just a subset of that. Plus, I had been putting together some Web pages for a while.

This book proved to be a much bigger challenge than I thought. It's one thing to use HTML—it's quite another to put it on paper. Still, with the encouragement of Kim Spilker, that wacky acquisitions editor , I managed to get some semblance of order to this book. Kim gets big thanks for pushing me a bit harder on this work.

Ann Zupan, my co-author and very good friend, thank you for working with me on this project. Your design insight and working familiarity with the HTML made this book so much easier!

Lorraine Cooper, the project editor, keeps giving me these strange looks every time we talk, like I'm going to have a fit. Thank you for putting up with my silliness!

My wife and daughters, as always, get all of my love and thanks for putting up with my incomprehensible HTML techno-babble these few weeks, just as they were getting used to Linux techno-babble.

—Brian Proffitt

As humbly as I can manage, I'd like to thank Brian Proffitt for believing in my abilities and pulling me in for this book. It was a lot of fun!

Special thanks also go to one of my closest friends, Mark Keehn, who never once doubted me or my abilities. His encouragement has always made it easier for me to shine. And his veterinary advice helps keep my pups from neglect, too! Thanks, Mark!

It may be silly, but I want to thank my little girls, who patiently wait for me to finish working on XHTML design and homework and studying and playing games. Even with a mightily distracted mom, Ursa and Brie manage to amuse themselves well, and then sit quietly for photographs while wearing weird things on their heads. Who could ask for better dogs?

—Ann Zupan

About the Authors

In his disguise as mild-mannered **BRIAN PROFFITT**, one of the authors lives in Indianapolis, Indiana, with his gorgeous wife and two beautiful daughters.

The author of three books on Sun StarOffice and *Install, Configure, and Customize Red Hat Linux 6.1* (Prima, 2000), Brian spends his copious free time (ha!) taking flying lessons, waving his arms in any conversation, and generally just confusing the heck out of his friends.

Brian's co-author has even less fame, if that's possible, but **ANN ZUPAN** hopes to someday be at the center of the universe in Danville, Indiana. She collects dragons and plays computer role-playing games, finds time to take her Irish Wolfhound to conformation shows (and occasionally win!), and may someday earn her master's degree in computer science engineering.

Contents at a Glance

Contents

Introduction

An XHTML book?

What the heck is XHTML?

Here's the really short answer that we give to people at parties: XHTML is a subset of the Extensible Markup Language (XML) that is designed to behave like HTML, only with cooler stuff. XHTML is the latest tool in developing Web pages.

And why should you care? Simple, my friends: the sheer volume of people on the Internet is going to drive many people into the online world, looking to set up their first Web page.

It is reported that between 1988 and 1998, only 10 percent of U.S. households had Internet access. Of those, 15 percent have made their own Web pages. It is predicted that in the 10-year period of 1998 to 2008, Internet access in U.S. households will reach 90 percent penetration. That means that the number of people likely to put together a Web page at home will grow by *nine times* in 10 years. That's not counting corporate Web sites, either.

That's a lot of pages.

XHTML and the need to use it are not going away anytime soon.

This book guides you through the true code that lies just behind those cute little Web pages you surf to every day, whether it be the new XHTML or older HTML language. This may seem odd. After all, there are plenty of really good tools like NetFusion, FrontPage, and HotDog that will let you put together a page just as you would a document in a word processing program. Why mess with the source code?

For two reasons. First, when you understand the source code, you understand the mechanics of your Web page in much greater detail and can implement changes with much greater control.

The second reason is a bit more far-reaching, but just as valid. You see, XHTML is a markup language with its origins in a much more complex parent language, XML, which in turn is derived from an even more complex language called SGML. As time goes on, XHTML and its relative XML are becoming increasingly complex—slowly approaching the level of detail of SGML. When this happens, the whole way we put documents together will change. We will be able to track and utilize documents based on their content so much faster and elevate information sharing to a whole new level. This means that the code behind the pages is becoming even more important because it is directly tied into this new context-oriented way of publishing.

So, even if you use a nice front-end HTML editor, it pays to know the code. If not now, then very soon.

Who Should Read This Book?

This book is great for the first-time Web page author. Even if you have a passing familiarity with HTML, the uniqueness of HTML 4.0 and XHTML 1.0 means you need to learn quite a few new things.

This book is also a good buy for programmers who are learning how to generate Web pages on the fly using all the great programming tools on the market today. Just knowing the code may not be enough. You'll want your pages to look great as well as function well.

This book will also serve as an excellent reference. Whenever you venture into new XHTML territory, you will be able to quickly see how to use the elements and entities that make up this markup language.

Helpful Hints

The book contains other helpful elements, as well, which offer insight and key information related to the topic being discussed.

TIP	**NOTE**	**CAUTION**
Tips tell you about new and faster ways to accomplish a goal.	Notes delve into background information regarding a given topic.	Cautions give you warnings about what not to do when using XHTML.

HTML
XHTML

This sidebar explains the differences between XHTML and HTML in detail.

BROWSER
BROWSER

Many times, one browser handles XHTML differently from another. This sidebar highlights those differences and gives you methods to work around them.

The appendixes provide quality reference information and a complete list of elements and entities for XHTML.

PART I

Stone Knives and Bearskins

1

Tag, You're It

Markup text has come a long way from its humble beginnings. Discover how XHTML can take ordinary text and display it on the Internet using nothing but simple little tags.

In this chapter, you'll learn how to do the following:

- Decipher an XHTML tag
- Identify a tag's attributes
- Apply certain types of tags

In the beginning, there was ASCII text: 256 fun and exciting characters. They were not very exciting to look at; conventional wisdom had decreed they appear in a `monospaced typeface like this one`. There were no other typefaces, no way to mark emphasis, no way to change type size.

In other words, blah.

Then came word processors, and, slowly, the ability to add such features to text became available. On the screen and in printed copies of documents, you could see **bold**, *italic*, and other kinds of text features. What was going on within the program itself was that a markup was being applied every time a new text attribute appeared. If you wanted boldface type, for example, this invisible markup would, in effect, tell the program reading and displaying the file that the next word should be bold.

The problem was none of these word processors used the same markup techniques. There was no *standard*. Microsoft used one method for Word, and WordPerfect (and Corel after it) used another method for WordPerfect. Of course the upshot of all this was that you needed a different application to read each type of document.

Also, this type of markup was geared toward defining the look of anonymous passages of text. For example, this content-oriented markup did not pay attention to the fact that the title of this chapter was the title: it just dictated that this certain collection of letters would be 24-point text in a Helvetica font. This does not seem such a bad thing, until someone decides the chapter titles all need to be 36-point Times New Roman. With content-oriented markup, you would have to go into each chapter and change the size and font of each chapter title.

In 1986, an international standard was published called Standard Generalized Markup Language (SGML). SGML was a context-oriented markup language. Instead of controlling anonymous passages of text, SGML placed controls on the structure of the document using tags. The `<title>` tag always contained a chapter title. You dictated the basic look of text within the `<title>` tag with what's known as a Document Type Definition (DTD). The DTD said that unless altered, text in the title tag would be a certain font, size, and color. Period.

Three years later, a scientist named Tim Berners-Lee who worked at CERN (European Laboratory for Particle Physics) in Switzerland started working on the underpinnings of what would become the World Wide Web. This early system was hypertext-based, meaning that links to documents would be created within other documents, which in theory would eliminate the need to continually hunt for related documentation. It was touchy at first, however, because files being shared still had proprietary markups (such as Macintosh's WriteNow application) encoded in them, which made sharing sometimes difficult. But soon after, Berners-Lee combined his hypertext idea with the SGML concept and essentially created a new DTD for the Hypertext Markup Language (HTML). After some revisions of the HTML standard, a new DTD was introduced to the world for the Extensible Hypertext Markup Language (XHTML), which will be the focus of this book.

Tag Structure

When a DTD defines a tag, it defines the look and placement of the contents of a tag, which is the text contained between the opening and closing tags of an XHTML tag.

> **NOTE**
> This combination of starting tag, text content, and closing tag is often referred to as an *element*.

What does a tag look like? Tags can be identified by the presence of angled brackets. Within the brackets is the code that identifies the tag. (The code is established by the DTD.)

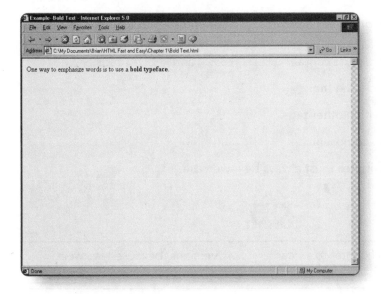

Take a look at the next sentence.

```
One way to emphasize words is
to use a <b>bold typeface</b>.
```

In the text version, you can see two sets of brackets, each of which contains a lowercase "b." In the screen at left, however, both of the <b> tags are nowhere to be seen, and the words "bold typeface" are in a bold font.

This is because the browser used in the figure has read the XHTML file, discerned the tags, referenced the XHTML DTD, and applied what the DTD says to do with text contained in the <b> tag: make it bold.

> **NOTE**
>
> DTDs are contained internally within browsers, so there is no need to include them with every document. It's a good thing, too—they're pretty big documents.

You can see from the start that XHTML is not difficult to use. There are, though, some rules of the road that you will need to remember as you create your own XHTML documents.

Tag Syntax

In every language, certain rules apply. In spoken languages, these rules are called grammar. In computer-based languages, they are referred to as syntax.

XHTML is no exception. Tags have their own syntax that must be followed so that a browser can understand what the document is trying to portray. Browsers are fairly tolerant of errors—they display anything without regard to how awful it looks. But you do not want a garbled mess of a Web page just because you forgot one little rule.

The following five basic principles apply to the creation of XHTML documents:

- All XHTML documents must contain <html>, <body>, and <title> tags.
- All tags must have a closing tag.
- Tags can be nested within other tags.
- Tags must be XHTML-compliant.
- All tags and their attributes *must* always be lowercase.

This last principle runs counter to all earlier HTML versions, because tags were formerly not case-sensitive.

A further discussion of the `<html>`, `<body>`, and `<title>` tags, listed in the first principle, is conducted in Chapter 2, "Document Structure." For now, let's explore the other principles.

A closing tag tells the browser to stop applying the tag's properties to the document. If, for example, you typed the following, "Course" would be italicized.

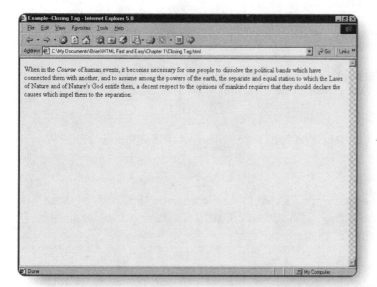

```
When in the <i>Course</i> of
human events, it becomes
necessary for one people to
dissolve the political bands
which have connected them with
another, and to assume among
the powers of the earth, the
separate and equal station to
which the Laws of Nature and
of Nature's God entitle them,
a decent respect to the
opinions of mankind requires
that they should declare the
causes which impel them to the
separation.
```

But look what happens if the closing tag is missing.

```
When in the <i>Course of
human events, it becomes
necessary for one people to
dissolve the political bands
which have connected them
with another, and to assume
among the powers of the
earth, the separate and equal
station to which the Laws of
Nature and of Nature's God
entitle them, a decent
respect to the opinions of
mankind requires that they
should declare the causes
which impel them to the
separation.
```

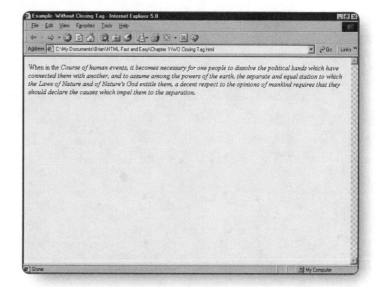

You can see the problem. This would also happen if only the "/" were missing from the second `<i>` tag. It's the slash that delineates the tag as closing.

Not all tags need closing tags within HTML documents. Most browsers, for example, start a new paragraph when they encounter a new `<p>` (paragraph) tag, even if there is no closing `</p>` tag. In XHTML, however, you must always use closing tags.

This even applies to tags that historically have never used closing tags, such as the `<hr>` (horizontal rule) tag, which could appear in HTML documents just as:

`<hr>`

Because of the absolute need for closing tags in XHTML, the proper method to create this element is:

`<hr></hr>`

Fortunately, XHTML does allow for a shortcut. Self-contained tags such as these can be closed with a shorthand method that consists of inserting a forward slash within a single appearance of the tag, like this:

`<hr/>`

This type of notation satisfies the requirement for the closing tag. Some HTML browsers may not like this notation, but you can get around the issue by inserting a space before the slash mark:

`<hr />`

Tags can also be nested. This is not to say they will settle down and have kids. In this case, nesting refers to the act of containing one set of tags within another.

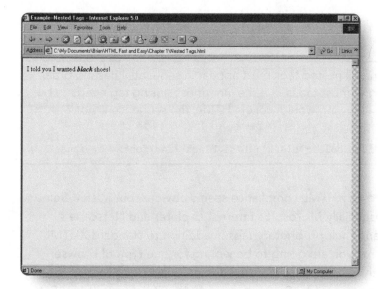

```
I told you I wanted <font
color="black"><b><i>black</i>
</b></font> shoes!
```

You can nest quite a large set of tags in an XHTML document. Just be cautious with them, because it can be easy to forget to add a tag in a large nesting situation.

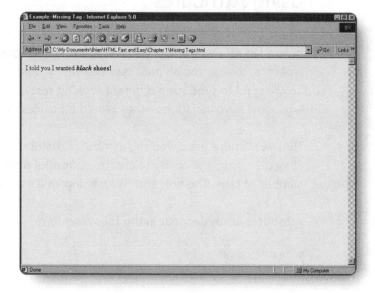

```
I told you I wanted <font
color="black"><b><i>black</i>
</font> shoes!
```

To be XHTML-compliant, all nested tags must appear in sequential nesting order. This means that if the innermost tag is `<i>`, the innermost closing tag needs to be `</i>`. Thus, though the following would work in HTML, the sequence is *not* XHTML-compliant:

```
I told you I wanted <font color="black"><b><i>black</i></font></b> shoes!
```

The final principle regarding XHTML compliance seems obvious, but it isn't. Some commercial browsers (especially Microsoft's Internet Explorer and Netscape's Navigator) can understand their proprietary tags in addition to standard XHTML tags. Unless you know that you are going to be writing for one type of browser client only, however, such as within a corporate intranet, avoid using these proprietary tags as much as possible. See Appendix A, "XHTML Element and Entity List," for more information on the official XHTML tags.

Using Attributes

When a tag is placed within a document, it contains a default set of attributes defined in XHTML's DTD. The `<b>` tag presents a bold version of the current typeface, the `<i>` tag an italic representation, and so on. Some tags, however, can be changed to produce a different-looking result than the original tag. In fact, some tags *must* have variations—they would be useless without them.

These variations are called tag attributes. Attributes are the real power in XHTML. They give users the ability to create wonderful new effects with a fairly limited number of tags. The only trick is knowing which attributes work with which tag.

Attributes always appear in the following form:

```
object="value"
```

An attribute's *object* is the aspect of the tag that gets modified. For instance, one tag that usually needs an attribute is the <font> tag. This tag, which is examined in more detail in Chapter 5, "Touching Up Text," controls many aspects of how text appears in an XHTML document. It can handle text size, typeface, and color—all at once if need be. These are the <font> tag's objects.

The *value* of an attribute is the specific characteristic assigned to the object. This can be a numeric value or an alphabetic word or word combination. When using the <font> tag, for instance, one legal use of attributes would be as follows:

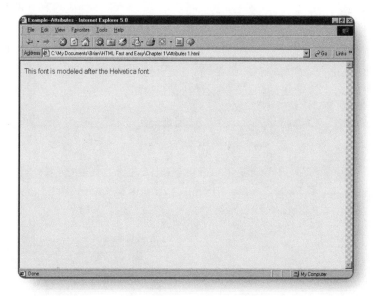

```
<font face = "arial">This
font is modeled after the
Helvetica font.</font>
```

Recall that all attributes must be lowercase to be XHTML-compliant.

This element tells the browser client to override any default typeface settings it might have and display this passage of text with the Arial typeface.

Tags can also have more than one attribute assigned to them:

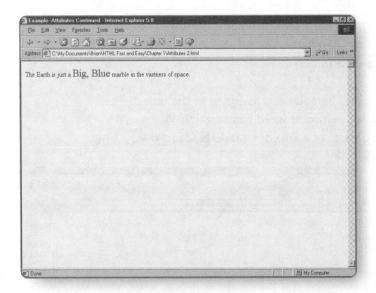

The Earth is just a <font size
= +2 color="blue">Big, Blue
</font> marble in the vastness
of space.

And, because you learned in the last section that you can nest tags, you can combine the attributes of one tag with those of another to provide some interesting results.

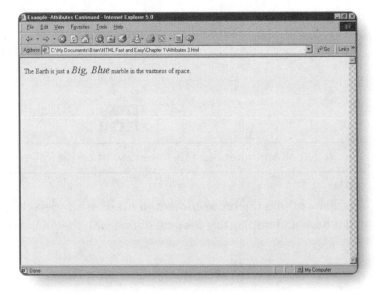

The Earth is just a <font
size = +2 color="blue">
Big, Blue</font>
marble in the vastness of
space.

All attribute values must be contained within quote marks. This means that you cannot minimize attributes within an XHTML document.

Minimizing attributes was a perfectly legal way of taking shortcuts in HTML 4.0 documents. In the `<hr>` tag, for example, one of the attributes is `noshade`. `noshade` is one of those attribute objects that has no value—it's a value unto itself. In HTML 4.0, you could minimize the appearance of this attribute by just typing the following:

```
<hr noshade>
```

In XHTML, however, the compliant method of generating this tag element is the following:

```
<hr noshade = "noshade" />
```

Even though `noshade` is its own value, it must still be written in this manner in XHTML documents.

One thing to remember about attributes: they only affect the element they are in. If you use an attributed tag in one part of your document, it will have only its default properties the next time it appears. This is known as *local attribution*. You can apply global attributes to some tags for your entire document, which is covered in Chapter 2, "Document Structure."

Using Some Tag Types

Now that you know the basic anatomy of an XHTML tag, let's take a look at some of the types of tags that you will use.

XHTML documents are typically divided into two sections: head and body. The head section contains elements that help identify the document and how it is perceived and displayed by the browser. The body section contains the elements that make up the primary content of the document.

In XHTML, another section *must* appear before the head section: the DOCTYPE section, which identifies exactly what type of document is about to be read by the browser. This element *should* appear in HTML documents as well, but it is *imperative* for XHTML pages because it alerts the browser to reference the correct DTD. DOCTYPE is discussed further in Chapter 2.

Head Tags

Marking off a particular section within an XHTML document is pretty simple: it's done with tags. In fact, you could easily say that the head section is synonymous with the `<head>` element.

The `<head>` element contains several tags that give information about the document. Though a majority of these elements do not appear to the browser user, they are nonetheless important for document identification and organization. These elements include the following:

- `<title>`

- `<base>`

- `<link>`

- `<meta>`

Chapter 2 delves more fully into each of these elements, but here is an example to start the ball rolling:

```
<head>
<title> XHTML Fast & Easy Web Development </title>
      <base href    = "http://www.prima-tech.com/" />
      <meta name    = "Keywords"
            content = "HTML, XMTML, tutorial" />
      <meta name    = "Copyright"
            content = "2000 Prima Tech Publishing, Inc." />
</head>
```

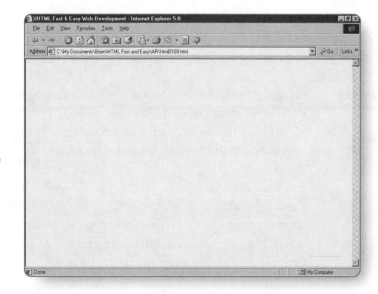

You can see that for all of the code, very little of this information appears in the browser. The content of the `<title>` element appears in the border of the browser application, but that's about it.

Still, some useful stuff is going on here. The first `<meta>` element tells any Internet search engines basically what this document is about, and the second `<meta>` element imprints the copyright information within the document.

Remember that the main goal of the `<head>` element is to contain information about the document, and everything else will appear in the `<body>` element.

Body Tags

Body tags make up the bulk of XHTML elements, and we will be spending much of the book looking at them. You can break elements that appear in the `<body>` element into four main categories:

- Block
- Inline
- Links
- Images

Block-level elements handle blocks of text within a document. Paragraphs certainly fall into this category, as do lists and headings. The main characteristic of a block-level element is that it starts a new line of text.

On the other hand, the definition of inline elements is those elements that affect text within blocks of text. You have already seen some of these elements, such as `<b>` and `<i>`. These elements, and others like them, never start a new line of text; they only alter what is within a text block.

Link elements, such as `<a>` and `<link>`, are what make the World Wide Web work. These specialized inline elements are the main connection points between documents on the Web. Even though they are inline elements, their unique nature means they are handled differently from other elements, as you will learn in Chapter 7, "Putting the Hyper in Hypertext."

As soon as the first graphical browser was created, a tag was created to handle the display of the new proliferation of images on the Internet. The `<img>` element is neither a block nor an inline element, though it can behave as both if need be. When graphics are used, `<img>` is the element to use, which is why it has its own chapter in this book: Chapter 8, "Images on the Web."

Conclusion

We have just scratched the surface of the capabilities of the XHTML language set, but by now you should have a good idea of what makes up an XHTML element, as well as how an attribute is used. Now when we toss these terms around in the rest of the book, you'll know what the heck we're talking about.

In Chapter 2, we'll start delving into the specific elements of the `<head>` element. You'll learn all about the four main head section elements, as well as how to use the `<!DOCTYPE>` element to create an XHTML-compatible document.

2

Document Structure

A lot of information is contained within an XHTML document. Its very structure is designed to help provide information to browsers in the most efficient manner possible.

In this chapter, you'll learn how to do the following:

- Create your document's type
- Incorporate XML capabilities in your XHTML document
- Set text and background attributes globally
- Make your page easy for search engines to find
- Give your page a title

Think back to your English classes in high school. If this brings back any unpleasant memories, we're sorry. But keep with it for a moment. Think past all those book reports and poetry contests and focus on how to write a report.

Got the memory? Good, you're about to use those skills again. (Just think how pleasant it will be now that you don't have all that teen angst.)

When documents are created (at least in the modern English language), they typically follow this order: introduction, body, and conclusion. This structure is probably familiar to you; it shows up in one form or another in newspaper articles, novels, and even television news scripts.

This kind of structure is called *content structure*. Most well-written Web documents also follow this model. When people discuss the *structure* of an XHTML document, they may actually be referring to the document *content*.

The document structure of this chapter, for example, consists of paragraphs, lists, headings, and graphics. Any of these structural items can appear in any order within the chapter. On their structural level, they are like bricks in a wall—who cares where a certain brick sits in a wall? On the content level, however, of course the order of these elements makes a difference. You wouldn't want to see the conclusion paragraphs at the start of this chapter, right?

In XHTML documents, the document structure is more closely connected with the content. Certain elements must appear in a certain order. These elements are those that are used in the head section of an XHTML document. Although not visually stimulating, the head-section elements are the most important elements within an HTML, XHTML, or any other SGML-based document.

The first, and most important, purpose of the head section is to identify the type of document you are presenting. Browsers care about this kind of thing, you see.

The head section has other useful facets, and we'll cover them all.

Putting the Document Together

There are things in this world we hardly ever see but would have a hard time living without. Air is a big one. The people who magically fill the vending machines—there's another. So much infrastructure supports you in your daily life, it's mind-boggling. You can't track it all.

So it is when you use the Internet. Nearly every page you visit has invisible HTML and XHTML code that helps browsers and other Internet tools find and display that page. And with the millions and millions of Web sites, those Internet tools need all the help they can get.

Establishing the Document Type

Whenever a browser reads an XHTML page, the browser requires additional information to assist it in figuring out what all the tags mean. This additional information is provided in a document called a Document Type Definition (DTD).

What the DTD does is simple: it quickly and plainly defines how a browser displays the contents of an XHTML document. This is usually done internally: most top-of-the-line browsers have the necessary DTDs built into their specifications. If a client is using a less robust or older browser, however, and the browser tries to display an HTML 4.01 or XHTML 1.0 document, the browser has difficulty displaying some or all of the page. This is why it's a good idea to add a solid reference to the DTD (including where to find the DTD on the Internet) within your documents. In this manner, older browsers can quickly find the DTD and (ideally) apply it to the document being loaded.

When an HTML document is created, the DTD it needs to reference is contained within the `<!DOCTYPE>` element. In XHTML 1.0, three specific DTDs can be referenced:

- Strict
- Loose (Transitional)
- Frameset

A strict XHTML document is one that conforms exactly to the XHTML 1.0 standard. Only elements within the standard are contained within the document, such as the following:

```
<!DOCTYPE html PUBLIC "-//W3C//DTD XHTML 1.0 Strict//EN"
"http://www.w3.org/TR/xhtml1/DTD/strict.dtd">
<html>
  <head>
    <title>Strict XHTML Document</title>
  </head>
  <body>
    <h1>In the Beginning...</h1>
    <p>This is the first paragraph.</p>
    <p>It is cleverly followed by another paragraph.</p>
  </body>
</html>
```

This Strict definition is typically used for documents that make use of Cascading Style Sheets (CSS), which are covered in Chapter 15, "Designing with Style (Sheets)." These documents typically conform very well to the Strict XHTML definition, if only because CSS methods were built for Strict XHTML documents.

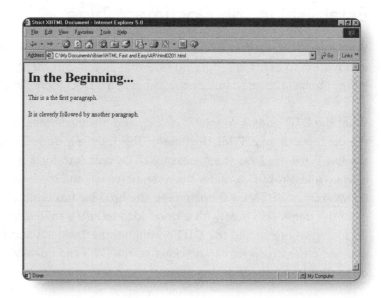

Note that the appearance of the `<!DOCTYPE>` element in the previous example does not seem to follow some of the previously stated XHTML rules. Take a look at the following line:

```
<!DOCTYPE html PUBLIC "-//W3C//DTD XHTML 1.0 Strict//EN"
"http://www.w3.org/TR/xhtml1/DTD/strict.dtd">
```

First, the start of this element is unique in that there's an exclamation point immediately following the first bracket. This serves as a universal symbol to all SGML-type document readers (including Web browsers) that this is the tag that is about to tell the reader software how to display the remainder of the document.

For this reason and this reason alone, you must have the `<!DOCTYPE>` element as the first in a document, even before the `<html>` element.

The `PUBLIC` attribute informs the browser that the document's DTD is a public standard, as opposed to a private set of instructions.

The information in the quotation marks is called the formal public identifier (FPI). In this example, the FPI tells the browser that the DTD is the W3C's DTD for XHTML 1.0 in the English language. After the FPI is the actual Web address of the DTD document.

You might have noticed that the `<!DOCTYPE>` element does not follow the rules of capitalization established for XHTML elements. This exception is allowed because until the element does its job, the browser does not know whether the document is an HTML, XHTML, or some other kind of document. Once the XHTML document type is declared, however, all XHTML rules apply.

Another XHTML DTD is the Loose DTD, also known as the Transitional DTD. This DTD is the most commonly defined DTD for HTML on the Web today. It is very likely this will be the most-used DTD for XHTML, for a couple of reasons, as illustrated in the next example.

```
<!DOCTYPE html PUBLIC "-//W3C//DTD XHTML 1.0 Transitional//EN"
"http://www.w3.org/TR/xhtml1/DTD/transitional.dtd">
<html>
  <head>
    <title>Transitonal XHTML Document</title>
  </head>
  <body>
    <marquee>The Marquee element is a browser-specific tag.</marquee>
    <p>Some browsers have created their own tags, despite what the standards
are. The Marquee tag above is one such element. A Strict DTD document would not
be able to display this element.</p>
     <p>Also, since quite a few browsers do not support cascading style sheets
yet, it is sometimes necessary to use presentational tags that are part of the
older HTML standards, such as the <font size=+1 color="maroon">Font</font>
tag.</p>
  </body>
</html>
```

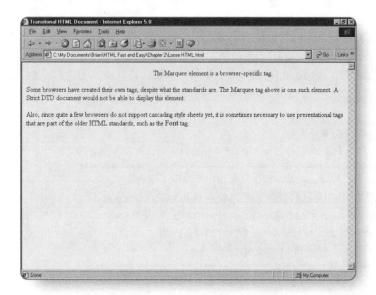

The content of the previous example gives you a good idea of why using the Loose DTD is necessary. Browser-specific elements, which are an unnecessary addition to the Internet, can't be displayed in a Strict DTD document. Nor can older elements that have been deprecated or phased out of HTML 4.0. The Transitional DTD is a nice compromise to both problems.

The final DTD in XHTML is the Frameset DTD. This definition is used whenever you have a document with frames in it. Although you examine frames in more detail in Chapter 11,"You've Been Framed," here is an example of the correct DTD to use:

```
<!DOCTYPE html PUBLIC "-
//W3C//DTD XHTML 1.0
Frameset//EN"
"http://www.w3.org/TR/xhtml1/
DTD/frameset.dtd">
<html>
  <head>
    <title>Frameset XHTML
Document</title>
  </head>
<frameset framespacing="0"
border="5" cols="165,*">
    <frame name="menu"
src="nav.html">
    <frame name="content"
src="main.html">
</frameset>
</html>
```

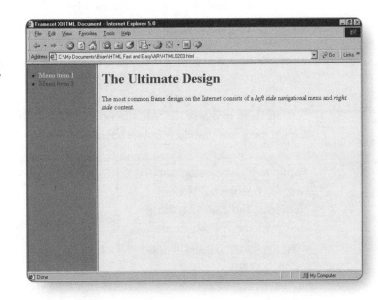

If you want to know whether your document follows its declared DTD standard, you can have an application automatically check your document. This type of application is called a *validator*.

The best validator to use, of course, is W3C's validator, which can be found at **http://validator.w3.org/**. All you have to do is type the address of your Web page, and the validator informs you of your document's compliance, as seen in the accompanying figure.

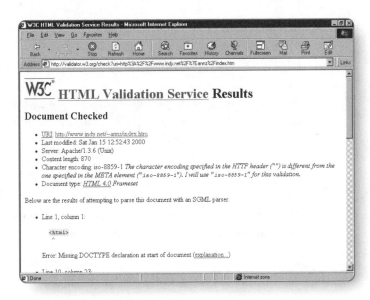

The Biggest Container of Them All

After the document type is declared, you must create the container element to house your document's content. This container element is known as the `<html>` element, and, although it does not look like much, it is one of the four elements that must be in every XHTML document. The `<!DOCTYPE>` element was the first, and it must be immediately followed by the `<html>` element.

Within the `<html>` element are two more large container elements, the `<head>` and the `<body>` elements, which are examined in more detail later in this section.

> ### CAUTION
> Because the `<html>` element is the container of the entire XHTML document, it is vital that the `</html>` tag be the very last tag.

But first, examine one special attribute that the `<html>` element can have, especially in an XHTML document: the XML namespace.

Declaring an XML Namespace

XHTML 1.0 has been described as a reworking of HTML 4.0 within the Extensible Markup Language (XML). In other words, XHTML is not really a new version of HTML. It's really a way of utilizing the HTML elements within XML.

This might need more explanation, because all this alphabet soup can get confusing. XML is another subset of SGML, which we talked about in Chapter 1. It is completely unrelated to HTML in that it was never derived from HTML but rather HTML's parent language, SGML.

XML was created to be a fully content-oriented markup language. Elements created in XML DTDs fully match all of a document's structure, not just the loose head and body structure of HTML documents.

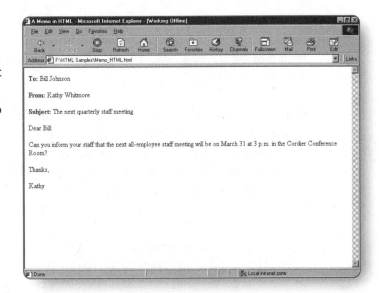

For those of you who just said "Huh?" when you read that last passage, here's an example. Say you want to create a memo online. Now, in the business world today, memos follow a specific form: a line for To, another for From, another for Subject, and so on. In HTML, such a document might look like this:

```
<html>
  <head>
    <title>A Memo in HTML</title>
  </head>
  <body>
    <p><b>To:</b> Bill Johnson</p>
    <p><b>From:</b> Kathy Whitmore</p>
    <p><b>Subject:</b> The next quarterly staff meeting</p>
    <p>Dear Bill:</p>
    <p>Can you inform your staff that the next all-employee staff meeting will
be on March 31 at 3 p.m. in the Cordier Conference Room?</p>
    <p>Thanks,</p>
    <p>Kathy</p>
  </body>
</html>
```

In an XML document that referenced the appropriate DTD, you could achieve nearly the exact same thing with this set of code.

```
    <TO>Bill Johnson</TO>
    <FROM>Kathy Whitmore</FROM>
    <SUBJECT>The next quarterly staff meeting</SUBJECT>
    <SALUTATION>Dear Bill:</SALUTATION>
    <TEXT>Can you inform your staff that the next all-employee staff meeting
will be on March 31 at 3 p.m. in the Cordier Conference Room?</TEXT>
    <CLOSING>Thanks,</CLOSING>
    <SIGNATURE>Kathy</SIGNATURE>
```

This might not seem such a huge advantage, until you realize that each of these elements can be styled independently of one other. If you want to change the format of the memo's header lines, you simply change the DTD of the document to reflect your changes.

You can also search for these elements independently, which is an excellent way of conducting searches. If you are searching a collection of HTML documents, looking for memos sent to Bill Johnson from Kathy Whitmore, your search parameter is rather lengthy. If you are searching a collection of XML documents formatted like the previous example, you only have to search for all instances of Bill appearing in the <TO> element and Kathy in the <FROM> element.

Displaying XML documents, particularly those with data content, becomes a lot more simple, too. If you want to display the contents of your database, such as in an online ordering tool, using XML elements can avoid a lot of code geared for displaying that data.

So, why isn't everyone using XML? The simple truth is, you don't always need this kind of control over the content of your Web pages. Yet this will likely change as more documents appear online. But instead of jumping way over to XML and having to learn a whole new markup language, a proposal for XHTML was made.

Essentially a subset of XML, XHTML is a hybrid that combines the best features of HTML with XML's capability to create custom elements. This extensibility gives Web designers new tools with which to play.

XHTML also has the capability to be modularized. More and more these days, Web sites are accessed by tools other than Web browsers. Handheld personal digital assistants (PDAs), cellular phones, and TV set-top devices are just a few items that you can use to surf the Web right now. If you have ever tried to view a Web page on a cell phone, however, you know how cumbersome it can be. To get around the limitations of these new surfing devices, XHTML can be modularized. Thus, if a super-powerful Web browser hits a Web page, the full content is displayed. If a PalmPilot requests the page, the device automatically filters out what it can't display and displays the rest of the page accordingly.

To make use of these extensible and portable elements, you need to declare an XML namespace. This declaration tells the browser reading your document that to find the display parameters for the extensible tags in the XHTML document, it needs to reference an XML schema at another location on the Internet for the extensible elements. An XML schema is just another DTD, only this time for whatever elements you want to use, not just those within HTML. In the memo example, you want to reference a schema that contains those special memo elements you used.

NOTE

Ultimately, it is hoped that XML schemas will completely replace the DTDs of SGML.

In a basic XHTML document, the namespace declaration appears in the `<html>` element as the attribute `xmlns` (for XML namespace).

```
<!DOCTYPE html PUBLIC "-//W3C//DTD XHTML 1.0 Transitional//EN"
"http://www.w3.org/TR/xhtml1/DTD/transitional.dtd">
<html xmlns:memo="http://www.bkp.org/schema">
```

This example assigns the namespace to a schema located on another Web site and associates it with a local part: memo. Now, every time an element contains memo, the document reader applies the element's attributes based on what the reader finds in the schema. With this knowledge, you can rework the memo example like this:

```
<!DOCTYPE html PUBLIC "-//W3C//DTD XHTML 1.0 Transitional//EN"
"http://www.w3.org/TR/xhtml1/DTD/transitional.dtd">
<html xmlns:memo="http://www.bkp.org/schema">
  <head>
    <title>An XHTML Memo</title>
  </head>
  <body>
    <memo:to>Bill Johnson</memo:to>
    <memo:from>Kathy Whitmore</memo:from>
    <memo:subject>The next quarterly staff meeting</memo:subject>
    <memo:salutation>Dear Bill:</memo:salutation>
    <p>Can you inform your staff that the next all-employee staff meeting will
be on March 31 at 3 p.m. in the Cordier Conference Room?</p>
    <memo:closing>Thanks,</memo:closing>
    <memo:signature>Kathy</memo:signature>
</html>
```

Because this does not reference a true schema, however, this can't be displayed effectively. But you can see that all the normal HTML tags remain as is, whereas the new extended elements all contain memo.

This is really just the tip of the iceberg, because there is a lot more functionality within namespaces. You are encouraged to read the W3C's XML namespace document at **http://www.w3.org/TR/REC-xml-names/** for more information.

Getting Your Head Together

After the `<html>` element is started, the next element that should appear in the document is the `<head>` element. Like the `<html>` element, the `<head>` element is a required element within any XHTML document.

> **CAUTION**
>
> The problem with this attribute is that little exists in the way of standards for metadata profiles, so it is not recommended you do anything with the `profile` attribute at this time.

The `<head>` element is a fairly straightforward container element that has only one optional attribute of its own. The `profile` attribute is used within the `<head>` element when you want to reference a profile of information for your document.

What the `<head>` element contains, however, are the most powerful elements to be found in an XHTML document.

Six active elements can appear within the `<head>` element:

- `<base>`
- `<link>`
- `<meta>`
- `<script>`
- `<style>`
- `<title>`

Two of these elements, `<link>` and `<style>`, are associated with the creation and use of style sheets, so we postpone discussion of them until Chapter 15. Likewise, the `<script>` element is examined further in Chapter 14, "Adding Applets to Your Web Site."

This leaves us with three elements to discuss here: `<base>`, `<meta>`, and, most important, `<title>`.

Giving Your Page a Title

Every document should have a title. Even if it's "grocery list," you have automatically given every document around you some kind of name. It's part of human nature. You see something new, and you slap a label on it.

So it is with Web documents. Since the earliest browsers were used, XHTML has provided a way to display the title of a document in the title bar of the browser. This technique has the advantage of getting the title out of the document, so that no matter how far down you scroll within the document, the title of the Web page is always visible.

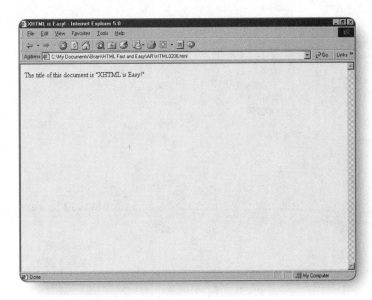

This technique is accomplished using the `<title>` element. The next example shows how easy it is to use.

```
<html>
  <head>
    <title>XHTML is Easy!</title>
  </head>
  <body>
    <p>The title of this document is "XHTML is Easy!"</p>
  </body>
</html>
```

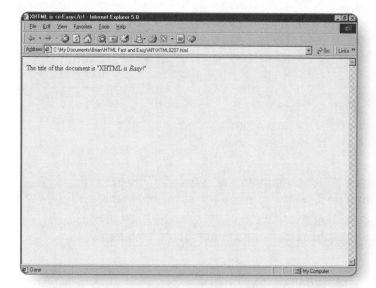

Unfortunately, a straightforward text display is all you can do with the `<title>` element. Adding additional presentational fonts does not work, because the rules for displaying text in a browser's title bar are very restricted. Take a look at this example to see what we mean:

```
<html>
  <head>
    <title>XHTML is <i>Easy</i>!</title>
  </head>
  <body>
    <p>The title of this document is "XHTML is <i>Easy</i>!"</p>
  </body>
</html>
```

You can see that using nested tags in the `<title>` element simply does not work. Still, using a title is a nice and simple way to keep your pages organized for visitors.

In an XHTML document, the `<title>` element must be the first element that appears within the `<head>` element.

`meta` Tags: For Your Eyes Only

The `<meta>` element is an optional XHTML element, but one you should strongly consider using. In a nutshell, the `<meta>` element defines information about a document that is not always included in the visible document content. This information is usually referred to as *metadata*.

Metadata enables users to describe and read about key information regarding the document's creation and status. This is useful when you have a Web page that is almost entirely graphical or is made up of frames. Using metadata enables you to still index and organize the content of your Web pages.

Metadata is also useful for Internet search engines. Most Internet search engines, such as Lycos and Excite, systematically scan all the Web pages they can find and index them into categories. These indexed sites can then be located far more easily when a search-engine user looks for that page's particular category. This is reason enough to use the <meta> element. With millions of Web pages out there, you definitely want the search engines to find your site.

The <meta> element has two primary attributes: name and content. You use these attributes in conjunction with one another, listing the name attribute first. For instance, if you wanted to identify the formatter of a Web page, you could use the following:

```
<meta name = "Formatter"  content = "Brian Proffitt">
```

You can use as many <meta> elements as you want, one for each value of the name attribute. These values are as follows:

- Author
- Classification
- Copyright
- Description
- Formatter
- Generator
- Keywords
- Rating
- Robots

These values are pretty self-explanatory. The Rating value is a content rating used to assist Web filters to screen out potentially offensive content. Generator indicates the type of HTML tool used to create the page.

Keywords and Description are the two name values that should be used to assist Internet search engines find and index your pages. The following example contains <meta> tags excerpted from NASA's Voyager Project home page at **http://vraptor.jpl.nasa.gov/voyager/voyager.html**.

```
<head>
<title>Voyager Project Home Page</title>
<meta name="description" content="The Official Voyager Project Home Page
straight from the Jet Propulsion Laboratory. Explore images of Jupiter,
Saturn, Uranus, and Neptune taken by Voyager 1 & 2. Find out Voyager's Message
to the Universe.  Learn about the science instruments on-board. Full of links
to other NASA and Space Exploration sites.">
<meta name="keywords" content="voyager, space, spacecraft, jupiter, saturn,
uranus, neptune, universe, outer space, instruments, JPL, NASA, project,
plasma, energy, particles, magnetomenter, radioisotope thermoelectric
genetator, planetary radio astronomy, plasma wave antenna, low energy charged
particle, photopolarimeter, infrared spectrometer ultraviolet spectrometer,
cosmic ray subsystem, plasma investigation, mag, pra, pwa, lecp, uva, crs,
pls">
</head>
```

You might expect this page would be easy to find if you typed "voyager" or "NASA voyager" into your favorite search engine, and you'd be right. But NASA's Web designers want this page to come up in other searches, too. In the accompanying image, the Voyager Web site is found even when you type something as seemingly unrelated as "magnetomenter" into Yahoo.com. Thus, the Keywords value has done its job.

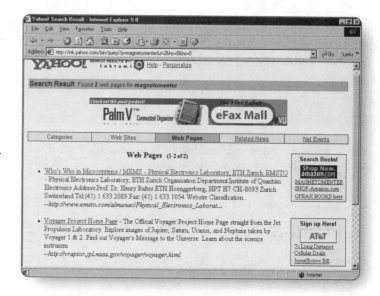

One other attribute belongs to the `<meta>` element: `http-equiv`. This attribute can be used in place of the `name` attribute and is used to deliver messages to any software reading your Web page.

You can use the `http-equiv` attribute to inform a search engine's automated Web surfer (usually referred to as a robot or spider) not to index certain things on your pages. This is sometimes necessary when you have slow Web site connection and you don't need to be further slowed by all of these automated search agents downloading your Web pages.

In the following example, robots and spiders may look at this page and index it, but they may not follow the links away from this page and index those pages.

```
<meta name="Robots" content="index,nofollow">
```

Table 2-1 reveals the four content values supported by many robots today.

Table 2-1 Robot `meta` Values

Value	Description
NOFOLLOW	No links from the page may be followed or indexed.
NOIMAGECLICK	Only allows indexed images to be reached from the Web page. Robots cannot directly access the image.
NOIMAGEINDEX	Only the page's text may be indexed.
NOINDEX	Nothing on the page may be indexed.

If you have ever come to a link that's been moved to another page, you might have been automatically redirected to that new page without lifting a finger. This is also something the `http-equiv` attribute can do for you. In the following code, the client browser is redirected to a new URL after a delay:

```
<META HTTP-EQUIV = "Refresh" Content = "60; URL =
http://www.bkp.com/index.html">
```

BROWSER
BROWSER

If you use this redirect <meta> element, be sure to leave an old-fashioned link on the old Web page. At this time, only Internet Explorer and Netscape Navigator support this functionality.

BROWSER
BROWSER

In Internet Explorer, you can achieve an interesting special effect by using the Page-Enter and Page-Exit values for `http-equiv`. Simply build these two <meta> elements into your Web page.

```
<meta http-equiv="Page-Exit" content="RevealTrans(Duration=5,Transition=12)">
<meta http-equiv="Page-Enter" content="RevealTrans(Duration=4,Transition=2)">
```

The type of transition effect is controlled by the numeric value of the `Transition` and the length of the change by `Duration`. Play around and see what you like!

Establishing Home Base

The `<base>` element is not often used. In these fast-paced times, it should be. The `<base>` element establishes the Internet location (also known as the URL) of the page you have just built.

This URL declaration enables you to create links in a much faster manner, as you see in Chapter 7, "Putting the Hyper in Hypertext." Without getting too far ahead of ourselves, if the document and the document's Web server know where the document is on the Internet, it becomes an easy matter for the server to locate any linked files *in relation to* the first document.

Not only does this decrease surfing time, it also gives you the advantage of quickly being able to move your entire Web site to another Web server. Once the files are moved, simply change the `<base>` element in your site's home page.

The syntax of the `<base>` element is pretty simple.

```
<head>
  <title>Using the Base Tag</Title>
  <base href="http://ww.bkp.com/Index.html">
</head>
```

Conclusion

Now that you have examined the head of an XHTML document, it's time for a quick look at the body, which is where most of the actual page content appears. Until now, the document's information was mostly internally-oriented.

In Chapter 3, "Building a Better Body," you learn that the `<body>` element is not just a big container tag—it contains several powerful attributes of its own that can give your documents a unique look in no time flat.

3

Building a Better Body

In the scheme of XHTML document creation, the <body> element is often not given enough credit. Many times, it is used simply as a big container element, dutifully holding all the block- and text-level elements of the document.

This is certainly an acceptable use for the element—after all, that's why it was originally made. You can do a lot more with the <body> element, however. You knew there'd have to be; why else would we devote a whole chapter to one element?

In this chapter, you'll learn how to do the following:

- Change the color of your page's background
- Add a background picture or texture to your document
- Set text and link colors globally
- Use the load attributes to start scripts

You might be surprised to learn that the `<body>` element can control colors within your XHTML document. Although this might not be an obvious association, the `<body>` element was once the *only* way to introduce color into a Web document.

Today, cascading style sheets handle most of the color options for a document more efficiently. Style sheets control tone and hue down to the element level, whereas the `<body>` element only manages color at the document level.

Still, for those times when using a CSS is not feasible, the color attributes of the `<body>` element are a simple way of styling your XHTML document.

A Page Full of Color

You have to admire the creators of XHTML for building color capabilities into Web documents. Reading black on white can get a little monotonous (excluding this book, of course). It is especially hard on your eyes when you are reading it on a monitor screen. The eye has enough trouble focusing on virtual letters on a glass screen as it is.

Beyond the physical sense, it's just a psychological advantage to display color on your Web site. Colors trigger emotional responses in almost every culture. Red can depict anger or warmth. Green can illustrate life and vibrancy, whereas blue comes across to many as a cool, soothing color. Color, therefore, can convey a lot of meaning on your Web site when used in moderation.

Before we discuss styles, let's get into the mechanics of bringing color to your page's background. The `<body>` element has two background-related attributes: `bgcolor` and `background`.

The first attribute, `bgcolor`, can have either a color name or a six-digit hexadecimal number representing the RGB value of the color.

RGB stands for Red, Green, and Blue. In the color model used by XHTML, all colors are just a mixture of one of these three colors. The color values of each component color can range from 0 to 255. The color value for pure blue is 0 Red, 0 Green, and 255 Blue. The RGB values in XHTML, however, are represented by a six-digit number: two for Red, two for Green, and two for Blue. What happens when the color value for any of these is higher than 99? That's where the hexadecimal part comes in. We all use base-10 math (decimal), probably because of the number of fingers on our hands. In base-10 math, anything over 99 items is going to be at least a three-digit number. In base-16 math, which is what hexadecimal math is, you can go up to the base-10 number 255 and still only have a two-digit number. So, in base-16 math, the base-10 sequence 8-16 would be 8, 9, A, B, C, D, E, F, 10.

TIP

Confused? No need to be. There is a great RGB color conversion site at **http://www.stardot.com/~lukeseem/hexed.html**. Also, those of you using Windows can use the scientific mode of your Calculator application to enter a base-10 number and then click the Hex radio button to get its base-16 equivalent.

Using RGB values is not hard once you have determined the proper value.

```
<html>
  <head>
    <title>Web Page Color</title>
  </head>
  <body bgcolor = "#00FFFF">
    <p>This Web page has a nice pale blue background color to soothe the
savage Web beast.</p>
  </body>
</html>
```

In the preceding example, the Red value is 0 and the Green and Blue values are both 255. This combination creates a color known as aqua. The hexadecimal value for this RGB value is 00FFFF. Also notice the RGB value always is preceded by a pound sign (#).

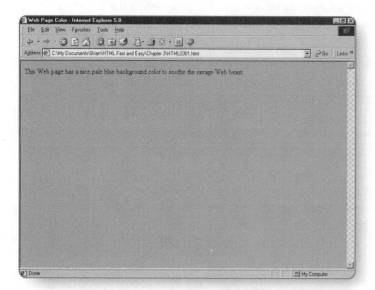

As you can see from the example, this does not look bad with black text because the contrast between text and background is strong. Watch what happens, however, when a darker background is used with black text.

```
<html>
  <head>
    <title>A Walk on the Dark Side</title>
  </head>
  <body bgcolor = "#000080">
    <p>This Web page has a dark blue background color to make you squint.</p>
  </body>
</html>
```

TIP

When creating your pages, it's a good idea to have someone else look at them before you publish them. You are not always the best judge of what's legible on a page, because you already know what's written there.

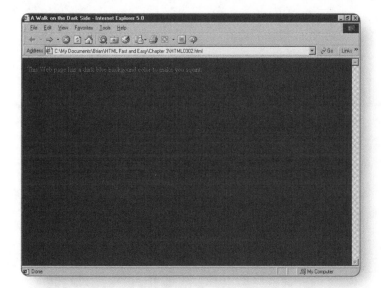

Hard to read, isn't it? It is important to make sure your pages are always legible, even if it means altering a beloved design. Otherwise, why is the page out there?

If you do not want to bother with deducing RGB values and then converting them into hexadecimal format (always a party activity for a Saturday night), you can use one of 16 English-named colors that are recognized by XHTML. Table 3-1 lists these colors and their equivalent RGB values.

Table 3-1 HTML Default Colors

Color	Value	Color	Value
Aqua	00FFFF	Navy	000080
Black	000000	Olive	808000
Blue	0000FF	Purple	800080
Fuchsia	FF00FF	Red	FF0000
Gray	808080	Silver	C0C0C0
Green	008000	Teal	008080
Lime	00FF00	White	FFFFFF
Maroon	800000	Yellow	FFFF00

Using these colors is a bit easier than the RGB values, because there is no higher-level math to do.

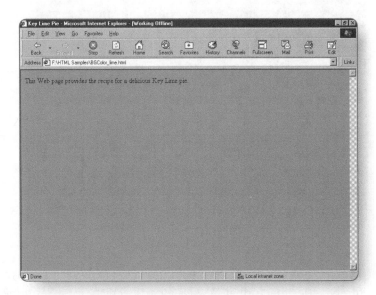

```
<html>
  <head>
    <title>Key Lime
Pie</title>
  </head>
  <body bgcolor = "lime">
    <p>This Web page provides
the recipe for a delicious
Key Lime pie.</p>
  </body>
</html>
```

The really nice thing about using RGB colors is that you have a choice of over 16 million for your Web page without requiring your page's visitors to download anything extra. When you use the background attribute, an additional file has to be downloaded, but if you play your cards right, it won't be a problem for your readers.

The background attribute has only one kind of value: a URL that points to the graphics file you want to use as a background. A background graphics file can be any size or shape. Whatever its appearance, the background image is tiled on the entire Web page behind the text when the Web page calls for it. This tiling effect lets you use a very small graphics file to achieve a big effect—all without giving your visitors a huge file to download.

```
<html>
  <head>
    <title>Background Check</title>
  </head>
  <body background = "softgrid.gif" bgcolor = "gray">
    <p>This background is not too distracting from this text.</p>
  </body>
</html>
```

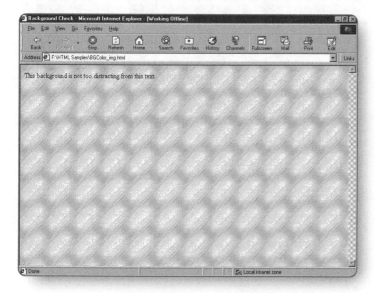

The URL points to a file in the Images subdirectory called softgrid.gif. This image file is only two kilobytes in size, barely a blip even for a 14.4 modem. Because it is tiled, it fills the page with multiple instances of itself and creates a nice effect.

BROWSER
BROWSER

You might notice that we left in a `bgcolor` attribute in the `<body>` element. This is because some browsers might not have the capability to display background images. Also, a user might have turned off his or her image display in the browser's preferences or the image file might not be available due to an error on your part. By having a background color set, you give your page a fallback position for design.

If we warned you to be careful with the contrast between background colors and text, the warning holds doubly true for background images. Not only is color contrast a factor, but you now have to be aware of how patterns interfere with or complement the text on your page.

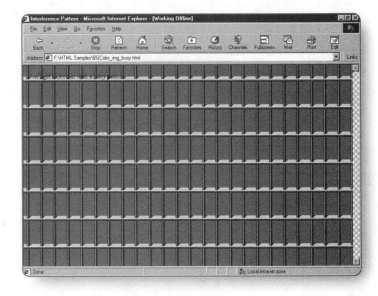

```
<html>
  <head>
    <title>Interference Pattern</title>
  </head>
  <body background = "/images/bars.gif" bgcolor = "gray">
    <p>Don't get locked in with a busy pattern.</p>
  </body>
</html>
```

To get a background, you can make one with a desktop graphics tool. Or, more easily, simply download a freeware or shareware image file from any of the myriad background Web sites on the Internet. The two backgrounds just used were from the very cool Backgrounds 4 Us site at **http://www.ecnet.net/users/gas52r0/Jay/ backgrounds/back.htm**, which is a shareware site. Use your favorite Internet search engine to find a wealth of sites with other backgrounds for downloading.

If you find a background you really like but are afraid it will not contrast properly with your text, fear not. There's a way out of this conundrum. If your background is too dark, you can simply make your text lighter, as you learn in the next section.

BROWSER vs BROWSER

Internet Explorer has an additional browser-specific attribute for the `<body>` element you can use to manipulate backgrounds. The `bgproperties` attribute can make a background graphic hold in one place so that text scrolls independently of the static graphic. This is achieved with the attribute's one and only value, `fixed`:

```
<html>
  <head>
    <title>Fixed Background</title>
  </head>
  <body background = "/images/softgrid.gif" bgproperties = "fixed" bgcolor =
"gray">
    <p>You can fix any background graphic into place. Use faint graphics in
this manner for a cool "watermark" look.</p>
  </body>
</html>
```

This attribute can only be used when a background graphic is present, and it only works in Internet Explorer browsers. Other browsers ignore the attribute.

Colorful Characters

It's funny how text of a certain color can send waves of panic through you. Back in school, whenever the teacher brought out the red pen, you just knew it was your paper he or she was marking up. Red meant trouble.

When colors are used properly, they can bring a lot of attention to your Web site. Not only can you color backgrounds, but you can bring color to your document's text and its hyperlinks as well.

Coloring Text

When you color text, you use the `text` attribute of the `<body>` element. For the `text` attribute, you can use either the hexadecimal RGB value or one of the 16 color names, just as with `bgcolor`.

```html
<html>
  <head>
    <title>Text Colors</title>
  </head>
  <body bgcolor = "#808080" text = "ff0000">
    <h1>Ohio State Fan Page!</h1>
  </body>
</html>
```

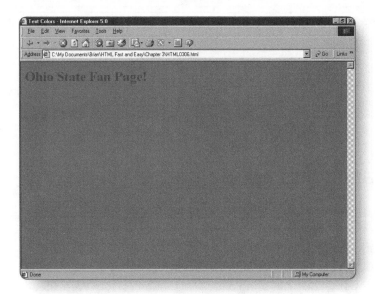

When you use colors, make sure you use colors that work well together and give your text enough contrast so that it can be read.

```html
<html>
  <head>
    <title>Low-Contrast Ahead</title>
  </head>
  <body bgcolor = "#000000" text = "800000">
    <p>Black and maroon can work well together, but not like this.</p>
  </body>
</html>
```

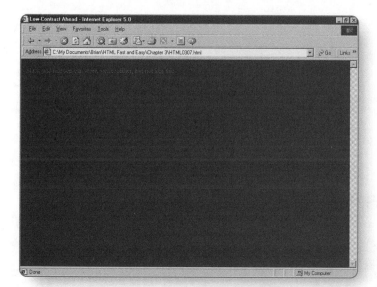

Obviously, these colors don't work well together.

Don't be afraid to experiment, especially if you like a certain combination of colors. After all, this is a lot cheaper than using pen and paper!

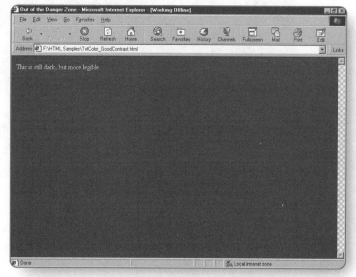

```html
<html>
  <head>
    <title>Out of the Danger Zone</title>
  </head>
  <body bgcolor = "#800000" text = "ffffff">
    <p>This is still dark, but more legible.</p>
  </body>
</html>
```

Colored text can even break through a cluttered background, as you can see in the next example:

```html
<html>
  <head>
    <title>Build Your Site One Brick at a Time</title>
  </head>
  <body background = "bricks.gif" bgcolor = "red" text = "yellow">
    <p>The proper use of color can help you make a solid Web site.</p>
  </body>
</html>
```

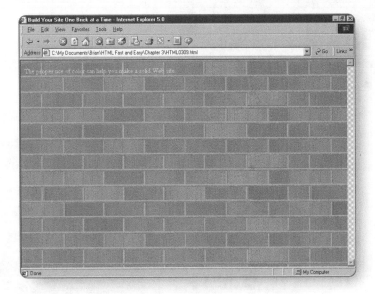

Coloring Links

As you surf the Web, you probably notice that the hyperlinked text that links one page to another often appears in a different color than the rest of the text in the document. Links are colored to indicate their status and to be seen more easily. Usually, if no special color scheme is declared within the document, there are three link conditions and colors:

- Unclicked links are blue.

- Active (clicked-on) links are red.

- Visited links are purple.

The three attributes that correspond to these link types are link, alink, and vlink, respectively. You do not have to assign any color values with these attributes if you want your pages to keep the default link colors. If you want to get creative, experiment all you want—just make sure your color scheme is consistent across all of your site's pages. Color values with these attributes are assigned with either the color names or an RGB value. Just remember, you now have to coordinate the color contrast among five areas.

```
<html>
<head>
<title>Biographies On-Line</title>
</head>
<body bgcolor="#000080" text="#FFFFFF" link = "FFFF00" alink = "FF0000" vlink
= "00FF00">
<h1 align="center">Famous Authors</h1>
<p>Click on the links below to view brief biographies of your favorite authors
throughout history.</p>
<blockquote><a href = "http://www.bkp.com/homer.htm">Homer</a><br>
<a href = "http://www.bkp.com/will.htm">William Shakespeare</a><br>
<a href = "http://www.bkp.com/swift.htm">Jonathon Swift</a><br>
<a href = "http://www.bkp.com/twain.htm">Mark Twain</a><br>
</blockquote>
</body>
</html>
```

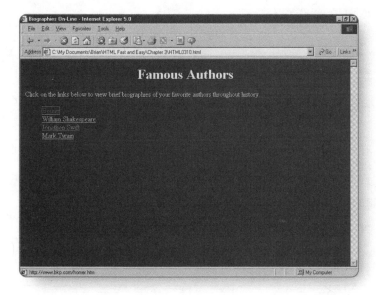

You can have a lot of fun with the color options provided by XHTML. Though all of this capability is duplicated within style sheets, it is still a nice way to get color across to those browsers unable to use CSS technology.

The `<body>` element has another set of attributes that can be used in place of CSS. Although not color-related, they are neat to use if you can. The `leftmargin`, `rightmargin`, `topmargin`, and `bottommargin` attributes establish a fixed border around the edge of the Internet Explorer browser window. The values used are the numeric pixel values. So, a value of 30 in any of these attributes would create a 30-pixel-wide border between the text and graphics and the browser's window edge.

```
<html>
  <head>
    <title>No Margins for Error</title>
  </head>
  <body leftmargin = "30" rightmargin = "30" topmargin = "30" bottommargin =
"30">
  </body>
</html>
```

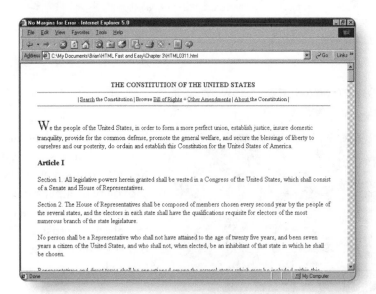

This attribute only works in Internet Explorer browsers. Other browsers ignore the attribute.

Starting Scripts

The <body> element has two additional attributes, and they have nothing to do with color. Onload and onunload are attributes designed to start scripts when a page is initially loaded or unloaded.

The advantage of this approach is that you can have the page start doing something for the reader as soon as the page appears completely in his or her browser, as in the next example. Don't worry about the stuff in the <script> element; we've just condensed it. Observe the onload attribute in the <body> element and the effect it has on the displayed Web page and the status bar immediately below it:

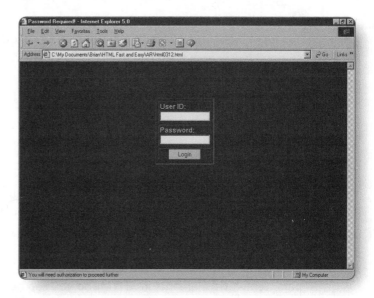

```
<html>
<head>
<title>Password Required!</title>
<center>
<script language="JavaScript">
<!--start script…
<!–…end script
</script>
</head>
<body>
<body bgcolor="black" onload="window.status=('You will need authorization to
proceed further');">
<p align="center"><br><font size="5"
face="arial"><u><b>Login</b></u></font></p>
<form id="InfoInput">
<center>
<table border="3" cellpadding="2" cellspacing="5" bgcolor="black"
bordercolor="red" bordercolorlight="blue" bordercolordark="red">
<td><font size="3" color="turquoise" face="arial"><b>User
ID:</b></font><br><input size="15" name="id" maxlength="12" type="text"></td>
```

```
<tr><td><font size="3" color="turquoise"
face="arial"><b>Password:</b></font><br><input type="password" size="15"
name="pass" maxlength="12"></td></tr>
<td align="center"><input type="button" value="   Login    "
onclick="Authorize()"></td></tr></table>
<br>
</body>
</html>
```

You learn more about scripting in Chapter 14, "Adding Applets to Your Web Site,"
so don't worry about the mechanics of what we've just shown you. Just file this
away for those times when you need to create a Web page that needs scripting run
whenever it is loaded or unloaded.

Conclusion

In this chapter, you have taken a brief foray into the world of the <body> element.
With just a few attributes, you can see how simple it is to dramatically change the
look and feel of your Web pages.

In Chapter 4, "Block Tags and You," you begin to examine the more detailed
paragraph-level elements in XHTML so you can begin to manipulate the actual
information your page is trying to present.

4

Block Tags and You

Until now, you have worked with XHTML elements that deal with managing your Web page at the document level. But when most folks sit down and write something, they are more concerned about the things going on at the word, sentence, and paragraph levels. XHTML has outstanding capabilities for managing things at these levels, beginning with a group of elements referred to as *block tags*.

In this chapter, you'll learn how to do the following:

- Manage paragraphs in your document
- Use headings to properly outline your document
- Utilize special block tags to mark quotes and contact information
- Take advantage of preformatted text
- Align text and headings
- Insert horizontal rules

Block tags are a fairly large group of XHTML elements designed to handle text at the paragraph level. By paragraph level, we're talking about paragraphs, headings, and addresses, etc.—any group of text beyond sentences. Using block tags is more intuitive to most XHTML users than, say, using elements in the head section. Now these elements are coming down to a more earthly level.

Organize Your Text

Writing, in theory, is not that hard. The trick is to get what's in your head on paper or, in this case, the screen. You don't have to be flowery or fancy. Just figure out what you want to say and say it.

Related words and sentences, as you know, are grouped in paragraphs. There is good reason for this. In earlier days, readers had trouble reading lengthy, unbroken text. Their eyes would get lost following the characters across a page, which meant the reader would sigh in frustration, back up to a passage of text that he or she remembered reading, and start over again.

When text was broken up into shorter passages, however, things started working better. The reader's eyes were less strained and he or she was more able to keep track of the words on the printed page. This principle also applies to electronic documents—even more so, given the greater fatigue eyes experience when reading text on a monitor instead of paper.

In XHTML, four elements can provide this kind of grouping:

- `<p>` Paragraph
- `<pre>` Preformatted text
- `<blockquote>` Stand-alone quotes
- `<address>` Stand-alone contact information

The following sections detail the capabilities of each of these elements.

Building Paragraphs

Using the <p> element might not seem such a big deal. After all, you have been using paragraphs since grade school, and it can't be that complicated.

This is essentially correct. Using <p> is very simple, as this example demonstrates:

```
<html>
  <head>
    <title>Using the Paragraph Element</title>
  </head>
  <body>
    <p>One of the interesting effects of using elements in XHTML is how the
elements deal with extra white space. In short, they ignore it.</p>
    <p>For instance, if you were to insert an inordinate amount of space
between two paragraphs, such as this one and the following paragraph, a
browser would display the same amount of space between paragraphs that it
always does.</p>




    <p>You see? The spacing is the same when you look at the browser.</p>
  </body>
</html>
```

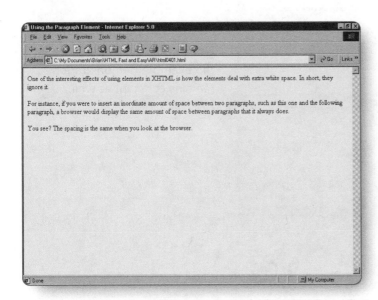

To delineate a paragraph, all you need to do is enclose the paragraph content within the <p> element.

It's actually even easier than this. In HTML, the `<p>` element is one of those elements with an optional end tag. This means you can achieve the same effect with the previous example even after taking out the `</p>` tag.

```
<html>
  <head>
    <title>Using the Paragraph Element, sans End Tag</title>
  </head>
  <body>
    <p>One of the interesting effects of using elements in XHTML is how the
elements deal with extra white space. In short, they ignore it.
    <p>For instance, if you were to insert an inordinate amount of space
between two paragraphs, such as this one and the following paragraph, a
browser would display the same amount of space between paragraphs that it
always does.


    <p>You see? The spacing is the same when you look at the browser.
  </body>
</html>
```

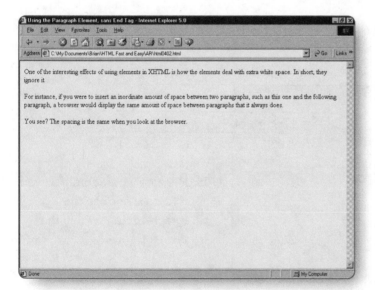

Notice that the white space in the example demonstration remains constant as well.

In XHTML documents, end tags are always required for all elements, so you *cannot* neglect the `</p>` tag.

Only one attribute is associated with the <p> element: the `align` attribute. As its name implies, the `align` attribute lets you set the alignment of the element's content. This attribute is discussed later in this chapter in the "Aligning Text" section.

Using Preformatted Text

As you read in the previous section, XHTML tends to ignore issues such as extra white space, either between or within elements. This is a good policy, because it makes it easier to maintain a level of presentation sanity on the Internet.

There might be times, though, at which you need the ability to use white space as part of your presentation. A good example is the presentation of some script right on your Web page:

```
<html>
  <head>
    <title>The Robot Section</title>
  </head>
  <body>
<pre>
function updown(isdn) {
if (isdn) {
    document.f[('pl'+pos)].src = image_directory + 'ball.gif';
}
else {
    document.f[('pl'+pos)].src= image_directory + 'square.gif';
    }
}
function dopc() {
document.f.st.value = stage;
if (cnt <= stage) {
    pcbusy = true;
    userturn = false;
    document.f.s.value = "Robot's Turn";
    setTimeout("pos=Math.floor((Math.random()*8)+1); updown(true)",500);
    setTimeout("updown(false) ; pcclicks[cnt]=pos; cnt++; dopc()",1200);
}
</pre>
  </body>
</html>
```

As you can see, this excerpt of script is displayed with all the correct white space and line breaks. It is also displayed in a monospaced font, which ensures that the alignment of the text is correct. Compare what happens if you try to control the appearance of the font and the line breaks separately:

```html
<html>
  <head>
    <title>The faux Robot Section</title>
  </head>
  <body>
<font face="courier"><p>
function updown(isdn) {<br />
if (isdn) {<br />
    document.f[('pl'+pos)].src = image_directory + 'ball.gif'; <br />
}<br />
else {<br />
    document.f[('pl'+pos)].src= image_directory + 'square.gif'; <br />
    }<br />
}<br />
function dopc() {<br />
document.f.st.value = stage; <br />
if (cnt <= stage) {<br />
    pcbusy = true; <br />
    userturn = false; <br />
    document.f.s.value = "Robot's Turn";<br />
    setTimeout("pos=Math.floor((Math.random()*8)+1); updown(true)",500); <br
/>
    setTimeout("updown(false) ; pcclicks[cnt]=pos; cnt++; dopc()",1200); <br
/>
}
</p>
</font>
  </body>
</html>
```

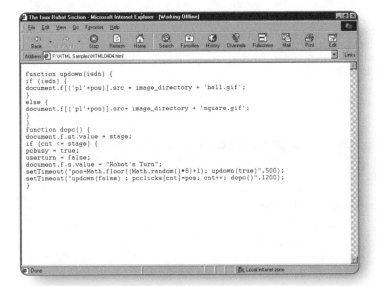

```
function updown(isdn) {
if (isdn) {
document.f[('pl'+pos)].src = image_directory + 'ball.gif';
}
else {
document.f[('pl'+pos)].src= image_directory + 'square.gif';
}
}
function dopc() {
document.f.st.value = stage;
if (cnt <= stage) {
pcbusy = true;
userturn = false;
document.f.s.value = "Robot's Turn";
setTimeout("pos=Math.floor((Math.random()*8)+1); updown(true)",500);
setTimeout("updown(false) ; pcclicks[cnt]=pos; cnt++; dopc()",1200);
}
```

Whereas it is not hard to duplicate the look of the contents of the `<pre>` element, the problem remains of the spacing and the tediousness of adding all those extra line-break tags. (You learn more about this in the "Creating Hard Rules in a Hard World" section of this chapter.)

Using the `<pre>` element is a quick way to display text in a specific way without the need to create special positioning tags.

Quote It!

Whenever you get a bunch of people together to discuss something important, invariably one of them falls back upon the words of someone else to support his or her argument. People like to quote other people, particularly famous people. It seems to lend credence to what they say.

In XHTML, you can bolster your own arguments with the `<blockquote>` element.

```
<html>
  <head>
    <title>Compromise in a Marriage</title>
  </head>
  <body>
<h1>Marriage: The Great Tug-of-War</h1>
<blockquote>The Japanese have a word for it. It's judo - the art of conquering
by yielding. The Western equivalent of judo is, 'Yes, dear.'<br />
-- J.P. McEvoy, American writer</blockquote>
```

```
<p>In today's society, it has become increasingly popular to cash in the chips
at the first sign of trouble in a marriage. Many sociological reasons have
been put forth as to why the divorce rate is at an all-time high, but the
simple truth may be that in today's empowered society, it's become too easy
for us not to compromise.</p>
</font>
  </body>
</html>
```

You can see in the example how the text passage contained within the `<blockquote>` element is indented. This indentation is a traditional method of setting off cited quotes even within printed material.

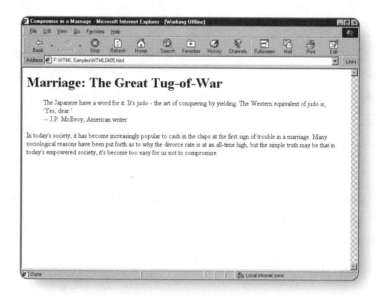

TIP

If you are not using style sheets, the `<blockquote>` element is a handy way to indent passages of text, even if it is not quoted material.

The `<blockquote>` element has one attribute, which has allowed it to remain part of the strict XHTML protocol. The `cite` attribute provides the Internet address of the source of the quotation, typically in the status bar of a compatible browser. This gives users the chance to research topics related to the quote. This should not be confused with the `<cite>` element, which styles an inline citation.

**BROWSER
VS
BROWSER**

If you choose to use the `cite` attribute, be aware that some browsers do not display the URL that is generated by `cite`. It is always a good idea to include the information, however, because a reader can still obtain the URL by viewing the source code.

Using the `cite` attribute is easy; the value of the attribute is simply the URL to be displayed.

```
<html>
  <head>
    <title>Compromise in a Marriage</title>
  </head>
  <body>
<h1>Marriage: The Great Tug-of-War</h1>
<blockquote cite = "http://www.bkp.com/quotes">The Japanese have a word for
it. It's judo - the art of conquering by yielding. The Western equivalent of
judo is, 'Yes, dear.'<br />
-- J.P. McEvoy, American writer</blockquote>
<p>In today's society, it has become increasingly popular to cash in the chips
at the first sign of trouble in a marriage. Many sociological reasons have
been put forth as to why the divorce rate is at an all-time high, but the
simple truth may be that in today's empowered society, it's become too easy
for us not to compromise.</p>
</font>
  </body>
</html>
```

Addressing in XHTML

In publishing, when someone gets credit for writing something, he or she gets the byline for the work. The byline is the person's name and perhaps title. Also, a section of the work might be devoted to how to contact the author if the author so desires.

This practice is a bit of formality in the publishing world, but it is more essential in the realm of online publishing. Authors and creators of Web pages often do not have the luxury of having a professional editor review their work. To compensate, they provide contact information for users in hopes that these users will provide feedback about their pages. Of course, many times this feedback is less than constructive. Still, it's worth sifting through the dirt to find that one golden nugget of feedback.

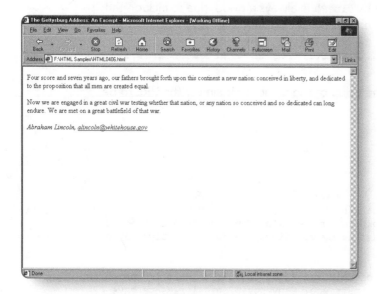

The element used to contain this contact information is <address>. It contains no attributes, so it's fairly straightforward to use. The <address> element is often used with active e-mail links to help facilitate the contact. Here's an example:

```
<html>
  <head>
    <title>The Gettysburg Address: An Excerpt</title>
  </head>
  <body>
<p>Four score and seven years ago, our fathers brought forth upon this
continent a new nation:  conceived in liberty, and dedicated to the
proposition that all men are created equal.</p>
<p>Now we are engaged in a great civil war testing whether that nation, or any
nation so conceived and so dedicated can long endure.  We are met on a great
battlefield of that war.</p>
<address>Abraham Lincoln, <a href = "mailto:
alincoln@whitehouse.gov">alincoln@whitehouse.gov</a></address>
  </body>
</html>
```

> **TIP**
>
> The `<address>` element also can be used to convey contact information for a portion of a document, such as within a form.

Outline Your Document with Headings

When developing documents of any great length, writers often have to break the work into sections. In a very large work, such as a book, the information is further divided into chapters and even sections of chapters. This helps the reader by organizing the information in manageable chunks. Sectioning off topics also assists the author in writing by ensuring a more logical flow of information.

Sections are indicated by headings. Headings are those large-type passages of text that announce the beginning of a new section. This is not a new concept to a lot of you. Some confusion might lie, however, in the differences between the six levels of headings you can use in XHTML.

Here are the heading elements in XHTML (in order by size, from largest to smallest): `<h1>`, `<h2>`, `<h3>`, `<h4>`, `<h5>`, and `<h6>`. They surround the heading text like any other container element.

```
<html>
  <head>
    <title>Block Tags and You</title>
  </head>
  <body>
<h1>Organize Your Text</h1>
<p>Writing, in theory, is not that hard. The trick is to get what's in your
head on paper or, in this case, the screen. You don't have to be flowery or
fancy. Just figure out what you want to say and say it.</p>
<p> Related words and sentences, as you know, are grouped in paragraphs. There
is good reason for this. In earlier days, readers had trouble reading lengthy,
unbroken text. Their eyes would get lost following the characters across a
page, which meant the reader would sigh in frustration, back up to a passage
of text that he or she remembered reading, and start over again. </p>
  </body>
</html>
```

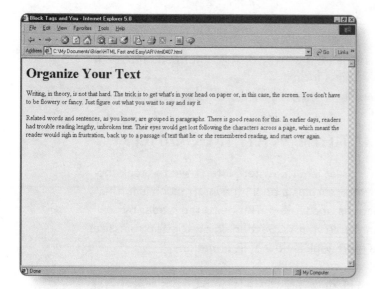

It's easy to see how the heading elements distinguish the heading from the rest of the text.

A lot of people get mixed up when they try to use the numbers in the heading elements as sequential markers of where the heading appears in the text. They think <h1> should surround the first heading in the document, <h2> the next heading, and so on. This is not always the case. The numbers in the heading elements signify the *level* of the heading. This can be illustrated with an outline of this chapter:

```
<html>
  <head>
    <title>Block Tags and You: An Outline</title>
  </head>
  <body>
<h1>Organize Your Text</h1>
<h2>Building Paragraphs</h2>
<h2>Using Preformatted Text</h2>
<h2>Quote It!</h2>
<h2>Addressing in XHTML</h2>
<h1>Outline Your Document with Headings</h1>
<h1>Applying Basic Layout Techniques</h1>
<h2>Aligning Text</h2>
<h2>Creating Hard Rules in a Hard World</h2>
  </body>
</html>
```

This is an outline because the topics are sectioned off into top-level headings (within the <h1> element), and with subtopics falling under subheadings (<h2> elements and lower).

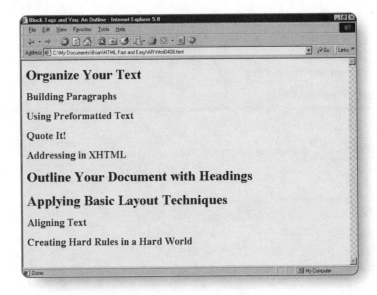

To help illustrate this further, see how the outline looks if you use the sequential heading method:

```
<html>
  <head>
    <title>Block Tags and You: A Bad Outline</title>
  </head>
  <body>
<h1>Organize Your Text</h1>
<h2>Building Paragraphs</h2>
<h3>Using Preformatted Text</h3>
<h4>Quote It!</h4>
<h5>Addressing in XHTML</h5>
<h6>Outline Your Document with Headings</h6>
<h6>Applying Basic Layout Techniques</h6>
<h6>Aligning Text</h6>
<h6>Creating Hard Rules in a Hard World</h6>
  </body>
</html>
```

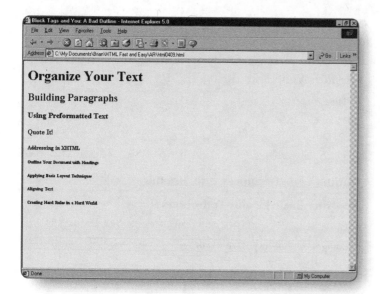

Not so good, is it? The author, you note, has also run out of numbers for the headings.

The best way to create a document with logical headings is to design the outline first. Then you can see how the headings work. When creating outlines, you need to make sure of a few things:

- Never have a stand-alone subheading.

- Always have your heading levels in logical order.

- Always have text after a heading. Never have two headings right next to each other.

When you have a stand-alone subheading, you have one subheading within a higher topic level. This does not work well in a document because you should have more than one subtopic to justify the addition of another level to your outline. For instance, if the following were the chapter's outline, the presence of the single <h2> element at the end of the chapter should make the author rethink the outline a bit.

```
<html>
  <head>
    <title>Block Tags and You: An Outline</title>
  </head>
  <body>
<h1>Organize Your Text</h1>
<h2>Building Paragraphs</h2>
<h2>Using Preformatted Text</h2>
```

```
<h2>Quote It!</h2>
<h2>Addressing in XHTML</h2>
<h1>Outline Your Document with Headings</h1>
<h1>Applying Basic Layout Techniques</h1>
<h2>Aligning Text</h2>
  </body>
</html>
```

Either the <h2> heading should be dropped and its related material merged into the preceding <h1> element's text or the <h1> element should be removed and the lone <h2> element promoted to <h1>. Either way, the stand-alone head (also sometimes referred to as a dangling head) needs to go.

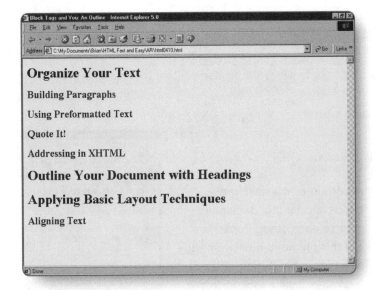

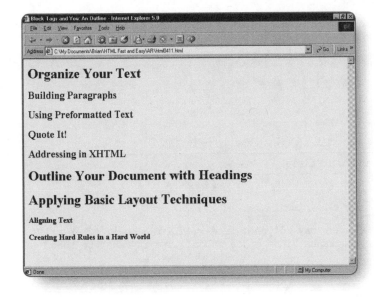

When you design an outline, make sure that you don't skip a heading level. This happens more often than you think, especially when headings are added while the document is being written (another good reason to do the outline first). This example shows a skipped heading level.

```
<html>
  <head>
    <title>Block Tags and You: An Outline</title>
  </head>
  <body>
<h1>Organize Your Text</h1>
<h2>Building Paragraphs</h2>
<h2>Using Preformatted Text</h2>
<h2>Quote It!</h2>
<h2>Addressing in XHTML</h2>
<h1>Outline Your Document with Headings</h1>
<h1>Applying Basic Layout Techniques</h1>
<h3>Aligning Text</h3>
<h3>Creating Hard Rules in a Hard World</h3>
  </body>
</html>
```

Another error is having two heads appear in a document next to each other. Publishers call this phenomenon jammed or banging heads, and it is not desirable. Take a look at this example to see what we mean:

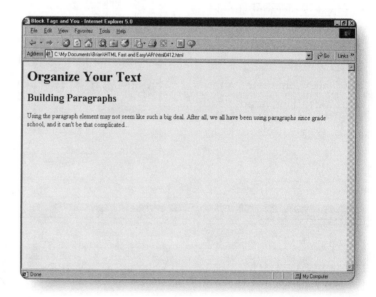

```
<html>
  <head>
    <title>Block Tags and You</title>
  </head>
  <body>
<h1>Organize Your Text</h1>
<h2>Building Paragraphs</h2>
<p>Using the paragraph element may not seem like such a big deal. After all,
we all have been using paragraphs since grade school, and it can't be that
complicated...</p>
  </body>
</html>
```

Without introductory material after the `<h1>` element, the stark positioning of the `<h2>` element gives this document an unprofessional look. Even if it's just a sentence or two, always have some text appear after a heading!

The heading elements all share the `align` attribute, which you'll read more about in the "Aligning Text" section below.

If you follow these simple guidelines, your headings will give your pages a well-organized look and feel.

Applying Basic Layout Techniques

This section of the chapter introduces you to some of the basic layout capabilities of XHTML. Layout is what publishers call positioning the text on the page or screen. Many software tools are on the market to accomplish sophisticated layouts in many formats, XHTML included.

For really great layouts, it is better to use a cascading style sheet in your document. CSS technology has really added a vast amount of control over Web page layout.

But, as is said throughout this book, not every browser can handle CSS. In those cases, you need to fall back on the tried and true capabilities of plain old XHTML.

Aligning Text

One of the most commonly used methods of Web page layout is the alignment of text and images. Chapter 8, "Images on the Web," discusses the ins and outs of image alignment. For now, however, concentrate on the alignment of block elements.

When aligning block elements such as `<p>` or any of the heading elements, the attribute to use is `align`. Within these elements, `align` defines horizontal alignment.

CAUTION

In other elements, such as `<img>` or the table elements, `align` has different capabilities. Make sure you remember what `align` does in each instance.

Because `align` affects horizontal alignment when used in block elements, it can have one of just four values: `left`, `center`, `right`, and `justify`. When text is left-aligned, it appears as most text appears in English documents: with a straight left margin and a ragged right margin.

```html
<html>
  <head>
    <title>The Gettysburg Address: An Excerpt</title>
  </head>
  <body>
<p align = "left">Four score and seven years ago, our fathers brought forth
upon this continent a new nation:  conceived in liberty, and dedicated to the
proposition that all men are created equal.</p>
<p align = "left">Now we are engaged in a great civil war testing whether that
nation, or any nation so conceived and so dedicated can long endure.  We are
met on a great battlefield of that war.</p>
  </body>
</html>
```

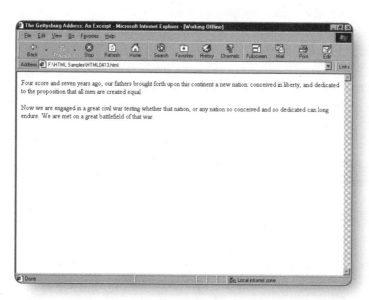

The center value does just what it says: it centers the text in the marked paragraph on the Web page.

```
<html>
  <head>
    <title>The Gettysburg Address: An Excerpt</title>
  </head>
  <body>
<p align = "center">Four score and seven years ago, our fathers brought forth
upon this continent a new nation:  conceived in liberty, and dedicated to the
proposition that all men are created equal.</p>
<p align = "center">Now we are engaged in a great civil war testing whether
that nation, or any nation so conceived and so dedicated can long endure.  We
are met on a great battlefield of that war.</p>
  </body>
</html>
```

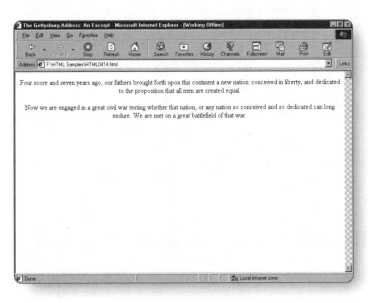

The `right` value aligns text along a straight right margin, leaving a ragged left margin.

```html
<html>
  <head>
    <title>The Gettysburg Address: An Excerpt</title>
  </head>
  <body>
<p align = "right">Four score and seven years ago, our fathers brought forth
upon this continent a new nation:  conceived in liberty, and dedicated to the
proposition that all men are created equal.</p>
<p align = "right">Now we are engaged in a great civil war testing whether
that nation, or any nation so conceived and so dedicated can long endure.  We
are met on a great battlefield of that war.</p>
  </body>
</html>
```

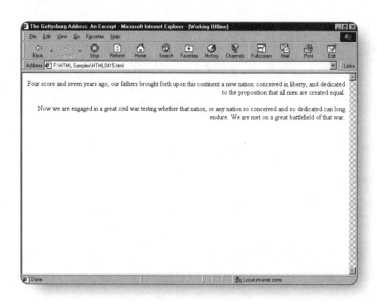

Sometimes you might not like the way a ragged margin looks. You can fix this using the justify value of align, as shown in the next example:

```
<html>
  <head>
    <title>The Gettysburg Address: An Excerpt</title>
  </head>
  <body>
<font size="5"><p align = "justify">Four score and seven years ago, our
fathers brought forth upon this continent a new nation:  conceived in liberty,
and dedicated to the proposition that all men are created equal.</p>
<p align = "justify">Now we are engaged in a great civil war testing whether
that nation, or any nation so conceived and so dedicated can long endure.  We
are met on a great battlefield of that war.</p></font>
  </body>
</html>
```

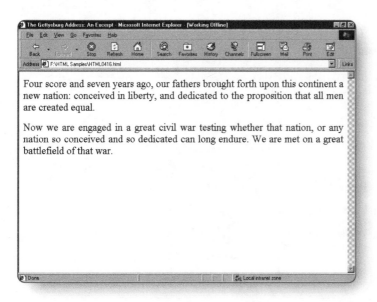

You can use the `align` attribute with interesting effect in any of the block elements, including the headings.

```html
<html>
  <head>
    <title>Block Tags and You: An Outline</title>
  </head>
  <body>
<h1>Organize Your Text</h1>
<h2 align = "right">Building Paragraphs</h2>
<h2 align = "right">Using Preformatted Text</h2>
<h2 align = "right">Quote It!</h2>
<h2 align = "right">Addressing in XHTML</h2>
<h1>Outline Your Document with Headings</h1>
<h1>Applying Basic Layout Techniques</h1>
<h2 align = "right">Aligning Text</h2>
<h2 align = "right">Creating Hard Rules in a Hard World</h2>
  </body>
</html>
```

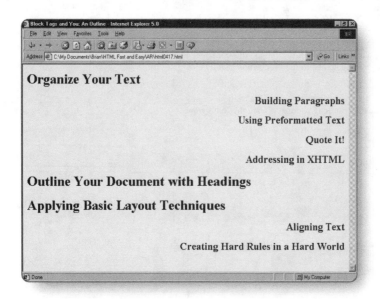

Creating Hard Rules in a Hard World

One final block element has not been discussed yet. This is due partly to the unique nature of the element. Although it is a block element by classification, it is not, by any means, a text element.

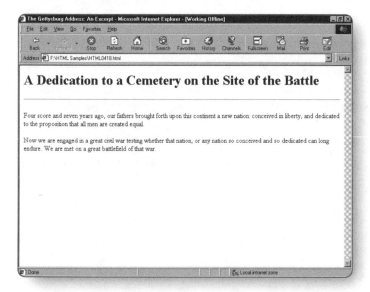

This is the <hr> element. This element's nomenclature is derived from the term horizontal rule, which is what it creates. Adding a rule to a document is pretty easy.

```
<html>
  <head>
    <title>The Gettysburg Address: An Excerpt</title>
  </head>
  <body>
<h1>A Dedication to a Cemetery on the Site of the Battle</h1>
<hr />
<p>Four score and seven years ago, our fathers brought forth upon this
continent a new nation:  conceived in liberty, and dedicated to the
proposition that all men are created equal.</p>
<p>Now we are engaged in a great civil war testing whether that nation, or any
nation so conceived and so dedicated can long endure.  We are met on a great
battlefield of that war.</p>
  </body>
</html>
```

Because the `<hr>` element is not a container, there is no need to use an end tag in an HTML 4.0-compliant document. In XHTML, however, an end tag must always be present. This can be accomplished using the shorthand marker `<hr />`.

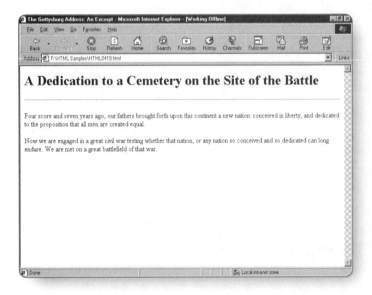

The `<hr>` element has several attributes that can be used to place and size the element. One attribute readily familiar to you is the `align` attribute. Because it is within a block element, `align` has the same four values in `<hr>`, as seen in the following example:

```
<html>
  <head>
    <title>The Gettysburg Address: An Excerpt</title>
  </head>
  <body>
<h1>A Dedication to a Cemetery on the Site of the Battle</h1>
<hr align="center" />
<p>Four score and seven years ago, our fathers brought forth upon this
continent a new nation:  conceived in liberty, and dedicated to the
proposition that all men are created equal.</p>
<p>Now we are engaged in a great civil war testing whether that nation, or any
nation so conceived and so dedicated can long endure.  We are met on a great
battlefield of that war.</p>
  </body>
</html>
```

The size of the line is determined by its thickness and its width across the page. The thickness (weight) of the line is managed by the size attribute. The value for the size attribute is numeric and represents the number of pixels in height the line will be. Thus, if you want to display a 20-pixel-high line, you specify the following:

```
<html>
  <head>
    <title>The Gettysburg Address: An Excerpt</title>
  </head>
  <body>
<h1>A Dedication to a Cemetery on the Site of the Battle</h1>
<hr size="20" />
<p>Four score and seven years ago, our fathers brought forth upon this
continent a new nation:  conceived in liberty, and dedicated to the
proposition that all men are created equal.</p>
<p>Now we are engaged in a great civil war testing whether that nation, or any
nation so conceived and so dedicated can long endure.  We are met on a great
battlefield of that war.</p>
  </body>
</html>
```

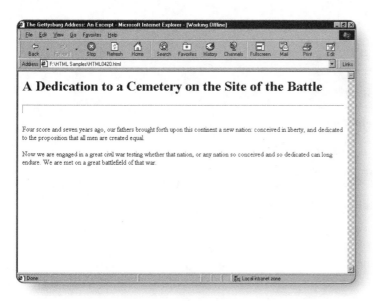

Style sheets usually handle the width of an <hr> element. You can use the `width` attribute directly when you are not using a CSS. Values of `width` can be displayed in terms of pixels or in terms of percentage of screen width. It is highly recommended you use the percentage value, because different users set up their browsers at different sizes. Watch what happens to a 500-pixel-long line when it's displayed in a browser window only 400 pixels wide:

```
<html>
  <head>
    <title>The Gettysburg Address: An Excerpt</title>
  </head>
  <body>
<h1>A Dedication to a Cemetery on the Site of the Battle</h1>
<hr width="500" />
<p>Four score and seven years ago, our fathers brought forth upon this
continent a new nation:  conceived in liberty, and dedicated to the
proposition that all men are created equal.</p>
<p>Now we are engaged in a great civil war testing whether that nation, or any
nation so conceived and so dedicated can long endure.  We are met on a great
battlefield of that war.</p>
  </body>
</html>
```

Now observe the effect if you set the width to cover 80 percent of the screen in the same browser:

```
<html>
  <head>
    <title>The Gettysburg Address: An Excerpt</title>
  </head>
  <body>
<h1>A Dedication to a Cemetery on the Site of the Battle</h1>
<hr width="80%" />
<p>Four score and seven years ago, our fathers brought forth upon this
continent a new nation:  conceived in liberty, and dedicated to the
proposition that all men are created equal.</p>
<p>Now we are engaged in a great civil war testing whether that nation, or any
nation so conceived and so dedicated can long endure.  We are met on a great
battlefield of that war.</p>
  </body>
</html>
```

You see? The browser window can be any size, and the line doesn't run off the screen!

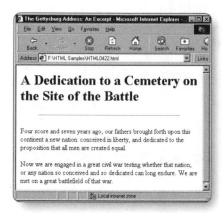

The final attribute of the `<hr>` element is the `noshade` element. Though not readily apparent, the figures in this section have a shadow effect under the rule. The `noshade` attribute gets rid of that:

```html
<html>
  <head>
    <title>The Gettysburg Address: An Excerpt</title>
  </head>
  <body>
<h1>A Dedication to a Cemetery on the Site of the Battle</h1>
<hr width="80%" noshade />
<p>Four score and seven years ago, our fathers brought forth upon this
continent a new nation:  conceived in liberty, and dedicated to the
proposition that all men are created equal.</p>
<p>Now we are engaged in a great civil war testing whether that nation, or any
nation so conceived and so dedicated can long endure.  We are met on a great
battlefield of that war.</p>
  </body>
</html>
```

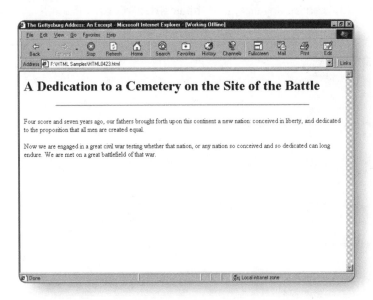

In XHTML, all attributes must have a value, even if it is a stand-alone attribute, such as noshade. To be XHTML-compliant, the attribute must appear as noshade = "noshade".

Conclusion

When dealing with block elements, you control the more basic organizational elements of the Web document. This is a pretty big step in document presentation. XHTML doesn't stop there, though.

In Chapter 5, "Touching Up Text," you learn about a whole new level of control in an XHTML document: the presentation of words and sentences in your Web document.

5

Touching Up Text

Words can convey new meanings just by the way they are displayed. This is often done with the application of various attributes, such as `bold` and `italic`.

In this chapter, you'll learn how to do the following:

- Use inline elements to give text `bold`, `italic`, and other attributes
- Size document text using different inline-element tools
- Enhance the structure of your document

In the olden days, when typewriters were king and word processors a distant future, getting boldface type onto paper was a cumbersome routine. Click! Backspace. Click! Click! Backspace. Not fun at all. Italics were impossible to get on a regular typewriter—but you could always get your type in red, provided you had a dual-ink ribbon.

Why rehash these distant and unpleasant memories? Mostly it's to illustrate how relatively easy it is to use a markup language today. Many people complain that once you move beyond the paragraph level of detail, XHTML can become a bit tedious. On some levels, this is an accurate, if unfortunate, assessment.

At the individual word and character level, XHTML elements are referred to as *inline elements*. Inline elements are used the same way as all other elements, but in a much more focused form. Using them properly can require a little extra work, but no more so, for example, than selecting text in a word processing document and clicking a Bold icon. Regardless, it's certainly a lot easier than using the old typewriter sitting in your parents' attic.

Like so many things that happen when extra care and work are involved, the results of using these inline elements are well worth the effort.

Basic Text Presentations

When you read text on a page, you are usually looking at a plain typeface, or font, as it is otherwise known. A font has a basic or unmodified appearance, just like the text in this sentence. When attributes are applied to the font, however, it takes on a slightly different appearance. **For example, when the bold attribute is applied to this passage, it looks like this.** *Italics is another attribute,* <u>as is underlining</u>.

> **NOTE**
>
> Some fonts are designed to appear as if an attribute has already been applied (Arial Black, for instance). These are specialized fonts that are usually employed by sophisticated desktop publishing applications.

When a font has an attribute applied to it, it retains its basic look and feel but displays an additional feature, such as extra-thick characters when bold is applied.

In the next sections, we take a quick look at four of the most common font attributes and a look at a unique font style.

Boldly Go...

Bold text is displayed in an XHTML document by the use of the <b> element. This is not exactly a news flash, because the <b> element is one of the most commonly used and well-known of the XHTML elements.

What is not so well known about the <b> element is that it is one of the few inline elements that has *not* been deprecated in XHTML. That is because despite the rapidly growing use of cascading style sheets and phrasal elements to apply attributes to text based on context, there are still valid uses for the <b> element.

NOTE

A *phrasal* element is an XHTML element that is applied to text based solely on context. These elements are also referred to as *logical* elements, and inline elements are sometimes known as *physical* elements.

For more information on phrasal elements, see Chapter 6, "Phrasing the Right Element."

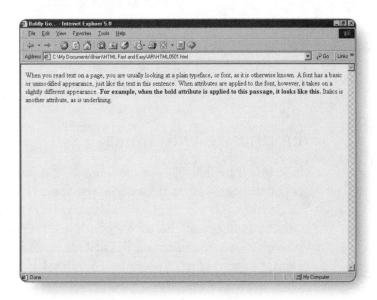

Using <b> is a simple process. Because this element has no attributes, you simply have to place the <b> container tags on each side of the passage you want boldfaced.

```
<p>
When you read text on a page, you are usually looking at a plain typeface, or
font, as it is otherwise known. A font has a basic or unmodified appearance,
just like the text in this sentence. When attributes are applied to the font,
however, it takes on a slightly different appearance. <b>For example, when the
bold attribute is applied to this passage, it looks like this.</b> Italics is
another attribute, as is underlining.
</p>
```

Try not to break a sweat with this, okay?

Because XHTML is meant to be a context-oriented markup language, it is not appropriate (by the strictest definitions of XHTML) to use the <b> tag when an appropriate phrasal element is available (such as <strong>). For a passage of text where no such phrasal element exists, you must use <b>. Vectors in mathematical equations are one example where the <b> element should be used.

```
<p>
If vectors <b>u</b> and <b>v</b> are at right angles in relation to each
other, <b>u</b> &perp; <b>v</b>.
</p>
```

Emphasize with Italics

Italic text is traditionally used for emphasis, as well as for citations of various types of publications, such as books or newspapers.

Like the <b> element, the <i> element should not be used exclusively for italic text. When it is used for emphasis, the XHTML standard recommends you use one of the phrasal elements first. If no phrasal or logical element will apply, you must use the inline, physical elements.

Using the <i> element is just as easy as using the <b> element, as you can plainly see in the next example.

```
<p>
When you read text on a page,
you are usually looking at a
plain typeface, or font, as
it is otherwise known. A font
has a basic or unmodified
appearance, just like the
text in this sentence. When
attributes are applied to the
font, however, it takes on a
slightly different
appearance. <b>For example,
when the bold attribute is
applied to this passage, it
looks like this.</b>
<i>Italics is another
attribute</i>, as is
underlining.
</p>
```

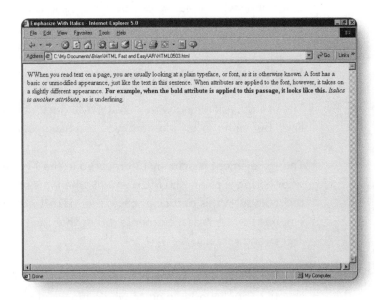

Though using <i> in this manner would work in an XHTML document, the <i> element is more appropriate to use when no phrasal elements, like <em>, are applicable.

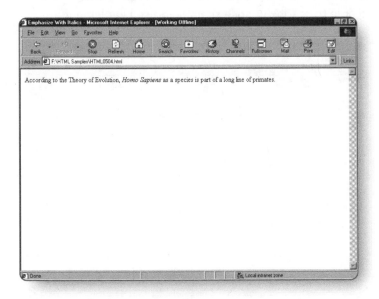

```
<p>
According to the Theory of
Evolution, <i>Homo Sapiens</i>
as a species is part of a long
line of primates.
</p>
```

The <i> element has no unique attributes, but like all other inline elements, it can contain the common `class` or `ID` attributes. These attributes are used with cascading style sheets, which are covered in Chapter 15, "Designing With Style (Sheets)."

Underlining Your Message

The use of underlining within an XHTML document is typically reserved for hyperlinks, but with the <u> element, you can have your regular text and underline it too.

The <u> element is actually deprecated in the XHTML standard. Deprecation is what happens to an XHTML element when it is replaced by newer elements or technology. In this particular case, the XHTML standard prefers users to indicate emphasis with phrasal elements rather than <u>. Recommended elements include <cite> and <strong>.

If you need to underline text within a document, you are encouraged to use style sheets to apply underlining to whole blocks of text or excerpts. This technique is described Chapter 15.

In the meantime, if you need to use the <u> element because you are concerned about browsers not being able to read your style sheets, you still implement it.

```
<p>
When you read text on a page,
you are usually looking at a
plain typeface, or font, as
it is otherwise known. A font
has a basic or unmodified
appearance, just like the
text in this sentence. When
attributes are applied to the
font, however, it takes on a
slightly different
appearance. <b>For example,
when the bold attribute is
applied to this passage, it
looks like this.</b>
<i>Italics is another
attribute</i>, <u>as is
underlining</u>.
</p>
```

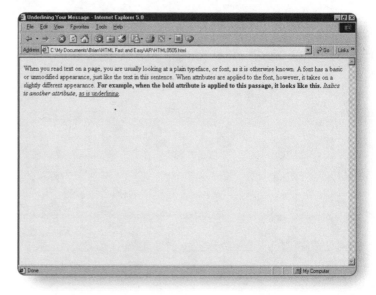

Strikethrough the Text

When editors want to mark text to be deleted in a document, they usually draw a straight line through it. When this is done electronically (and believe us, editors do this a lot!), an editor applies a strikethrough attribute to the text. The need to do this in an XHTML document is, admittedly, rather rare. After all, many Web pages are static in nature and not designed to be edited after they are put up for display. It is for this reason that the strikethrough elements have been deprecated.

More than one inline element can affect strikethrough text: `<s>` and `<strike>`. Each creates exactly the same effect, as you can see in the next example.

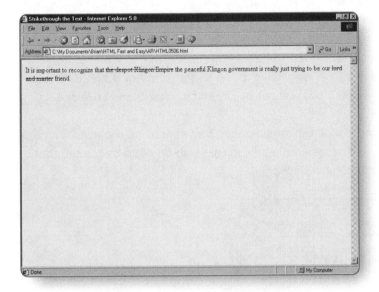

```
<p>
It is important to recognize
that <s>the despot Klingon
Empire</s> the peaceful
Klingon government is really
just trying to be our
<strike>lord and
master</strike> friend.
</p>
```

BROWSER
BROWSER

Because you have a choice, you should use the `<strike>` element instead of the `<s>` element. Older versions of Netscape support `<strike>` but not `<s>`. Your odds of creating an incorrect display are therefore lower if you use `<strike>`.

If you use either of these elements to denote editorial comments, you should shift to the phrasal element equivalent, which is `<del>`. It is also recommended you use CSS methodology to create the strikethrough effect instead of these deprecated elements.

Using Monospaced Fonts

When you (or your ancestors) used that typewriter, you were usually setting text on the page that was in a fixed-width font. This means that there is exactly the same spacing between every letter. If you look at this paragraph, you will see that there are variations in the spacing between letters, which saves a lot of space on the page.

Typewriters are mostly gone now, but their legacy remains. Fixed-width text, also known as monospaced text, has a lot of use in Web pages. Because of its uniform spacing, it is ideal for displaying programming code. Programmers use text alignment to help them follow program structure and flow, which is most easily accomplished by using a monospaced font.

The inline element originally designed to handle this task is the `<tt>` element ("tt" stands for teletype text). We say "originally" because this element is one of those deprecated ones that are being phased out by phrasal elements and style sheets.

There are very few instances where a monospaced font cannot be replaced with the logical elements `<code>`, `<samp>`, or `<kbd>`. Still, in case you do need to use the font without any special meaning, here's how:

```
<p>
My old IBM Selectric was good
for writing those double-
spaced <tt>typewritten
reports</tt> in high school.
</p>
```

As you can see in the example, you are not applying an attribute to the current font in your document. The `<tt>` element actually changes the font to a new font. This is an important distinction.

Although a new font is displayed, you can apply any of the other inline elements in combination with `<tt>`, just as you can combine them with each other. So, you can create unique fonts with simple tools.

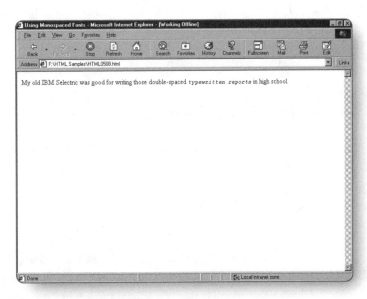

```
<p>
My old IBM Selectric was good
for writing those double-
spaced <i><tt>typewritten
reports</tt></i> in high
school.
</p>
```

Now that you have completed a survey of the inline attribute elements, it's time to explore the class of inline elements that controls how big of an impact your text will make. And we mean big.

Sizing Up Your Text

When Neil Armstrong first walked on the moon in 1969, journalists around the world went nuts. On television, Walter Cronkite actually welled up with emotion. Print journalists extolled in their various publications about the triumph of humankind over what was once an insurmountable goal. Newspapers proclaimed in bold 12-point type "Man Walks On Moon!" Whoops, that's not right. Twelve-point type? That's about the size of the text you're reading now.

No editor in his or her right mind would announce one of the most significant events in human history in small type. We all know this, because we all know that to get someone's attention, you have to make things stand out. In a newspaper, that means big type. Ninety-six-point big, at least.

In XHTML, whether the text needs to be huge or really small, you can adjust the size using three sets of elements. In the next sections, we examine the methodologies of each set.

The Font Foundation

When the <font> element was first introduced into the XHTML standard by Netscape, there was much rejoicing. It could handle so many aspects of text: color, typeface, and, yes, size. Like most innovative technologies, this element was soon marked for deprecation by the W3C.

The simple truth was that the <font> element was not the honeymoon people thought it would be. Ironically, it was the browsers' fault. Because of the ability of the user of a browser to set the color and font aspects of any given page, there were too many instances where the <font> element would cause confusion.

The attribute used for determining font size is, well, size. No one ever accused XHTML of being original. What is not obvious, though, are the types of sizing the <font> element can perform. Essentially, size can control text size in two ways: through absolute and relative sizing.

Absolute sizing uses the <font> element to assign one of seven sizes to the text contained with the element. By default, the <font> element has a default size of 3, so when you use that value on a page, you won't see a difference.

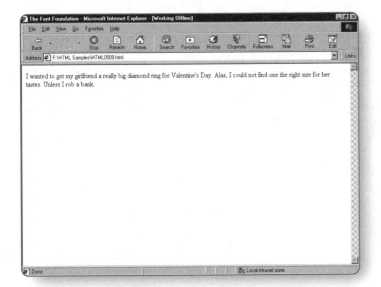

```
<p>
I wanted to get my girlfriend
a really <font
size="3">big</font> diamond
ring for Valentine's Day.
Alas, I could not find one the
right size for her tastes.
Unless I rob a bank.
</p>
```

If you adjust the absolute `size` value to a larger number, you will see a change in the text.

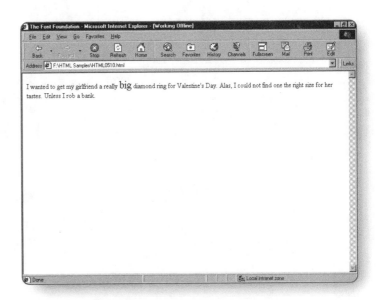

```
<p>
I wanted to get my girlfriend
a really <font
size="5">big</font> diamond
ring for Valentine's Day.
Alas, I could not find one
the right size for her
tastes. Unless I rob a bank.
</p>
```

The values of absolute size range from 1 to 7. The largest value is pretty big, as you can see in the next example.

```
<p>
I wanted to get my girlfriend
a really <font
size="7">big</font> diamond
ring for Valentine's Day.
Alas, I could not find one
the right size for her
tastes. Unless I rob a bank.
</p>
```

Because it breaks up the text dramatically, you should use large absolute sizes sparingly. The same holds true for reversing the process with size values less than 3.

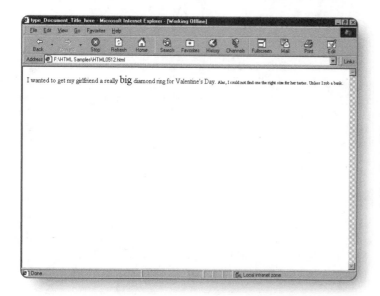

```
<p>
I wanted to get my girlfriend
a really <font
size="5">big</font> diamond
ring for Valentine's Day.
<font size="1">Alas, I could
not find one the right size
for her tastes. Unless I rob a
bank.</font>
</p>
```

Using relative size values is a slightly better way of handling text sizing. By using positive or negative size values, you can actually adjust the text based on the size of the text around it. For instance, if the default text size on the page is set at 3, a `size` value of `<font size="-2">` would display the contained text at an absolute size of 1. A value of +1 would set the text at an absolute value of 4. Using relative values, we can achieve the same effect as in the previous example:

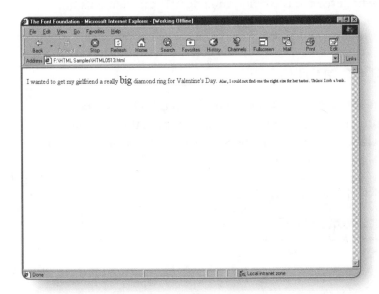

```
<p>
I wanted to get my girlfriend
a really <font
size="+2">big</font> diamond
ring for Valentine's Day.
<font size="-2">Alas, I could
not find one the right size
for her tastes. Unless I rob a
bank.</font>
</p>
```

There is, however, a catch to using relative sizes. If, for instance, the user of a browser has set his or her default text to be very large (perhaps he or she is near-sighted), adjusting the relative size of text passages can have disastrous results.

```
<p>
I wanted to get my girlfriend
a really <font
size="+2">big</font> diamond
ring for Valentine's Day.
<font size="-2">Alas, I could
not find one the right size
for her tastes. Unless I rob
a bank.</font>
</p>
```

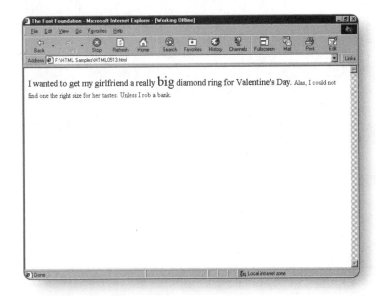

Given all of this trouble, is the `<font>` element ever appropriate for size? Using absolute values for the `size` attribute (`<font size=1>`, for example) is generally not a good idea. Relative values of `size`, such as `<font size="+1">` and `<font size="-1">`, usually work no matter what browser is reading the page. These elements are redundant, however, with the XHTML elements `<big>` and `<small>`.

Sizing Text, Big or Small

If you just want to size text to convey simple emphasis, you should use the more mild-mannered `<big>` and `<small>` elements. The effect of using these elements is the same as using the relative `size` values in the `<font>` element of "+1" and "-1", respectively. This can be seen in the following examples.

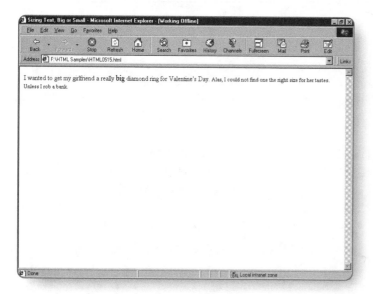

```
<p>
I wanted to get my girlfriend
a really <font
size="+1">big</font> diamond
ring for Valentine's Day.
<font size="-1">Alas, I could
not find one the right size
for her tastes. Unless I rob a
bank.</font>
</p>
```

You can use the `<big>` and `<small>` elements to achieve the same effect.

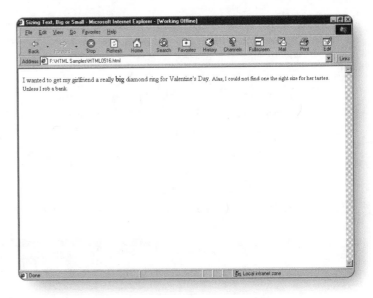

```
<p>
I wanted to get my girlfriend
a really <big>big</big>
diamond ring for Valentine's
Day. <small>Alas, I could not
find one the right size for
her tastes. Unless I rob a
bank.</small>
</p>
```

If this seems like six of one and a half-dozen of another, you would be right—except for the fact that the `<font>` element is deprecated and will not be as widely supported in the future. We recommend using the `<big>` and `<small>` elements for a more subtle approach and style sheets (if possible) for more sweeping size changes.

Super- and Subscripting

The English language, as any non-native speaker will tell you, is weird. Come on, they'll say, 25 definitions of the word "run"? Are you serious?

Another little quirk shows up in our writing when we use ordinal terms. Ordinal terms are words like first, second, third, and so on. In English, we sometimes shorten these terms to 1st, 2nd, and 3rd. Kooky. To create these shorthand ordinals, we need to use a typesetting device known as a superscript.

Many of you will recognize superscripts and their positional opposites, subscripts. Super- and subscripts are a part of "normal" literary works, too, not just math. Footnotes and endnotes are often denoted with superscripts.

The element responsible for adding superscripts to text is <sup>, and the subscript element is <sub>. Neither of these elements is deprecated, and both are solid components of XHTML. This is primarily because no phrasal equivalent exists for these elements. Superscripts and subscripts are pure presentation.

As you might expect, using the elements is not difficult. Just be sure you keep them straight—you can confuse these elements pretty easily.

```
<p>
Mortgage payments to the Bank
of the Internet must be made
before the 10<sup>th</sup> of
each month.
</p>
```

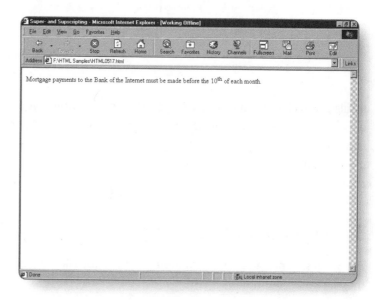

Likewise, the subscript element is a piece of cake.

```
<p>
Ozone is made up of the
O<sub>3</sub> molecule, which
is not breathable by us
O<sub>2</sub>-breathing
humans.
</p>
```

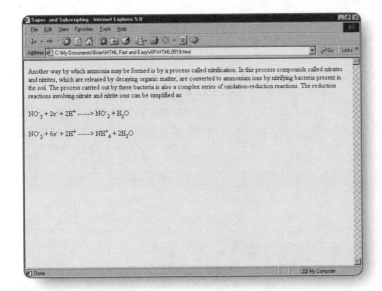

You can also use superscripts and subscripts simultaneously, which is handy when describing chemical reactions.

```
<p>
Another way by which ammonia may be formed is by a process called
nitrification. In this process compounds called nitrates and nitrites, which
are released by decaying organic matter, are converted to ammonium ions by
nitrifying bacteria present in the soil. The process carried out by these
bacteria is also a complex series of oxidation-reduction reactions. The
reduction reactions involving nitrate and nitrite ions can be simplified as:
</p>
```

```
<p>
NO<sup>-</sup><sub>3</sub> + 2e<sup>-</sup> + 2H<sup>+</sup> -----> NO<sup>-
</sup><sub>2</sub> + H<sub>2</sub>O
</p>
<p>
NO<sup>-</sup><sub>2</sub> + 6e<sup>-</sup> + 2H<sup>+</sup> ----->
NH<sup>+</sup><sub>4</sub> + 2H<sub>2</sub>O
</p>
```

Breaking Up Is Not Hard to Do

We have one final inline element to discuss —the line-break element <br>. As the name implies, <br> has one primary task: to break a current line of text at a particular point. Unlike the <p> element, <br> accomplishes this without starting a new paragraph or other block-level element.

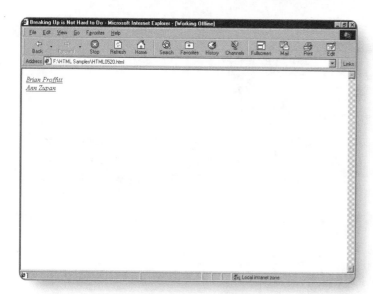

For example, line breaks are particularly useful when you want to create more than one line in the <address> element:

```
<address>
<a href = "mailto:bkproffitt@home.com">Brian Proffitt</a><br />
<a href = "mailto:annz@indy.net">Ann Zupan</a>
</address>
```

The <br> element is not a container tag, so in HTML there is no need for an end tag. In XHTML, the absolute need for an end tag means that an end slash must be inserted in every appearance of <br>.

The <br> element has one attribute: clear. The purpose of the clear attribute is to break block text and position it around floating elements on a Web page, such as an image or a table. Clear has three values: left, right, and all. If text is wrapping around an image, a line break with the clear="left" attribute will break the text to the next available left margin of the page. This would perhaps be made more clear by an illustration:

```
<h1>Cattleya Orchid</h1>
<p>
<img src="../corsageorchid.jpg" align="left">Cattleya Orchids are large,
flamboyant flowers each composed of 3 sepals, 2 large side petals and a
central flared tip.
<br clear="left" />
Flowers vary in size from 3-6 inches across and are available in the colors of
white, yellow and shades of lavender or pink and often have a contrasting
colored lip and throat. Cattleyas represent the ultimate corsage and wedding
orchid. Vase life averages 4-5 days when kept cool and sprayed with water and
are available year round with peak production during April and May.
</p>
```

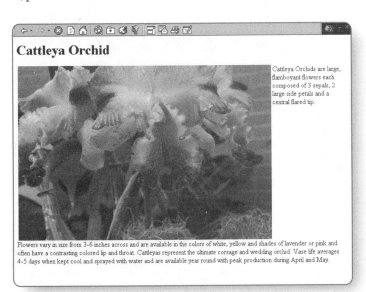

The <br> element has not been placed on the deprecated list, but style sheets duplicate many of its capabilities, so you will need to balance its usage accordingly.

CAUTION

Try not to use <br> to make aesthetic changes to text blocks and tables. Remember, different browsers will view your page in different font sizes, so any fancy alignments you try to make will be eliminated.

Conclusion

Inline elements can give you, the Web page author, precise control over everything in your Web page, even individual characters. But, like anything so detail-oriented, inline elements can be a big pain in the neck if they are overused. Use them in moderation.

Judicious use of inline elements is especially important as XHTML moves toward its context-oriented origins. As documents become increasingly content-oriented rather than presentation-oriented, the phrasal elements of XHTML will become more widely used. In the next chapter, "Phrasing the Right Element," we examine these phrasal elements to see just how they are an improvement over many of the deprecated inline elements.

6

Phrasing the Right Element

XHTML enables you to assign elements based on meaning or structure and then unify every appearance of the element in the document. In this manner, you can quickly make design changes to the document based on the type of phrase.

In this chapter, you'll learn how to do the following:

- Assign emphasis to text phrases
- Manage abbreviations and acronyms
- Mark up citations and quotes
- Illustrate code and mathematical variables

When a politician says something and then wants to retract it, he or she will likely say the statement was taken out of context. As we have seen in recent years in the United States, sometimes that works ("I did not have…"), and sometimes it doesn't ("Read my lips…"). Context is always a slippery thing in the political arena.

In an XHTML document, context is a bit more quantifiable. Within a document, certain phrases of the document have special meaning. To help illustrate this meaning, often the phrase is given a special presentation style. Emphasized phrases are presented in italic or bold form, for instance.

Delivering Strong Emphasis

Mothers have a way of emphasizing your name in such a way that you know you're going to get it. This is a subtle trick but very effective. And if they use your middle name as well, you're doomed.

Emphasis conveys meaning in the English language. We use it every day. Placing a particular amount of stress on a word or phrase can change the whole tone of a sentence. In writing, we display emphasis by either applying italics or bold to the text.

As you read in Chapter 5, "Touching Up Text," applying either of these effects is easy in XHTML, so why do it again with different elements?

To answer this question, examine the following example. Here is a passage of text with italic text used both for emphasis and to indicate the title of a book.

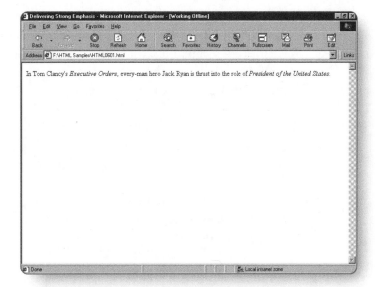

```
<p>
In Tom Clancy's <i>Executive
Orders</i>, every-man hero
Jack Ryan is thrust into the
role of <i>President of the
United States</i>.
</p>
```

Simple enough. Suppose, however, you decide that you want to display emphatic text as bold italic? Using this example, you would have to add the <b> element around every <i> element. Most search and replace tools in text editors and XHTML editors can handle this, leaving you with this:

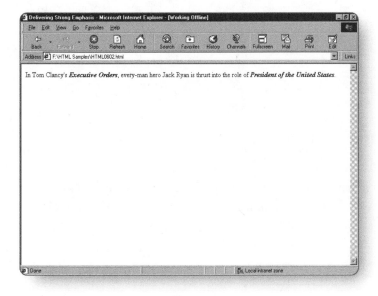

```
<p>
In Tom Clancy's
<b><i>Executive Orders</i>
</b>, every-man hero Jack Ryan
is thrust into the role of
<b><i>President of the United
States</i></b>.
</p>
```

But that's not right, is it? The title of the book is not emphatic in nature, so it should not be in bold italic type. This means you as the author will have to select which passages of text are truly being emphasized, which are just italic for presentation value, and then go through the entire document and make the necessary changes. That's the hard way.

Instead, you can assign emphasis elements to the emphatic phrases in the beginning of the process. Then you can use style-sheet technology to alter the appearance of text contained within just the emphasis elements.

If you wanted to keep the italic look to your emphatic text, you could use the `<em>` element, which by default displays its contents as italic text. Now the example would look like this:

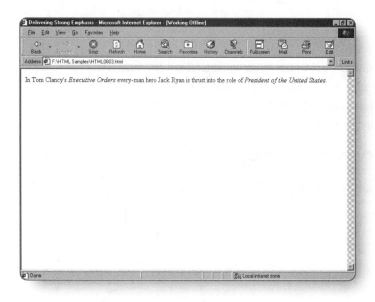

```
<p>
In Tom Clancy's <i>Executive
Orders</i> every-man hero Jack
Ryan is thrust into the role
of <em>President of the United
States</em>.
</p>
```

And, without giving too much away before Chapter 15, "Designing with Style (Sheets)," you can adjust the appearance of just your emphatic text with a single style-sheet command.

```
<html>
  <head>
    <title>Bold Italic Emphasis</title>
    <style type="text/css">
        em {font-style: italic, bold}
    </style>
  </head>
  <body>
<p>
In Tom Clancy's <i>Executive Orders</i> every-man hero Jack Ryan is thrust into the role
of <em>President of the United States</em>.
</p>
  </body>
</html>
```

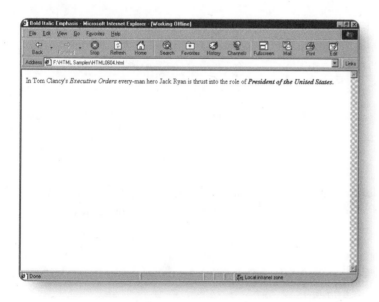

And *that* (we emphasize) is the greatest benefit of using phrasal elements to mark up your text!

The other emphatic element is <strong>. Like <em>, it should be used only around text you want to emphasize—*not* around characters you just want to make bold, which is the default display style for <strong>.

A good example of this type of usage is demonstrated in the following example.

```
<p>
Vector <b>x<sub>2</sub></b>
is <strong>perpendicular
</strong> to vector
<b>x<sub>1</sub></b>
</p>
```

You can clearly see the benefits of using phrasal elements. With just a little up-front work, you will give yourself much greater control over the presentation of your document.

There are, of course, additional phrasal elements in the XHTML lexicon, not just the ones used for emphasis. These are examined in the remainder of this chapter.

Using Other Phrasal Tags

Phrasal elements are XHTML's best innovation to date, more than making up for the stupid `<blink>` element in early versions of HTML that burned retinas by incessantly flashing text. When you use phrasal or logical elements, your documents will exhibit a much stronger structure based on context—which is what XHTML and its parent language XML are all about.

Marking Abbreviations and Acronyms

When printing with ink and presses in the olden days, it was often necessary to save ink by using fewer letters on the page. Saving ink is not such a big deal anymore, but we have gotten into the habit of abbreviating as many words as we can. If we're not abbreviating, we're applying an acronym. Double Income No Kid couples become DINKs. By the way becomes BTW. The United Nations Children's Fund becomes UNICEF, a word unto itself.

When you have a number of acronyms or abbreviations in your document, it is a good idea to enclose them within either the `<acronym>` or `<abbr>` elements.

Each of these elements has a single `title` attribute. The value of the `title` attribute is full presentation of the abbreviated word or the acronym's term, as you can see in the following example.

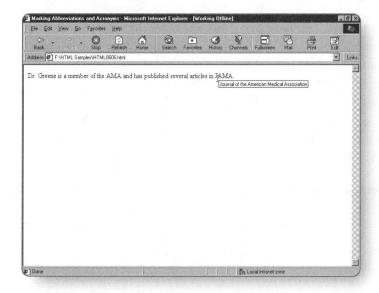

```
<p>
<abbr
title="Doctor">Dr.</abbr>
Greene is a member of the
<acronym title = "American
Medical Association">AMA
</acronym> and has published
several articles in <acronym
title = "Journal of the
American Medical Association">
JAMA</acronym>.
</p>
```

In the visual display, you can see that the effect of these elements is subtle. Notice that when the cursor is held over the JAMA abbreviation, for example, the full name of the publication appears as a pop-up tool tip. It is the value of the `title` attribute that is displayed.

Also, these elements have additional value. You may be scoffing at this, thinking that this is surely overkill. But it's not, and we'll tell you why.

First, using phrasal elements around the appropriate content is always good. If you wanted to apply a special format to just the acronyms in your Web page, you could just globally change the attributes of the `<acronym>` elements.

Second, it is important to recall that the World Wide Web has the word "World" in it—the first word, in fact. Many non-English speakers hit English-language Web pages. They may be using translation programs to read them. Marking up even seemingly simple abbreviations like Dr. and Mr. are a tremendous help to those translation programs. This type of markup also helps Internet search engines find your stuff. If someone types Journal of the American Medical Association into a search engine, the previous page will be located, even if the displayed text only says JAMA.

Defining Phrases

In some publications, particularly technical ones, the first time a certain technical term appears within a defining phrase, it is presented in a special way to say "Hey, look at me, I'm a special word!" That special word is usually defined away from the main body of the text as well, either in a sidebar or a glossary.

When constructing a Web page, you can use the <dfn> element to mark such defined terms. The <dfn> element has two jobs: marking defined words for later style changes and displaying the term in the default italic style.

```
<p>
XHTML is an
<dfn>extensible</dfn> markup
language because it allows for
the inclusion of new elements,
unlike HTML, which has a fixed
set of elements.
</p>
```

This may not seem like a big deal, especially to look at. But remember that you are trying to keep things organized by content, not just presentation.

Netscape Navigator does not support the `<dfn>` element. If you know this browser will view your pages, you might want to use presentational elements (such as `<i>`) to achieve the `<dfn>` display in Navigator.

Creating Editing Marks

When creating Web documents, there may be an instance or two where the content needs to be changed and displayed for others to see. As you learned in Chapter 5, `<s>` and `<strike>` are good presentational elements for creating edit marks in XHTML. Contextually, there is a better solution: the `<ins>` and `<del>` elements.

When you use the `<del>` element, you will see a strikethrough font effect on-screen.

```
<p>
To be or not to be, that is
the <del>answer</del>.
</p>
```

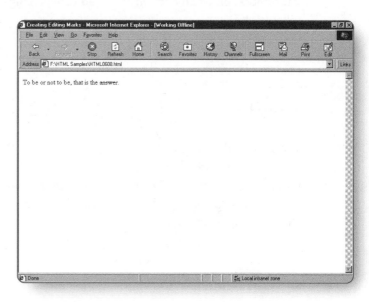

On many occasions you will need to use the `<ins>` element in tandem with `<del>`.

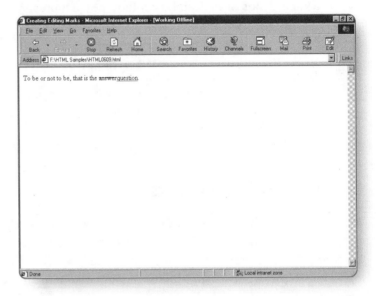

```
<p>
To be or not to be, that is
the <del>answer</del>
<ins>question</ins>.
</p>
```

Both of these elements have three attributes that enable you to keep additional information on when and why such editorial changes were made. They are as follows:

- `cite`

- `title`

- `datetime`

The `cite` attribute has a URL value, which can be the reference reason why the change was made. The `title` attribute has a text value that lets the author add a reason for the change. The `datetime` attribute is what it sounds like: the date and time the change was made. Used together, they convey a lot of information, as shown in the next example.

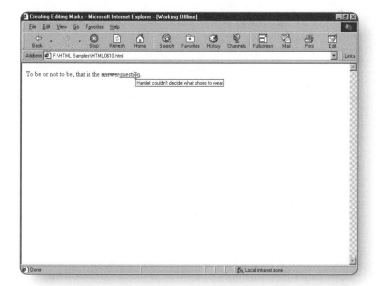

```
<p>
To be or not to be, that is
the <del cite="http://www.
shakespeare.com/hamlet/
famousquotes.html" title="Just
plain wrong" datetime="2000-
02-10t20:01:05-06:00">answer
</del><ins cite="http://www.
shakespeare.com/hamlet/
famousquotes.html" title=
"Hamlet couldn't decide what
shoes to wear" datetime="2000-
02-10t20:01:17-06:00">
question</ins>.
</p>
```

As you can see in the figure, only the `title` information appears on the actual Web page. For strict control over the editing of your pages, however, the additional `cite` information is kind of nice to have around.

BROWSER vs BROWSER

Netscape Navigator does not support the `<ins>` or `<del>` elements. If you know this browser will view your pages, you might want to use presentational elements (such as `<s>` and `<strike>`) to achieve the same effect in Navigator.

Adding Citations and Quotations

When you reference another publication in your document, it is known as a citation. Citations are usually displayed in the `<cite>` element as italic, but you can change this later if you want to by using style sheets. Revising an earlier example results in the example on the following page.

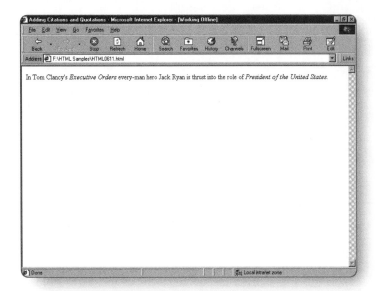

```
<p>
In Tom Clancy's <cite>
Executive Orders</cite> every-
man hero Jack Ryan is thrust
into the role of <em>President
of the United States</em>.
</p>
```

Nothing too tricky here. The `<cite>` element has no unique attributes, so it is a simple, pure phrasal element.

In Chapter 4, "Block Tags and You," we discussed the use of the `<blockquote>` element in XHTML. `<blockquote>`, however, sets quotations aside in their own separate element, which you may not always want. For inline quotations, use the `<q>` element like this:

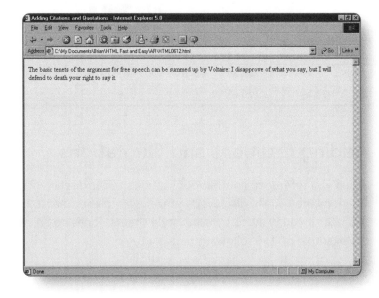

```
<p>
The basic tenets of the
argument for free speech can
be summed up by Voltaire:
<q>I disapprove of what you
say, but I will defend to
death your right to say
it.</q>
</p>
```

Note that the display for the `<q>` element's content does not vary from the text surrounding it. Like other phrasal elements, `<q>` is less concerned with the look of the text than its meaning.

`<q>` does have a single attribute, `cite`. The `cite` attribute, like the same attribute in `<ins>`, holds the value of a URL that contains the quoted material:

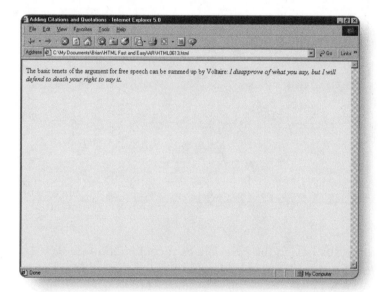

```
<p>
The basic tenets of the
argument for free speech can
be summed up by Voltaire: <q
cite="http://www.freedom.net">
I disapprove of what you say,
but I will defend to death
your right to say it.</q>
</p>
```

Displaying Code

One of the most dynamic learning tools in the world today is, of course, the Internet. Every day, millions of people get online not to buy kitschy things from eBay, but to learn something. That is, after all, the reason the Internet was originally created.

Discovering and sharing new coding methods is a major goal for dedicated Internet programmers. You can display code in XHTML documents by using `<code>`, a phrasal element that is well suited to the task.

When using `<code>`, text contained within the element is shown in a monospaced font, which is ideal for displaying code. There is, however, a hitch with using `<code>`. Unless `<code>` is contained by the `<pre>` element, any multiple spaces within the element are compressed to a single space. This is particularly bothersome, especially when trying to read such code.

```
<p>
The code needed to shake your
screen should read:
<code>
function shake(n) {
if (self.moveBy) {
for (i = 10; i > 0; i--) {
for (j = n; j > 0; j--) {
self.moveBy(0,i);
self.moveBy(i,0);
self.moveBy(0,-i);
self.moveBy(-i,0);
        }
      }
   }
}
</code>
</p>
```

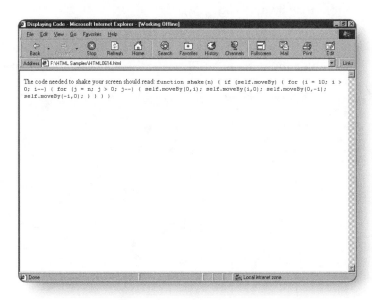

You can circumvent this effect by having the `<pre>` element contain the `<code>` element, which would "lock" multiple spaces in place.

```
<p>
The code needed to shake your
screen should read:
</p>
<pre>
<code>
function shake(n) {
if (self.moveBy) {
for (i = 10; i > 0; i--) {
for (j = n; j > 0; j--) {
self.moveBy(0,i);
self.moveBy(i,0);
self.moveBy(0,-i);
self.moveBy(-i,0);
        }
      }
   }
}
</code>
</pre>
```

Despite this quirk, using the <code> element will, in the long run, help you style your document.

Algebraic Variables in XHTML

When you write about programs and mathematics, sooner or later variables are bound to come up. Variables are usually displayed in italics, but (big surprise) XHTML has a phrasal element, <var>, to handle them too.

```
<p>
The Pythagorean Theorem states
that in a right triangle, the
sum of the square of the
adjacent side and square of
the opposite side is equal to
the square of the hypotenuse.
In other words,
<var>a</var><sup>2</sup> +
<var>b</var><sup>2</sup> =
<var>c</var><sup>2</sup>
</p>
```

Because of variables' unique nature, we strongly advise you to use the <var> element when you display variables. Variables, more so than most of the other phrases of text in a document, are easy to lose in the shuffle if they are not marked properly.

Conclusion

This concludes Part I. In Part II, "Paper and Pencil," Chapter 7, "Putting the Hyper in Hypertext," we'll begin to examine more advanced features of XHTML, including the most unique device of the entire markup language: links to other pages.

PART II

Paper and Pencil

7

Putting the Hyper in Hypertext

Now that you have plowed through the basic concepts of XHTML elements, it's time to start using the more advanced capabilities of XHTML. Specifically, let's examine what puts the "H" and the "T" in XHTML: the concept of hypertext.

In this chapter, you'll learn how to do the following:

- Use both absolute and relative hyperlinks
- Link to other sections of the same Web page
- Use the `<base>` element to improve relative links
- Link to other documents (not just English Web pages)

Hypertext is not as new as you might think. As early as July 1945, Vannevar Bush published an article in *Atlantic Monthly* about the future of publications entitled "As We May Think." His main premise was that since people rarely think in truly linear fashion, our vast storehouse of knowledge (which was starting its exponential skyrocket in the 1940s) would eventually have to reflect this nonlinear nature. He did not call this idea hypertext, nor did he ever imagine the existence of the World Wide Web. His ideas did include a sort of proto-Web-like thingamajig called the memex, however. Many of his fellow computer scientists were intrigued by this memex idea, but no one could come up with a practical application of the theory for 20 years.

In 1965, a man named Ted Nelson expanded on Bush's ideas and the new computer-aided instruction technology that was starting to come into existence. Computer-aided instruction navigated students through topics in a way that appealed to Nelson, who created an early form of a new technology called hypertext.

If someone ever asks you what hypertext is (and hopefully it will be Regis Philbin), you can answer with the short definition: a form of publication that allows interconnected links between topical documents, which facilitates nonlinear exploration of the subject matter.

And that would be your final answer.

Anchors Aweigh!

Think of an anchor. A big, heavy, metal thing designed to do one thing and do it well: hold a ship in place. Anchors are not something you would associate with a fast, nimble, agile thing also designed to do one thing: get someone on the way to somewhere else.

And yet, despite the paradoxical descriptions, it is true that in the realm of XHTML, the element that creates a hypertext link is called the anchor element, or <a> for short.

The <a> element is unique among all other XHTML elements. It alone has the capability to take the user to another Web page, be it located on the same Web site or in a computer in eastern Siberia. It does not matter where the link goes, as long as you have the right address.

You can create three kinds of hyperlinks with <a>. These are as follows:

- Absolute links
- Relative links
- In-text links

To assist you in building these myriad link types, <a> has quite a few attributes associated with it. In the next three sections, we examine these attributes to see how they can work for you.

Building Absolute Links

The most common type of link you can create with <a> is the absolute link. An absolute link is a hypertext connection that links directly to a fully addressed target document. It is easy to make an absolute link using the primary <a> attribute href, which stands for hypertext reference. The value of this attribute is always the URL of the document to which you want to link.

Say, for example, you have text about a topic and want to link a passage of that text to a related Web page.

```
<p>
On July 4, 1776, the Second Continental Congress, meeting in Philadelphia in
the Pennsylvania State House (now Independence Hall), approved the Declaration
of Independence. Its purpose was to set forth the principles upon which the
Congress had acted two days earlier when it voted in favor of Richard Henry
Lee's motion to declare the freedom and independence of the 13 American
colonies from England. The Declaration was designed to influence public
opinion and gain support both among the new states and abroad -- especially in
France, from which the new "United States" sought military assistance.
</p>
```

In this paragraph, you would like the reader to link to the actual text of the Declaration of Independence. The most logical place to have this link would be around the words "Declaration of Independence." So, you would have the `<a>` element enclose that passage.

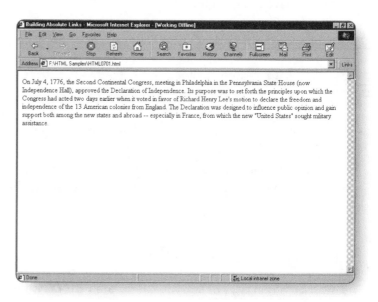

```
<p>
On July 4, 1776, the Second Continental Congress, meeting in Philadelphia in
the Pennsylvania State House (now Independence Hall), approved the
<a>Declaration of Independence</a>. Its purpose was to set forth the
principles upon which the Congress had acted two days earlier when it voted in
favor of Richard Henry Lee's motion to declare the freedom and independence of
the 13 American colonies from England. The Declaration was designed to
influence public opinion and gain support both among the new states and abroad
-- especially in France, from which the new "United States" sought military
assistance.
</p>
```

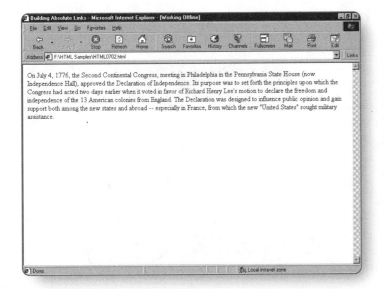

Nothing happened, right? That is because the <a> element must always have either the href or the name attribute in place for it to perform completely. You know the URL of a great page that displays the text of the Declaration, so you can use that as the href value.

```
<p>
On July 4, 1776, the Second Continental Congress, meeting in Philadelphia in the
Pennsylvania State House (now Independence Hall), approved the <a href =
"http://lcweb2.loc.gov/const/declar.html">Declaration of Independence</a>. Its purpose
was to set forth the principles upon which the Congress had acted two days earlier when
it voted in favor of Richard Henry Lee's motion to declare the freedom and independence
of the 13 American colonies from England. The Declaration was designed to influence
public opinion and gain support both among the new states and abroad -- especially in
France, from which the new "United States" sought military assistance.
</p>
```

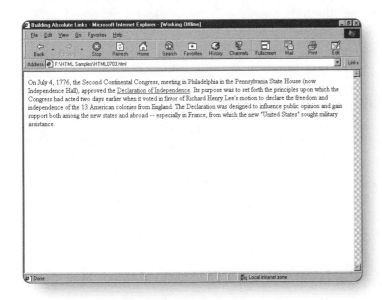

Now you'll notice the presence of an underline beneath the passage. If you were to click on the link, you would be taken to the appropriate page.

The amount of information in the value of `href` determines whether the link is absolute or relative. In an absolute link, the information is a full URL—even if the page is on the same Web site. The link used in the previous example is certainly an example of an absolute link.

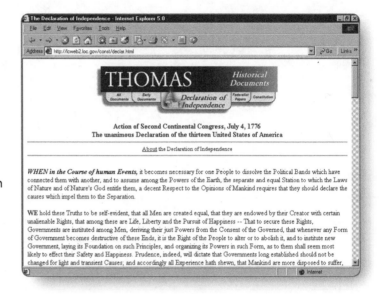

Typing in all of that information can be a bit tedious, though—particularly if the referenced Web page is actually on your Web site. That's where the relative link type comes in.

Building Relative Links

Everything is relative, Einstein said. He wasn't talking about your aunts and uncles but rather the belief that everything that goes on in the universe is observed through a particular frame of reference. Your own frame of reference decides how you view the universe relative to you. For instance, you are likely sitting still reading this book, hardly moving.

Nothing could be further from the truth. The Earth is revolving around you and orbiting that nice yellow star 93 million miles or so away. The yellow star, though, is careening through space at about 60 miles per second while this whole arm of the

Milky Way galaxy is whipped around the galactic center in an orbit of its own. Hope you don't get motion sickness.

The reason we're not all dizzy from this constant motion is that within our frame of reference (standing on the surface of the Earth), we are currently stationary *relative* to everything else in that same reference frame.

This rather dizzying concept can be applied to the World Wide Web as well. If another Web page is in the same frame of reference as the linking page (in other words, on the same Web site server), you can address the link with a URL relative to the original page. Hence the term relative link.

To understand this better, you have to wrap your brain around the very concept of the Web. Everything on the World Wide Web is just a bunch of files sitting in ordinary file directories and folders, just like the files on your PC. Everything. The files on the Web, however, are more accessible because they are sitting on special machines that let just about anyone on the planet read them and because they are written in a common, easy-to-access file format (HTML). So when we link to another Web page, we are really providing instructions to a reader's browser to open *this* file in *this* directory on *that* server.

If, for instance, the descriptive text we have been using were on the same Web site as the Declaration page and in the same file directory, the link would be very simple:

```
<p>
On July 4, 1776, the Second Continental Congress, meeting in Philadelphia in
the Pennsylvania State House (now Independence Hall), approved the <a href =
"declar.html">Declaration of Independence</a>. Its purpose was to set forth
the principles upon which the Congress had acted two days earlier when it
voted in favor of Richard Henry Lee's motion to declare the freedom and
independence of the 13 American colonies from England. The Declaration was
designed to influence public opinion and gain support both among the new
states and abroad -- especially in France, from which the new "United States"
sought military assistance.
</p>
```

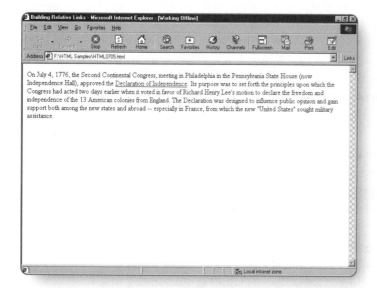

Visually, there is no difference. Unless the visitors to your site are paying attention to the links displayed in the status bar of the browser, they won't know if the file is in another country or sitting on the same server.

If the destination file is on another directory in the same Web server, you can still use relative links. You just need to provide a little more information in the <a> element. If the desired file were in a subdirectory of the const directory in which the file is sitting, the link would be structured in this manner:

```
<p>
On July 4, 1776, the Second Continental Congress, meeting in Philadelphia in
the Pennsylvania State House (now Independence Hall), approved the <a href =
"/congress/declar.html">Declaration of Independence</a>. Its purpose was to
set forth the principles upon which the Congress had acted two days earlier
when it voted in favor of Richard Henry Lee's motion to declare the freedom
and independence of the 13 American colonies from England. The Declaration was
designed to influence public opinion and gain support both among the new
states and abroad -- especially in France, from which the new "United States"
sought military assistance.
</p>
```

Now the link is pointing directly to the file in the subdirectory. It can be even more complicated should you wish it. If the file were in a directory in a completely different section of the directory tree, all you'd have to do is use the standard URL symbols to create the right href value.

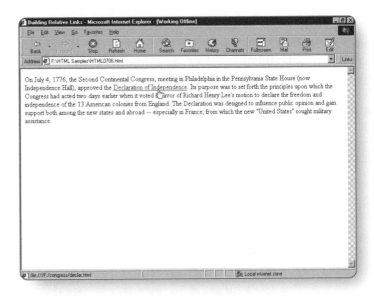

```
<p>
On July 4, 1776, the Second Continental Congress, meeting in Philadelphia in the
Pennsylvania State House (now Independence Hall), approved the <a href =
"../../documents/contcongress/declar.html">Declaration of Independence</a>. Its purpose
was to set forth the principles upon which the Congress had acted two days earlier when
it voted in favor of Richard Henry Lee's motion to declare the freedom and independence
of the 13 American colonies from England. The Declaration was designed to influence
public opinion and gain support both among the new states and abroad -- especially in
France, from which the new "United States" sought military assistance.
</p>
```

Again, outwardly, nothing is changed for the reader. This link directs the browser two directory levels up from where the current file sits and then down two other subdirectories to the declar.html file. At this point, you might be wondering if the full URL would have been faster to create. Probably so, but you should use relative links for another reason.

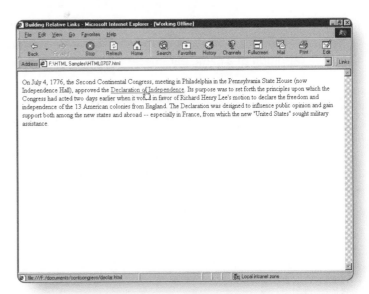

Whenever a Web site has to be moved to another location on the server or another server entirely, relative links can make the transition very easy. If you keep the same directory structure in your new location that was in the old, all of the relative links will function perfectly!

If you had only absolute links to same-server files in that situation, all of the links would have to change to reflect the files' new locations.

This is why we recommend the following guidelines when deciding what kind of link to use:

- Use absolute links when linking to any external server or Internet service.
- Use relative links to any files on your local server.

The next kind of link to use not only gets the right file, it also puts your readers in the exact spot on the page you want them to start reading.

Building In-Text Links

Unlike the other uses of the <a> element, linking to a specific location within a file is more than just creating a link to the destination page. You also need to create the link to "catch" the incoming reader.

When in-text links are built, they can be either absolute or relative in nature, using the same guidelines detailed in the previous sections. The major difference is the addition of a name parameter within the href value.

This parameter points the link directly to the correct spot on the destination page...provided there is an <a> element in that spot.

The U.S. Constitution is a fantastic document, but let's face it, it's big and a bit cumbersome to read. If your Web site were to point people to the beginning of articles and their sections of the Constitution, this could be a big help. So, first you need to create the name links:

```
<center><h1>THE CONSTITUTION OF THE UNITED STATES</h1></center>
<hr />
<p>
<font size="+3">W</font>e the people of the United States, in order to form a
more perfect union, establish justice, insure domestic tranquility, provide
for the common defense, promote the general welfare, and secure the blessings
of liberty to ourselves and our posterity, do ordain and establish this
Constitution for the United States of America.
</p>
<h3>Article I</h3>
<p>
Section 1. All legislative powers herein granted shall be vested in a Congress
of the United States, which shall consist of a Senate and House of
Representatives.
</p>
<p>
Section 2. The House of Representatives shall be composed of members chosen
every second year by the people of the several states, and the electors in
each state shall have the qualifications requisite for electors of the most
numerous branch of the state legislature
</p>
```

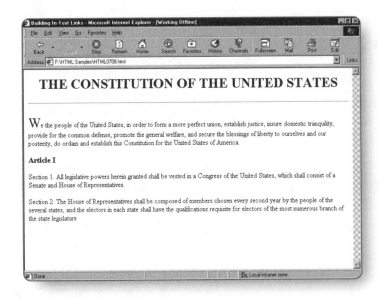

To create a name link, you need to use the name attribute of the <a> element. You do this by enclosing the passage of text you want readers to see first when they are connected to this page through your in-text links.

```
<center><h1>THE CONSTITUTION OF THE UNITED STATES</h1></center>
<hr />
<p>
<font size="+3">W</font>e the people of the United States, in order to form a
more perfect union, establish justice, insure domestic tranquility, provide
for the common defense, promote the general welfare, and secure the blessings
of liberty to ourselves and our posterity, do ordain and establish this
Constitution for the United States of America.
</p>
<a name = "a1"><h3>Article I</h3></a>
<p>
<a name = "a1s1">Section 1</a>. All legislative powers herein granted shall be
vested in a Congress of the United States, which shall consist of a Senate and
House of Representatives.
</p>
<p>
<a name = "a1s2">Section 2</a>. The House of Representatives shall be composed
of members chosen every second year by the people of the several states, and
the electors in each state shall have the qualifications requisite for
electors of the most numerous branch of the state legislature
</p>
```

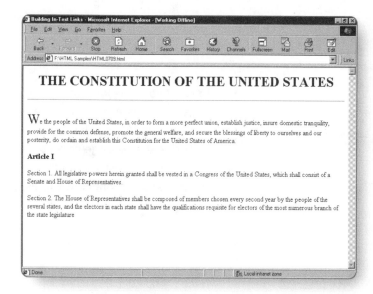

When you look at the figure representing this sample, you will likely notice the lack of underlining or colored text that normally denotes the presence of the <a> element. Those features are the properties of the href attribute. When the name attribute of <a> is used, the element is invisible to human readers. Browser software, however, can see it loud and clear.

Now it's time to build the links *to* this page:

```
<center><h1>THE CONSTITUTION OF THE UNITED STATES</h1></center>
<hr />
<h2>Article I</h2>
<p>
<b>Section 1.</b> The formation of Congress.
</p>
<p>
<b>Section 2.</b> The composition of the House of Representatives.
</p>
<p>
<b>Section 3.</b> The composition of the Senate.
</p>
```

Assuming the main Constitution file we are linking to is called const.html, the links to each of the articles and sections in that document would look like the following:

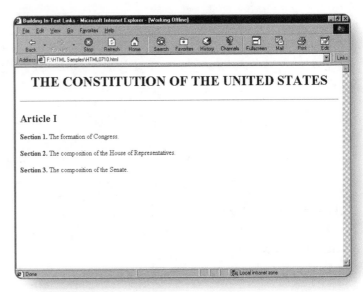

```
<center><h1>THE CONSTITUTION OF THE UNITED STATES</h1></center>
<hr />
<h2><a href = "const.html#a1">Article I</a></h2>
<p>
<b><a href = "const.html#a1s1">Section 1.</a></b> The formation of Congress.
</p>
<p>
<b><a href = "const.html#a1s2">Section 2. </a></b> The composition of the
House of Representatives.
</p>
<p>
<b><a href = "const.html#a1s3">Section 3. </a></b> The composition of the
Senate.
</p>
```

Now the links are visible in the document. The values of `href` still contain the file name of the destination file, now followed by a pound sign (#) and the appropriate value of the name links in that file.

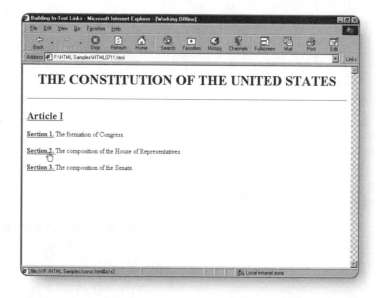

Clicking on the link for Section 2 of Article I, for instance, will result in this page display.

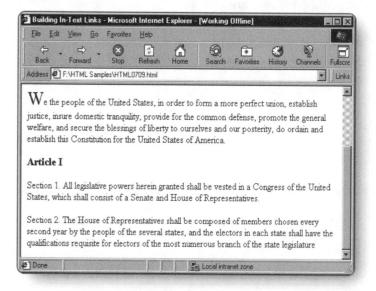

These links were relative links, but they could have just as easily been absolute. Using a full URL does not affect the name parameter one bit.

You can also link to other sections within the same document. If our handy index of Articles were at the top of the const.html document, we could still enable readers to jump to the specific articles.

```
<center><h1>THE CONSTITUTION OF THE UNITED STATES</h1></center>
<hr />
<h2><a href = "#a1">Article I</a></h2>
<p>
<b><a href = "#a1s1">Section 1.</a></b> The formation of Congress.
</p>
<p>
<b><a href = "#a1s2">Section 2. </a></b> The composition of the House of
Representatives.
</p>
<p>
<b><a href = "#a1s3">Section 3. </a></b> The composition of the Senate.
</p>
```

The href and name attributes are the majority of the <a> element functions. But, of course, there is more to it than just these basics, as you will learn in the next sections of this chapter.

TIP

If you are linking to an external page, check the source code for that page and see if that site's author used named links that you could use.

CAUTION

You must take care to avoid embedding an <a> element within another <a> element. This is particularly easy to do when using name links. If you need to place a name link at an already hyperlinked passage, just add the name attribute to the preexisting <a> element.

Creating Your Page's Hyperstructure

Not only can you create links to different sections of the same document, you can also design the underlying hypertext structure of your document. Doing this gives you excellent control over your pages and provides readers with nifty navigation tools as well.

Establishing a Base

As we mentioned before, relative links link to other documents in relation to the location of the current document. Most of the time, this is a straightforward process. The browser remembers the location of the open document and proceeds from there.

Sometimes, though, this might not work very well. A growing number of Web pages have multiple URLs to the same page. When Sun Microsystems bought Star Division in 1999 to acquire the latter's StarOffice product, Sun incorporated the old Star Division Web site into its own. If you type **http://www.stardivision.com** today, you will be instantly taken to the Sun site at **www.sun.com/staroffice**.

Other problems can occur when XHTML pages are e-mailed to people. A stand-alone XHTML file has no URL from which a browser can work.

It is possible in such a situation that any relative links off such pages might puzzle your browser. To make it very clear to incoming browsers where they are, use the `<base>` element.

The `<base>` element has two attributes: `href` and `target`. The latter is similar to the target attribute of `<a>`, which we will discuss in Chapter 11, "You've Been Framed."

When you want to use the `<base>` element, you must make sure it appears in the `<head>` element of your document. The `href` value is the exact URL of the current page. `<base>` has no closing tag, so be sure to use the shorthand closing tag modifier.

```html
<html>
<head>
<title>The U.S. Constitution</title>
<base href = "http://www.loc.gov/documents/conindex.html" />
</head>
<body>
<center><h1>THE CONSTITUTION OF THE UNITED STATES</h1></center>
<hr />
<h2><a href = "const.html#a1">Article I</a></h2>
<p>
<b><a href = "const.html#a1s1">Section 1.</a></b> The formation of Congress.
</p>
<p>
<b><a href = "const.html#a1s2">Section 2. </a></b> The composition of the
House of Representatives.
</p>
<p>
<b><a href = "const.html#a1s3">Section 3. </a></b> The composition of the
Senate.
</p>
</body>
</html>
```

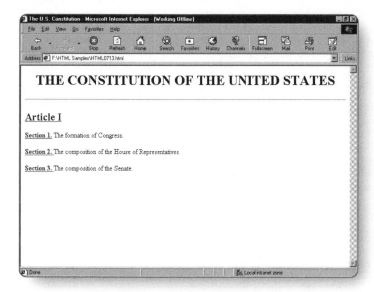

No major changes here, but your readers' browsers will be less confused, which is always a good thing.

Link with Tabs and Hot Keys

A more direct way of assisting your readers is to help them navigate within your Web page. There are ways of doing this without using direct hyperlinks, though the <a> element is still involved.

If your readers like using the Tab key to cycle through a software interface, they will love it if you apply the tabindex attribute to your links. In a nutshell, the tabindex attribute is a numeric value from 0 to 32767. The significance of this value is that it will set the tab stop for that link.

In this example, the tabindex attribute is used in conjunction with the name attribute:

```
<center><h1>THE CONSTITUTION OF THE UNITED STATES</h1></center>
<hr />
<p>
<font size="+3">W</font>e the people of the United States, in order to form a
more perfect union, establish justice, insure domestic tranquility, provide
for the common defense, promote the general welfare, and secure the blessings
of liberty to ourselves and our posterity, do ordain and establish this
Constitution for the United States of America.
</p>
<a name = "a1" tabindex = "1"><h3>Article I</h3></a>
<p>
<a name = "a1s1" tabindex = "2">Section 1</a>. All legislative powers herein
granted shall be vested in a Congress of the United States, which shall
consist of a Senate and House of Representatives.
</p>
<p>
<a name = "a1s2" tabindex = "3">Section 2</a>. The House of Representatives
shall be composed of members chosen every second year by the people of the
several states, and the electors in each state shall have the qualifications
requisite for electors of the most numerous branch of the state legislature.
</p>
```

No change is visible here, but now when a reader enters this page and presses the Tab key, he or she will immediately be taken to the beginning of Article I. The second time the Tab key is pressed, the page will jump to Article I, Section 1, and so on.

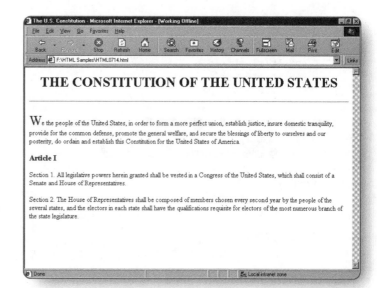

You can enhance keyboard navigation even more by creating *hot keys* that, when pressed, guide the reader straight to the appropriate link. This is done using the `accesskey` attribute. One great place to use this feature is in a long alphabetical index of material.

```
<h1>HTML 4.0 Tags</h1>
<p>&lt;a&gt;</p>
<p>&lt;abbr&gt;</p>
<p>&lt;acronym&gt;</p>
<p>&lt;address&gt;</p>
<p>&lt;area&gt;</p>
<p>&lt;b&gt;</p>
<p>&lt;base&gt;</p>
<p>&lt;bdo&gt;</p>
<p>&lt;big&gt;</p>
<p>&lt;blockquote&gt;</p>
<p>&lt;body&gt;</p>
<p>&lt;br&gt;</p>
<p>&lt;button&gt;</p>
<p>&lt;caption&gt;</p>
<p>&lt;cite&gt;</p>
<p>&lt;code&gt;</p>
<p>&lt;col&gt;</p>
<p>&lt;colgroup&gt;</p>
<p>&lt;dd&gt;</p>
```

```
<p>&lt;del&gt;</p>
<p>&lt;dfn&gt;</p>
<p>&lt;div&gt;</p>
<p>&lt;dl&gt;</p>
<p>&lt;dt&gt;</p>
<p>&lt;em&gt;</p>
```

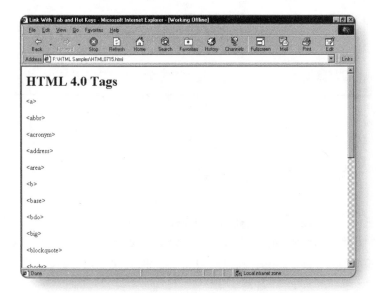

By adding <a> elements at the right locations in this handy list, you can create a very interactive index:

```
<h1>HTML 4.0 Tags</h1>
<p><a name = "a" accesskey = "a">&lt;a&gt;</a></p>
<p>&lt;abbr&gt;</p>
<p>&lt;acronym&gt;</p>
<p>&lt;address&gt;</p>
<p>&lt;area&gt;</p>
<p><a name = "b" accesskey = "b">&lt;b&gt;</a></p>
<p>&lt;base&gt;</p>
<p>&lt;bdo&gt;</p>
<p>&lt;big&gt;</p>
<p>&lt;blockquote&gt;</p>
<p>&lt;body&gt;</p>
<p>&lt;br&gt;</p>
<p>&lt;button&gt;</p>
<p><a name = "c" accesskey = "c">&lt;caption&gt;</a></p>
<p>&lt;cite&gt;</p>
<p>&lt;code&gt;</p>
<p>&lt;col&gt;</p>
<p>&lt;colgroup&gt;</p>
```

```
<p><a name = "d" accesskey = "d">&lt;dd&gt;</a></p>
<p>&lt;del&gt;</p>
<p>&lt;dfn&gt;</p>
<p>&lt;div&gt;</p>
<p>&lt;dl&gt;</p>
<p>&lt;dt&gt;</p>
<p><a name = "e" accesskey = "e">&lt;em&gt;</a></p>
```

No change is visible here, but when the reader presses the "e" key, for example, the screen scrolls down to the beginning of the elements starting with e in this list.

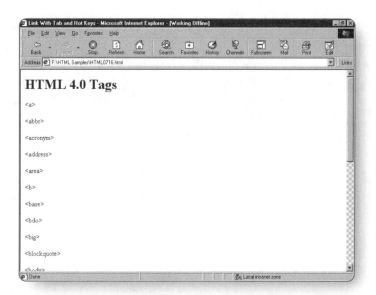

BROWSER
BROWSER

Even though the tabindex and accesskey attributes are fully XHTML-compliant, not all browsers can implement them (such as Internet Explorer). Be aware of this if you use them.

TIP

Should you decide to use the accesskey attribute, make sure you include instructions on using the feature on your Web page. Because it is invisible, readers won't know the feature is there for them to use unless you tell them.

You have a lot of choices in determining how you can assist readers of your Web page. Similarly, you have an incredible amount of choices on what types of documents you can link to your page. It isn't just an XHTML World Wide Web anymore.

Linking to Other Documents

In the beginning of the Web, way back in 1990, there were maybe fewer than 500 Web sites in the entire world. And of those sites, 99.9 percent of them were either HTML pages or images. XHTML was unheard of. Very little else was out there. Today, the story is much different.

Instead of a handful of Web sites, there are now millions. They are no longer strictly HTML or XHTML, either. You have your Shockwave pages, PDF pages, pages in different languages...how's a browser to keep track of it all?

In the next sections, you learn how XHTML coding can assist your browser in handling unusual files, including files not even on the World Wide Web!

Parlez-Vous What?

It is a conceit to think that every page on the Web is written in English. It is a trap that Americans and our British brothers fall into all too often. Needless to say, it aggravates the heck out of our global neighbors. Mostly they kindly put up with our arrogance because we're (a) good customers and (b) the home of Jerry Lewis.

As the Internet becomes a truly global phenomenon, you will find more pages that contain non-English content. You may find yourself linking to them as well. This might not seem like such a big deal to you. After all, the <a> element will link to any page on the Internet, right?

True, but not every other language uses the same alphabet as you do. French, German, and Spanish use characters similar to those used in English. Russian and

Greek use Cyrillic lettering. Japanese and Chinese don't even use phonetic characters. A browser built in the good old USA might have issues when coming across these pages. If you link to these types of pages, you can help the visiting browser a bit by informing it of the link's language and character set.

```
<h1>Recommended Electrical Engineering Institutions</h1>
<p>
<a href = "http://ece.www.ecn.purdue.edu/ECE/">Purdue University School of
Electrical Engineering</a>, West Lafayette, IN, US
</p>
<p>
<a href = "http://www.tue.nl/">Eindhoven University of Technology</a>,
Eindhoven, The Netherlands
</p>
<p>
<a href = "http://www.cc.ece.ntua.gr/">Institute of Communication and Computer
Systems</a>, Hellas, Greece
</p>
```

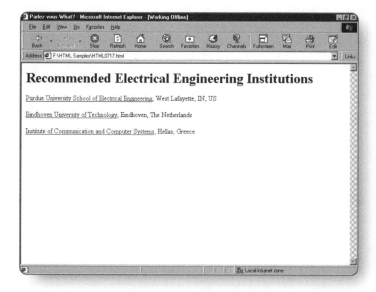

In this example, you have a short list of international institutions you might want to recommend, with the appropriate links already applied. You know that the last two links point to sites that are not in English. Now you can use the charset and hreflang attributes to provide additional information for browsers reading your Web page.

The hreflang attribute is the simpler of the two to understand. It is basically a two-letter code indicating the language of the target Web page. The second site on the list is in Dutch and the third site is in Greek, so the hreflang values for these languages need to be inserted.

```
<h1>Recommended Electrical Engineering Institutions</h1>
<p>
<a href = "http://ece.www.ecn.purdue.edu/ECE/">Purdue University School of
Electrical Engineering</a>, West Lafayette, IN, US
</p>
<p>
<a href = "http://www.tue.nl/" hreflang = "nl">Eindhoven University of
Technology</a>, Eindhoven, The Netherlands
</p>
<p>
<a href = "http://www.cc.ece.ntua.gr/" hreflang = "el">Institute of
Communication and Computer Systems</a>, Hellas, Greece
</p>
```

This change has no visual effects on the links themselves. The visiting browsers to your site are now alerted that these linked sites are in a different language.

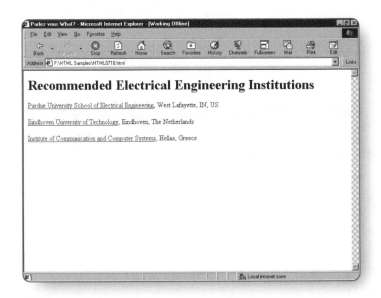

Table 7-1 provides a complete list of the available languages and their two-letter codes.

Table 7-1 HTML `hreflang` Values

Language Name	Language Code	Language Name	Language Code	Language Name	Language Code
Abkhazian	ab	Danish	da	Irish Gaelic	ga
Afar	aa	Dutch	nl	Italian	it
Afrikaans	af	English	en	Japanese	ja
Albanian	sq	Esperanto	eo	Javanese	jw
Amharic	am	Estonian	et	Kannada	kn
Arabic	ar	Faroese	fo	Kashmiri	ks
Armenian	hy	Fiji	fj	Kazakh	kk
Assamese	as	Finnish	fi	Kirghiz	ky
Aymara	ay	French	fr	Kirundi	rn
Azerbaijani	az	Frisian	fy	Kiyarwanda	rw
Bashkir	ba	Galician	gl	Korean	ko
Basque	eu	Georgian	ka	Kurdish	ku
Belarussian	be	German	de	Laotian	lo
Bengali	bn	Greek	el	Latin	la
Bhutani	dz	Greenlandic	kl	Latvian Lettish	lv
Bihari	bh	Guarani	gn	Lingala	ln
Bislama	bi	Gujarati	gu	Lithuanian	lt
Breton	br	Hausa	ha	Luxemburgish	lb
Bulgarian	bg	Hebrew	he	Macedonian	mk
Burmese	my	Hindi	hi	Malagasy	mg
Cambodian	km	Hungarian	hu	Malay	ms
Catalan	ca	Icelandic	is	Malayalam	ml
Chinese	zh	Indonesian	id	Maltese	mt
Cornish	kw	Interlingua	ia	Manx Gaelic	gv
Corsican	co	Interlingue	ie	Maori	mi
Croatian	hr	Inuktitut	iu	Marathi	mr
Czech	cs	Inupiak	ik	Moldavian	mo

Table 7-1 Continued

Language Name	Language Code	Language Name	Language Code	Language Name	Language Code
Mongolian	mn	Serbian	sr	Tibetan	bo
Nauru	na	Serbo-Croatian	sh	Tigrinya	ti
Nepali	ne	Sesotho	st	Tonga	to
Northern Sámi	se	Setswana	tn	Tsonga	ts
Norwegian	no	Shona	sn	Turkish	tr
Occitan	oc	Sindhi	sd	Turkmen	tk
Oriya	or	Singhalese	si	Twi	tw
Oromo	om	Siswati	ss	Uigur	ug
Pashto	ps	Slovak	sk	Ukrainian	uk
Persian	fa	Slovenian	sl	Urdu	ur
Polish	pl	Somali	so	Uzbek	uz
Portuguese	pt	Spanish	es	Vietnamese	vi
Punjabi	pa	Sudanese	su	Volapük	vo
Quechua	qu	Swahili	sw	Welsh	cy
Rhaeto-Romance	rm	Swedish	sv	Wolof	wo
Romanian	ro	Tagalog	tl	Xhosa	xh
Russian	ru	Tajik	tg	Yiddish	yi
Samoan	sm	Tamil	ta	Yorouba	yo
Sangho	sg	Tatar	tt	Zhuang	za
Sanskrit	sa	Telugu	te	Zulu	zu
Scots Gaelic	gd	Thai	th		

Pinning down the `charset` value is a little tricky. Unfortunately, there are the International Standards Organization's character sets, which is good, and a whole bunch of nonstandardized character sets for languages like Korean and Chinese, which is not so good. Without standardization, it's difficult to tell which value to use for `charset`.

Luckily, there is a good way to track down this information. If you plan to link an international page to your own, visit the page first with your browser and view that page's source XHTML with the appropriate tool on your browser.

Clicking on the third link in the previous examples, you would see this code excerpted from the beginning of the page.

```
<!doctype html public "-//w3c//dtd html 3.2//en">
<html>
<head>
    <meta http-equiv="Content-Type" content="text/html; charset=iso-8859-7">
    <title>E & CE Dept. - ICCS Computer Center WWW Server (Greek text, ISO-
8859-7 encoding)</title>
    <meta name="Author" content="Thomas H. Arvanitis">
</head>
<body background="/images/backg.gif">
```

If you look in the `<meta>` element near the top of the head section, you will see that the author has inserted the character-set information within the `content` attribute. We can use that value directly within the `charset` attribute of the `<a>` element in our original document. After similar research on the Eindhoven Web site, you will have these values in the `<a>` element:

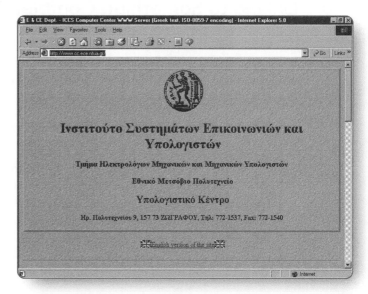

```
<h1>Recommended Electrical Engineering Institutions</h1>
<p>
<a href = "http://ece.www.ecn.purdue.edu/ECE/">Purdue University School of
Electrical Engineering</a>, West Lafayette, IN, US
</p>
<p>
<a href = "http://www.tue.nl/" hreflang = "nl" charset ="iso-8859-1">Eindhoven
University of Technology</a>, Eindhoven, The Netherlands
</p>
<p>
<a href = "http://www.cc.ece.ntua.gr/" hreflang = "el" charset ="iso-8859-
7">Institute of Communication and Computer Systems</a>, Hellas, Greece
</p>
```

NOTE

For a complete list of all of the standard and nonstandard character sets in use on the Internet today, read **ftp://ftp.isi.edu/in-notes/iana/assignments/character-sets**.

By alerting the browsers reading your page that there may be another character set to read, it will enable them to inform their users upon clicking if they can read the new page or whether the user needs a new character set installed on the computer first.

Linking to Something Completely Different

Not all links need to go to Web pages. Many links can be directed to other file types, such as image, sound, and multimedia files. These types of links are easy to build. Instead of filling in the absolute or relative address of an XHTML file, you simply write the URL to the other file.

CAUTION

If you have selected to present your information in a format other than XHTML, make sure you have selected a format that is either close to being universal or a format that a reader can get the tools to read fairly quickly. If you have a link to a PDF file, for example, provide a companion link to the Adobe Acrobat site so your readers can download that tool to read the file.

Many Web browsers have the capability of reading more than files on the World Wide Web. You can create links to files on other Internet services, such as file transfer protocol (FTP), Gopher (the non-graphical predecessor to the Web), and newsgroups. You can even create a link that will create a blank e-mail message for your readers to send.

Table 7-2 lists the most common non-Web Internet services you can access with the <a> element and examples of how to accomplish it.

Table 7-2 Internet Service Links

Service	Example Link
FTP	`<a href = "ftp://ftp.somewhere.net">`
Gopher	`<a href = "gopher://gopher.somewhere.net">`
Mail Message with Subject	`<a href = "mailto:email@somewhere.net?subject = New E-Mail">`
Mail Message	`<a href = "mailto:email@somewhere.net">`
Newsgroups	`<a href = "news:news.somewhere.net">`
Telnet	`<a href = "telnet://telnet.somewhere.net">`

Conclusion

You can see that the <a> element is certainly a very flexible and useful element in the XHTML bag of tricks. Though visually not very exciting, this element is the glue that holds the World Wide Web together.

If you want visual, hang on for the next chapter, where we'll start showing you how to use images to really liven up your Web pages!

8

Images on the Web

A picture is worth a thousand words? Why not 1,115? Or 26? The use of images on the World Wide Web is one of the biggest pluses of this medium, no matter how many words the images represent.

In this chapter, you'll learn how to do the following:

- Decide which image format you should use
- Position your images on the Web page
- Create links to and from images
- Use thumbnail images to enhance your site's look and efficiency

The first picture one of the authors of this book ever saw on the Internet was a picture of President Richard Nixon shaking hands with Elvis Presley in the White House. As the image slowly scrolled to fill the monitor of the Solaris workstation he was lucky enough to use way back in 1991, he remembers thinking, "Wow, cool."

With the advent of the first graphical Web browser, Mosaic, the dull academic world of the Internet was suddenly an interesting place to visit. True, in those days, there was not much to see, because this was right before the National Science Foundation transferred control of the Internet to private organizations. This transfer of control served to open the Web to commercial ventures, a decision that has given us some really tasteless Web sites but has also given us a lot of good sites.

Today, it is almost inevitable that Web sites have images. The images might be of ourselves, our products, or our families—anything we can imagine and capture. As you are building your Web site, however, you need to be aware that there is a right way and a wrong way to add images.

Choosing an Image

Images have an undeniable power to affect the human psyche. When we look at the Declaration of Independence, it should move us. After all, this piece of paper essentially told the largest empire in the world at the time to take a flying leap. But when you put a copy of this document next to the portrait depicting the signing of the Declaration of Independence, eyes will be drawn toward the painting every time.

That's because even though the brain says that the document is far more important in the grand scheme of things, eyes are always drawn to images over text. Ad agencies on Madison Avenue know this, and you, too, need to know how to use this effect to create appealing Web pages.

Images in an XHTML document are displayed within the `<img>` element. Several attributes can be used by this element, two of which are required: `src` and `alt`.

The src attribute is the heart of the <img> element. Its value is the URL of the image file that gets displayed. This value can be either a full absolute URL or a relative path name:

```html
<html>
<head>
<title>Ursa and Brie</title>
</head>
<body text="#9966FF" bgcolor="#FFFFFF">
<h1><font face="Comic Sans MS" color="#800080">Dogs!</font></h1>
<hr align="center" width="75%" />
<h3 align="center"><font face="Comic Sans MS" color="#800080">Brie's first
conformation show is coming!<br />
Her second show is next weekend. We hope you can all be there!</font></h3>
<p>
<font color="#9966FF" face="Comic Sans MS">At 6 months, Brie is now around 85
lbs. She's getting so big! Take a look at these great pictures taken around
Christmas.</font>
</p>
<p>
<img src="BrieXmas99.jpg" /><br />
<img src="BrieFlakeXmas99.jpg" /><br />
<img src="http://www.indy.net/~annz/images/Dogs/UrsaPuffBedXmas99.jpg" />
</p>
</body>
</html>
```

In the images near the bottom of the page, you can see that the src links to the files were both relative and absolute. So you can pull image files onto your Web page from anywhere on the Internet. This is very handy, particularly on the booming Web auction sites, which usually require you to link pictures into the auctioned item page because there isn't enough room on the actual auction site's servers.

CAUTION

Be very sure you have permission before you display images from another Web site on your own Web site. Not only is this a potential copyright problem, but you will also be adding new traffic to the image server. Displaying other people's images without permission is also rude because many Web site owners are charged more for a lot of traffic.

The other attribute you should use is `alt`. The `alt` attribute contains the text that will be displayed if someone surfs to your Web page with either a non-graphical browser (it does happen) or, more likely, a browser with the image display turned off to save time. By including text within the `alt` attribute, you can quickly describe the picture that would have displayed in that spot:

```
<p>
<img src="BrieXmas99.jpg" alt="How can you resist me?" /><br />
<img src="BrieFlakeXmas99.jpg" alt="I'm having a bad hair day!" /><br />
<img src="http://www.indy.net/~annz/images/Dogs/UrsaPuffBedXmas99.jpg"
alt="The illusion of gentility..." />
</p>
```

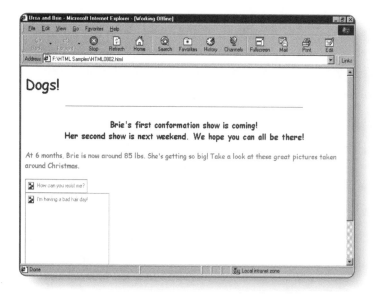

TIP

When using `alt`, try to use original descriptors instead of a reiteration of the image file name. Remember, the point is to entice people to download these graphics separately or turn their browser's image display back on.

> **NOTE**
>
> A little-used attribute similar to `alt` is `longdesc`. This attribute has the value of a URL (absolute or relative) that you can point people to for an even more detailed description of the image. This is a wonderful service for the visually impaired visitors to your Web site.

We need to back up briefly and cover something really important. Before you choose what images to show, you need to decide in what format the images are to be shown. It is not a good idea to just place files willy-nilly onto your page and hope for the best. Images, even the smaller ones, can take quite a bit of time to download, especially for readers surfing in to your page on a 28.8- or 56-K modem. You can make an image display as large as you want, but to keep your page's download time to a minimum, you must make the image's file size as small as possible.

You may have noticed that the three sample pictures are in the .jpg file format, indicating that they are JPEG images, one of the two most common image file formats on the Web today.

Another common file format is the Graphics Interchange Format, or GIF. GIF files use what is known as a "lossless" compression method to reduce their size to a manageable level. This means that pieces of information within an image are cataloged, and any redundant data are substituted with smaller "placeholder" data.

To demonstrate, say that data in an image appears as the following:

```
e7ryf23277094324djfrp27423277094324hf2hfo4i7523277094324
```

If you look carefully, you can see three instances of the data combination `23277094324`. In a GIF, we can substitute that data string with smaller data that represents the longer string. For instance, say this string is represented by `A`. Then the data is much smaller and still conveys the same thing to a GIF reader.

```
e7ryfAdjfrpAhf2hfo4i75A
```

This method means that no image data is lost, hence the term lossless.

Obviously, the more repetition an image has, the better it will compress. That is why GIFs are ideal to use when you have images with few colors and not a lot of detail, including black and white and grayscale.

```
<h1>GIF vs JPEG: Small-Color Images</h1>
<p>
<img src = "graph.jpg" />This JPEG image has a file size of 30,801 bytes.
<br clear="all" />
<img src = "graph.gif" />This GIF file with the same information has a file
size of only 3,341 bytes, and almost 90 percent reduction!
</p>
```

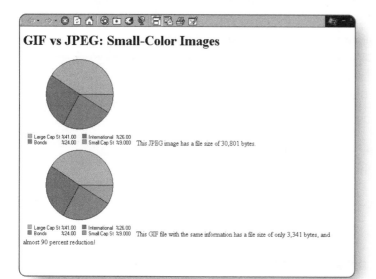

Using GIF images has a significant drawback: they can only display 256 colors at a time. Still, if you are using an image with fewer colors, such as a diagram or chart, this should not be an insurmountable problem.

JPEGs use an entirely different method of compression—the "lossy" compression method. Instead of compressing repetitious information, the lossy method literally tosses image data out of the original image. It does this by dividing the image into pixels, pitching a certain percentage of the image pixels, and then using mathematical algorithms to modify the remaining pixels and smooth out the blockiness left behind.

When done well, this method is great and reduces images without a lot of compromise in image quality.

```
<h1>GIF vs JPEG: Large-Color Images</h1>
<p>
<img src = "world.jpg" />This JPEG image has a file size of 18,308 bytes.
<br clear="all" />
<img src = "world.gif" />This GIF file with the same information has a much
larger file size of 91,142 bytes, an increase of about 400 percent!
</p>
```

The really neat thing about JPEGs is that many JPEG editors let you control the amount of compression applied to a JPEG image, which enables you to reduce the file size even further.

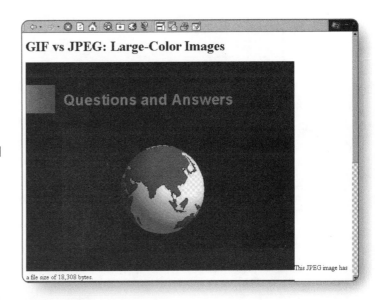

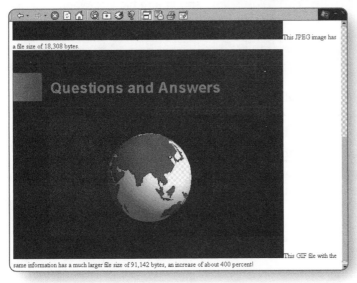

```
<h1>Compressing JPEGs</h1>
<p>
<img src = "BrieToymin.jpg" />This JPEG image has little to no compression.
The file size is 30,170 bytes.
<br clear="all" />
<img src = "BrieToymid.jpg" />This JPEG image has average compression with a
file size of 6,946 bytes.
<br clear="all" />
<img src = "BrieToymax.jpg" />This JPEG image has maximum compression with a
file size of 1,921 bytes.
</p>
```

From a file-size standpoint, it looks as if the maximum compression option is the best way to go. But look at the image again! It's completely pixelated—too much data was thrown out, and the algorithms could not piece the image back together effectively. You must, therefore, always strike a balance between image quality and image file size when working with JPEGs.

JPEGs are recommended for displaying photographs or any other image with many colors because they can show over 16 million colors.

Now that you have the basics of image display down, it's time to move on to the discussion of image placement on your page.

Displaying an Image

When you start displaying your images, you want them to appear on your page correctly. The best way to handle image placement is with tables, which you will learn how to create in Chapter 10, "Building Tables."

In the meantime, you can do some things to control your image layout, as you will see in the next section.

Image Alignment

Looking back at the dog Web page, we can see that some of the images are now off the screen. Instead of a vertical column, let's try a horizontal row.

```
<html>
<head>
<title>Ursa and Brie</title>
</head>
<body text="#9966FF" bgcolor="#FFFFFF">
<h1><font face="Comic Sans MS" color="#800080">Dogs!</font></h1>
<hr align="center" width="75%" />
<h3 align="center"><font face="Comic Sans MS" color="#800080">Brie's first
conformation show is coming!<br />
Her second show is next weekend. We hope you can all be there!</font></h3>
<p>
<font color="#9966FF" face="Comic Sans MS">At 6 months, Brie is now around 85
lbs. She's getting so big! Take a look at these great pictures taken around
Christmas.</font>
</p>
<p>
<img src="BrieXmas99.jpg" alt="How can you resist me?" /> <img
src="BrieFlakeXmas99.jpg" alt="I'm having a bad hair day!" /> <img
src="http://www.indy.net/~annz/images/Dogs/UrsaPuffBedXmas99.jpg" alt="The
illusion of gentility..." />
</p>
</body>
</html>
```

That looks a bit better. Now all of the images are on one screen.

We may be able to get more creative if we use the `align` attribute. `align` is deprecated in XHTML, but it is still handy to use. `align` has just five values: `left`, `right`, `top`, `middle`, and `bottom`. `left` and `right` are pretty easy to understand; each value places the image against the left or right margin of the Web page. The other three position the image relative to the baseline of the content next to it. Applying this to the images on our Web page, we get the following:

```
<p>
<img src="BrieXmas99.jpg" alt="How can you resist me?" align="top"/> <img
src="BrieFlakeXmas99.jpg" alt="I'm having a bad hair day!" /> <img
src="http://www.indy.net/~annz/images/Dogs/UrsaPuffBedXmas99.jpg" alt="The
illusion of gentility..." align = "bottom"/>
</p>
```

In the `<img>` element, there is no `center` value for `align`. You can get around this very easily by using a block element around the images and using the `center` value there.

```
<p align="center">
<img src="BrieXmas99.jpg" alt="How can you resist me?" align="top" /> <img
src="BrieFlakeXmas99.jpg" alt="I'm having a bad hair day!" /> <img
src="http://www.indy.net/~annz/images/Dogs/UrsaPuffBedXmas99.jpg" alt="The
illusion of gentility..." align = "bottom" />
</p>
```

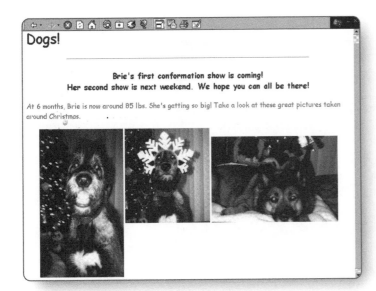

Again, block and inline elements can only offer you a partial solution; style sheets and tables can assist you in creating very accurate layouts for your Web page. Still, for simple straightforward placement of images, XHTML can do the job pretty well.

Image Sizing

Somewhere in your surfing travels, you have probably run across this phenomenon: a page starts to load, and big empty rectangles appear as placeholders where the images will go while the text appears in its entirety. Because the text is already there, you can start reading the page as the images continue to download.

TIP

The values of `height` and `width` are in pixels. Most image dimensions in pixels can be determined with most simple graphics viewers.

This effect is achieved by two attributes of the `<img>` element: `height` and `width`. The values of these settings tell the browser downloading your page images are coming, please make this much room for them. Using them is a sign of a good Webmaster.

Once you determine your figure's dimensions, simply add them to the appropriate `<img>` element:

```
<p align="center">
<img src="BrieXmas99.jpg" alt="How can you resist me?" align="top"
height="341" width="200" /> <img src="BrieFlakeXmas99.jpg" alt="I'm having a
bad hair day!" height="217" width="200" /> <img
src="http://www.indy.net/~annz/images/Dogs/UrsaPuffBedXmas99.jpg" alt="The
illusion of gentility..." align = "bottom" height="197" width="300" />
</p>
```

CAUTION

A strong word of caution here: many people try to use the height and width attributes to actually resize their images on the page. Don't attempt to do this. Web browsers will rarely compress an image correctly. You will probably end up with something that looks like an image in a funhouse mirror.

Linking from an Image

XHTML not only gives you the ability to link passages of text to other pages, but it also enables you to link images.

The linking of images can really cut down on the wordiness of your Web site. Many sites exclusively use icons or other images to help users navigate. You will be able to as well.

Linking images is as easy as adding the <a> element around the <img> element.

If, for instance, the author of the example Web page wanted to direct viewers to another Web page about her dog's breed, the page could be modified in the following way:

```
<html>
<head>
<title>Ursa and Brie</title>
</head>
<body text="#9966FF" bgcolor="#FFFFFF">
<h1><font face="Comic Sans MS" color="#800080">Dogs!</font></h1>
<hr align="center" width="75%" />
<h3 align="center"><font face="Comic Sans MS" color="#800080">Brie's first
conformation show is coming!<br />
Her second show is next weekend. We hope you can all be there!</font></h3>
<p>
<font color="#9966FF" face="Comic Sans MS">At 6 months, Brie is now around 85
lbs. She's getting so big! Take a look at these great pictures taken around
Christmas.</font>
</p>
<p>
<a href=" http://www.geocities.com/Petsburgh/Reserve/6442/index.html">
<img src="BrieXmas99.jpg" alt="How can you resist me?" align = "middle" />
</a>
```

```
<font color="#9966FF" face="Comic Sans MS">Click on me to see more info on
Irish Wolfhounds!</font>
</p>
</body>
</html>
```

You will notice the presence of a border around the image now. This indicates the image is linked. You may not like this border for aesthetic reasons. If you don't, you can easily remove it by setting the border attribute in <img> to 0:

```
<p>
<a href=" http://www.geocities.com/Petsburgh/Reserve/6442/index.html">
<img src="BrieXmas99.jpg" alt="How can you resist me?" align = "middle"
border="0" />
</a>
<font color="#9966FF" face="Comic Sans MS">Click on me to see more info on
Irish Wolfhounds!</font>
</p>
```

This kind of image link is simple to build and easy to use. Other types of image links actually allow you to link sections of an image to different URLs. This is called an imagemap, which we will examine in closer detail in Chapter 13, "Navigating with Images."

Conclusion

As far as XHTML is concerned, getting images on your page is easy. Of course, there are a lot of other factors to consider when using images, such as look, feel, and flow, just to name a few. You now have the basic tools you need to begin experimenting with images on your page.

In Chapter 9, "Making a List and Checking It Twice," you will learn the ins and outs of creating lists—without having to deal with all that pesky reindeer fur.

9

Making a List and Checking It Twice

Stock portfolios, TV guides, movie times. They're all examples of one of the most commonly used tools in language: the list.

In this chapter, you'll learn how to do the following:

- Create numbered lists
- Use alternate numbering schemes for lists
- Create bulleted lists using XHTML-generated bullets
- Apply custom bullets to lists
- Make definition lists

Your eyes open early in the morning, your ears assailed by some DJ telling you what a great day it's going to be. Unconsciously, you smack the snooze button and close your eyes again.

Ten minutes later, the cycle repeats, though now it's the Backstreet Boys you hear, which is enough of a scare to get you to sit up and hit the off button at the same time.

You sit, you rub your face, you think. And, if you're like most other people who have found yourself in this situation, you start reviewing what you have to do that day. You are on your way to making your first list of the day.

This list starts small and typically includes immediate goals: get up, head to the bathroom, that sort of thing. As the fog of sleep lifts, however, more of the day's planned events appear in your brain. By the time you're getting dressed, you probably know what things will need to be done and in what order. You might have written some of the more detailed stuff down somewhere.

People love to make lists. Lists help us order our thoughts and remember things our decidedly nonlinear brains might otherwise forget. One of the earliest features in the first versions of HTML included the capability to make lists, and this toolset has improved with time.

Using Numbered Lists

A lot of people use numbered lists, often in the wrong way. Sorry to nitpick, but it's true.

Numbered lists are supposed to be sequential in nature, meaning that each item is supposed to appear in a certain order. A good example is a how-to list; if the tasks are not done in the correct order, the whole project fails.

A grocery list, therefore, is not a numbered list. Nor is a list where the writer states he has three points to make and then lists them in a numbered list. Besides how-to lists, outlines are a good example of numbered lists. The topics necessarily fall in a certain order.

Order is the name of the game when creating a numbered list in XHTML. These lists are marked with the <ol> element, which stands for ordered list. Whenever any list is created in XHTML, there is always the overall list element, like <ol>, and the <li> element, which is assigned to the individual list items, as demonstrated here:

```
<h1>Searching Help in Star Office</h1>
<ol>
<li>Click on Search Help. The Search dialog box will open.</li>
<li>Click on the Index tab. The Index tab will come to the front. </li>
<li>Type the word or topic you are looking for in the top field. </li>
<li>Double-click on the appropriate topic in the center field. The help topics
will appear in the bottom field. </li>
<li>Click on the Help topic in the bottom field. The Display button will
activate. </li>
<li>Click on Display. The correct Help topic will appear.</li>
</ol>
```

When you create a list, the first list item (marked by <li>) starts its numbering at 1, or the alphabetic equivalent if you are using a numbering scheme other than decimal numbering (1,2,3…). To accomplish this, you can use the type value in the <ol> element. To create a list with capital Roman numerals, you can give type the value of I.

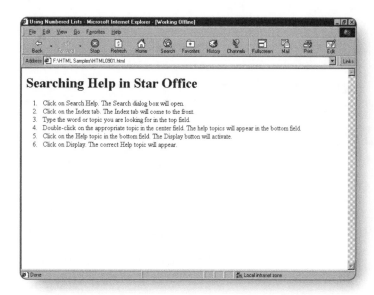

```
<h1>Searching Help in Star Office</h1>
<ol type="I">
<li>Click on Search Help. The Search dialog box will open.</li>
<li>Click on the Index tab. The Index tab will come to the front. </li>
<li>Type the word or topic you are looking for in the top field. </li>
<li>Double-click on the appropriate topic in the center field. The help topics
will appear in the bottom field. </li>
<li>Click on the Help topic in the bottom field. The Display button will
activate. </li>
<li>Click on Display. The correct Help topic will appear.</li>
</ol>
```

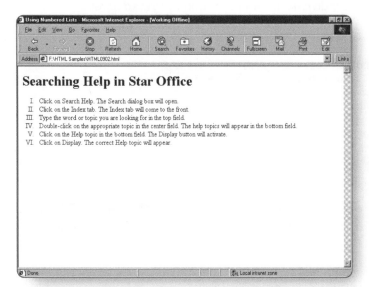

This attribute is officially deprecated within XHTML. Its functionality is duplicated within cascading style sheets, a technology we explore further in Chapter 15, "Designing with Style (Sheets)." You should always be prepared to use this attribute, however, because not every browser can read CSS-designed pages easily. There are other type values, which are listed in Table 9-1.

Table 9-1 Values for the type Attribute of the List Elements

type Value	Definition
1	Decimal numbers (1, 2, 3...)
i	Lowercase Roman numerals (i, ii, iii...)
I	Uppercase Roman numerals (I, II, III...)
a	Lowercase alphabetic (a, b, c...)
A	Uppercase alphabetic (A, B, C...)

You can also (if needed) use the `type` attribute within individual `<li>` elements to counteract the numbering scheme of the rest of the list:

```
<h1>Chapter 3: Building a Better Body</h1>
<ol type="I">
<li>A Page Full of Color</li>
<li>Colorful Characters</li>
<li type="a">Coloring Text</li>
<li type="a">Coloring Links</li>
<li>Starting Scripts</li>
</ol>
```

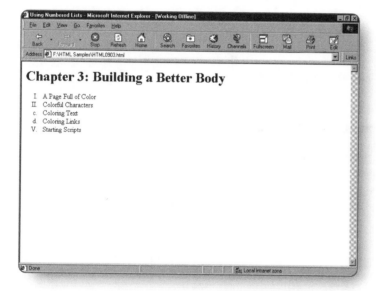

You can see that the changes you made work, but if you try to create subcategories in an outline with this method, you also can see there are some problems with it. The subcategories' numbering continues right along with the rest of the list's numbering.

You can make your life easier while creating outlines if you just nest lists. By inserting an entire list element within another, you can create a list of sub-items very quickly.

```
<h1>Chapter 3: Building a Better Body</h1>
<ol>
<li>A Page Full of Color</li>
<li>Colorful Characters</li>
<ol>
<li>Coloring Text</li>
<li>Coloring Links</li>
</ol>
<li>Starting Scripts</li>
</ol>
```

Now the subtopics are renumbered and even indented. Their numbering scheme still matches the main body of the list, but that can be fixed.

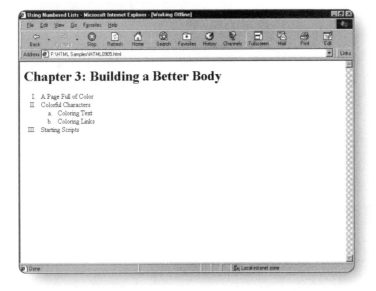

```
<h1>Chapter 3: Building a
Better Body</h1>
<ol type="I">
<li>A Page Full of Color</li>
<li>Colorful Characters</li>
<ol type="a">
<li>Coloring Text</li>
<li>Coloring Links</li>
</ol>
<li>Starting Scripts</li>
</ol>
```

Another deprecated value of the list elements is the `start` attribute, which lets users restart the numbering wherever they want. It is unfortunate this attribute is deprecated, because currently there is no CSS equivalent. We recommend you use `start` whenever you need to, deprecated or not.

When using this attribute, the value must be an integer no matter what the list type is. If, for instance, the Web page author wanted to include the chapter heading in the ordered list, he or she could use the `start` attribute in this manner:

```
<ol type="I" start ="3">
<font
size="5"><b><li>Building a
Better Body</li></b></font>
<ol type="A">
<li>A Page Full of Color</li>
<li>Colorful Characters</li>
<ol type="1">
<li>Coloring Text</li>
<li>Coloring Links</li>
</ol>
<li>Starting Scripts</li>
</ol>
</ol>
```

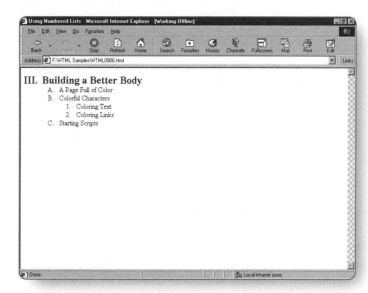

CAUTION

You can nest as many lists as you care to. Just be careful that you keep the start and end `<ol>` tags straight on your page; otherwise your list will become very disorganized very quickly.

If spacing on your page is a concern, you can use the `compact` attribute to bring your list items closer together. This attribute is simple to use, as you can see in the following example.

Remember that all stand-alone attributes, such as compact, must have the value accompanying the attribute to be valid in XHTML.

```
<h1>Searching Help in Star Office</h1>
<ol compact="compact">
<li>Click on Search Help. The Search dialog box will open.</li>
<li>Click on the Index tab. The Index tab will come to the front. </li>
<li>Type the word or topic you are looking for in the top field. </li>
<li>Double-click on the appropriate topic in the center field. The help topics
will appear in the bottom field. </li>
<li>Click on the Help topic in the bottom field. The Display button will
activate. </li>
<li>Click on Display. The correct Help topic will appear.</li>
</ol>
```

Now that you have reclaimed some screen real estate (though the effect is more noticeable in Netscape Navigator), you can add more information or graphics to your page.

Creating Nonsequential Lists

Most lists created in publications fall under the nonsequential or unordered list category. They are unordered because it does not matter in any real sense which item appears in what order in the list.

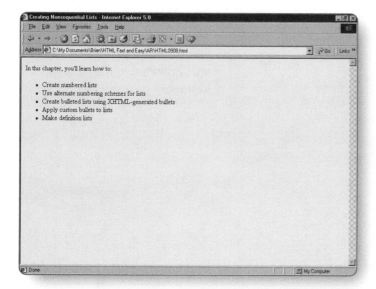

Unordered lists in XHTML are always bulleted, usually with a solid circle. The element used to create them is `<ul>`. Like ordered lists, the `<ul>` element works in conjunction with the `<li>` element to make the list.

```
<p>
In this chapter, you'll learn how to:
</p>
<ul>
<li>Create numbered lists</li>
<li>Use alternate numbering schemes for lists</li>
<li>Create bulleted lists using XHTML-generated bullets</li>
<li>Apply custom bullets to lists</li>
<li>Make definition lists</li>
</ul>
```

Not really difficult, is it?

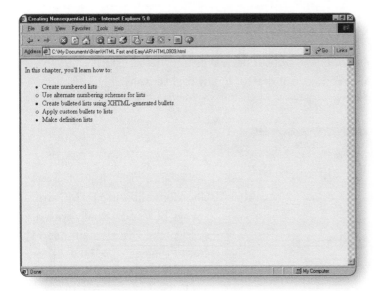

You can change the look of the bullets used for your list by taking advantage of the deprecated `type` attribute for `<ul>`. This attribute has three values, `disc` (the default), `circle`, and `square`, all of which are illustrated in the next example.

```
<p>
In this chapter, you'll learn how to:
</p>
<ul>
<li type="disc">Create numbered lists</li>
<li type="circle">Use alternate numbering schemes for lists</li>
<li type="square">Create bulleted lists using XHTML-generated bullets</li>
<li type="circle">Apply custom bullets to lists</li>
<li type="disc">Make definition lists</li>
</ul>
```

One of the neat features of this element is what happens when unordered lists are nested within each other.

```
<p>
In this chapter, you'll learn how to:
</p>
<ul>
<li>Create numbered lists</li>
<li>Use alternate numbering schemes for lists</li>
<ul>
<li>Create bulleted lists using XHTML-generated bullets</li>
<li>Apply custom bullets to lists</li>
</ul>
<li>Make definition lists</li>
</ul>
```

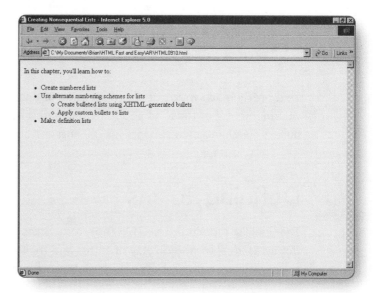

As you can see, the style of the bullets change depending on the level the list item is within the list. This feature has been replaced by the `list-style` component in style sheets.

Another deprecated but useful feature the `<ul>` element shares with ordered lists is the `compact` attribute, which is demonstrated here:

```
<p>
In this chapter, you'll learn how to:
</p>
<ul compact="compact">
<li>Create numbered lists</li>
<li>Use alternate numbering schemes for lists</li>
```

```
<li>Create bulleted lists using XHTML-generated bullets</li>
<li>Apply custom bullets to lists</li>
<li>Make definition lists</li>
</ul>
```

That pretty much wraps up the discussion of unordered lists, at least in terms of the `<ul>` element. For those of you feeling cheated because we did not cover graphical bullets, just hang on a second, it's coming up!

Defining Terms

The final list type in the XHTML repertoire is the definition list. As the name implies, this list is ideal for the display of terms and their definitions. Definition lists display neither bullets nor numbers, which makes them even more useful than this.

The `<dl>` element handles the formation of definition lists, as you might guess. The similarity between the other list types ends there, however. The list items in a definition list are not indicated by the `<li>` element. Rather, they are handled by the `<dt>` (definition term) and the `<dd>` (definition definition) elements.

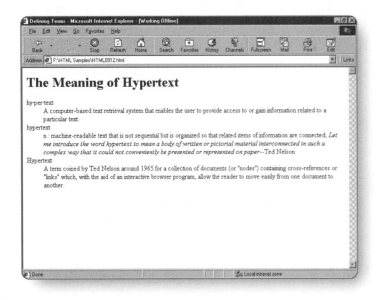

In this example, we have compiled a few definitions of one of our favorite words. Examine the code and the result carefully here and you should pick up the trick of using this list.

```
<h1>The Meaning of Hypertext</h1>
<dl>
<dt>hy&#183;per&#183;text</dt>
<dd>A computer-based text retrieval system that enables the user to provide
access to or gain information related to a particular text.</dd>
<dt>hypertext</dt>
<dd>n : machine-readable text that is not sequential but is organized so that
related items of information are connected; <cite>Let me introduce the word
hypertext to mean a body of written or pictorial material interconnected in
such a complex way that it could not conveniently be presented or represented
on paper</cite>--Ted Nelson</dd>
<dt>Hypertext</dt>
<dd>A term coined by Ted Nelson around 1965 for a collection of documents (or
"nodes") containing cross-references or "links" which, with the aid of an
interactive browser program, allow the reader to move easily from one document
to another.</dd>
</dl>
```

As with the other lists, the items within a definition list can be nested within other definition lists. The results aren't terribly dramatic, but they're visible nonetheless.

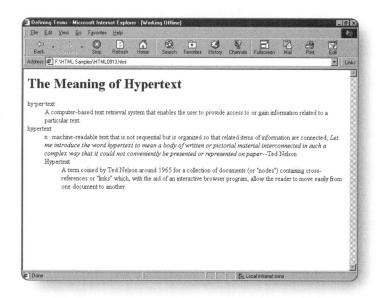

```
<h1>The Meaning of Hypertext</h1>
<dl>
<dt>hy&#183;per&#183;text</dt>
<dd>A computer-based text retrieval system that enables the user to provide
access to or gain information related to a particular text.</dd>
<dt>hypertext</dt>
<dd>n : machine-readable text that is not sequential but is organized so that
related items of information are connected; <cite>Let me introduce the word
hypertext to mean a body of written or pictorial material interconnected in
such a complex way that it could not conveniently be presented or represented
on paper</cite>--Ted Nelson</dd>
```

```
<dl>
<dt>Hypertext</dt>
<dd>A term coined by Ted Nelson around 1965 for a collection of documents (or
"nodes") containing cross-references or "links" which, with the aid of an
interactive browser program, allow the reader to move easily from one document
to another.</dd>
</dl>
</dl>
```

Because definition lists have no extra baggage-like bullets, you can achieve some interesting effects using images for your own custom bullets.

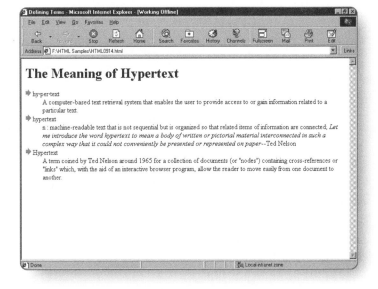

```
<h1>The Meaning of Hypertext</h1>
<dl>
<dt><img src="arrow.gif"> hy&#183;per&#183;text</dt>
<dd>A computer-based text retrieval system that enables the user to provide
access to or gain information related to a particular text.</dd>
<dt><img src="arrow.gif"> hypertext</dt>
<dd>n : machine-readable text that is not sequential but is organized so that
related items of information are connected; <cite>Let me introduce the word
hypertext to mean a body of written or pictorial material interconnected in
such a complex way that it could not conveniently be presented or represented
on paper</cite>--Ted Nelson</dd>
<dt><img src="arrow.gif"> Hypertext</dt>
<dd>A term coined by Ted Nelson around 1965 for a collection of documents (or
"nodes") containing cross-references or "links" which, with the aid of an
interactive browser program, allow the reader to move easily from one document
to another.</dd>
</dl>
```

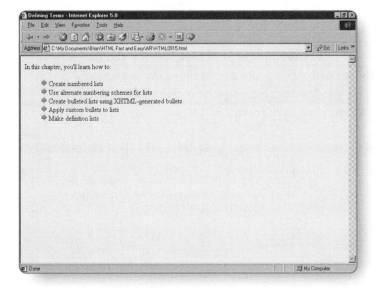

You can also use a special image with a non-definition list, such as our bulleted list example in the previous section. Instead of using the <ul> element to create your bulleted list, use the <dl> element with either the <dt> or <dd> element.

```
<p>
In this chapter, you'll learn how to:
</p>
<dl>
<dd><img src="arrow.gif"> Create numbered lists</li>
<dd><img src="arrow.gif"> Use alternate numbering schemes for lists</li>
<dd><img src="arrow.gif"> Create bulleted lists using XHTML-generated
bullets</li>
<dd><img src="arrow.gif"> Apply custom bullets to lists</li>
<dd><img src="arrow.gif"> Make definition lists</li>
</ul>
```

CAUTION

If your individual list items are lengthy, using the <dl> method with just the <dd> or <dt> elements might not work very well because of text wraparound. This wraparound flows under the bullet graphic without indenting, which is not a great look. There is, of course, a trick to get around this, which we cover in the next chapter, "Building Tables."

Conclusion

Creating lists is essential on today's Web pages, because lists are the fastest way to impart the information the visitors to your site are desperately seeking. By organizing your information into succinct list items, you give readers what they want and leave them ready to come back for more.

Another great way to organize your work is to use tables. In the next chapter, we'll show you that tables, perhaps regarded as the most cryptic of all XHTML constructs, really are not so bad after all.

10

Building Tables

When you have a little data you need to present to others, you will likely choose to place it in a list format. If you have a lot of data or data with many values, you will need to use a table to organize the data into a cohesive form.

In this chapter, you'll learn how to do the following:

- Create basic tables
- Know the primary elements for table creation
- Utilize relative and absolute widths for tables
- Use tables for layout

Creating tables in a word processor application is not very difficult these days. But, to be truthful, creating tables in XHTML is not exactly a walk in the park. This is not to say you should avoid using tables in your XHTML pages. On the contrary, the practical applications of tables on a Web page are fantastic.

To build tables, however, you need to know more than one or two XHTML elements. Once you have the elements mastered, you will be able to figure out the complexities of XHTML tables easily.

Tables 101: The Simple Stuff

A simple table has two components: rows and columns. In the intersection of those components is where the data resides. This intersection is called the cell. A table in XHTML is always created with these three elements in mind. In a markup language where spacing and rows make little to no difference in the displayed output, how *are* rows, columns, and cells created in XHTML?

Defining Table Elements

When you start making a table, you need to have a pretty good idea of what the table is supposed to look like. With this in mind, the first element you need to use is the `<table>` element. Within the `<table>` element, data is typically organized by rows, which are marked by the `<tr>` element. Data in cells is indicated by the `<td>` element.

With these three elements, we can build a rudimentary table.

```
<table>
<tr>
    <td>Apples</td>
    <td>Carrots</td>
    <td>Daisies</td>
</tr>
<tr>
    <td>Oranges</td>
    <td>Potatoes</td>
    <td>Orchids</td>
</tr>
 <tr>
    <td>Tomatoes</td>
    <td>Squash</td>
    <td>Strawberries</td>
</tr>
</table>
```

This example has created a three-by-three table of plants. Not a lot of meaning can be gleaned from this table from just this presentation. It's plant life; so what? This is why a lot of tables need headings at the top of their columns. This is done with the `<th>` element.

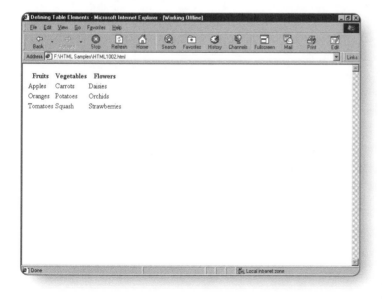

```
<table>
<tr>
    <th>Fruits</th>
    <th>Vegetables</th>
    <th>Flowers</th>
</tr>
<tr>
    <td>Apples</td>
    <td>Carrots</td>
    <td>Daisies</td>
</tr>
<tr>
    <td>Oranges</td>
    <td>Potatoes</td>
    <td>Orchids</td>
</tr>
 <tr>
    <td>Tomatoes</td>
    <td>Squash</td>
    <td>Strawberries</td>
</tr>
</table>
```

This is a little better, because the column heads give an idea of what this data means. The content of the `<th>` element is automatically given the bold attribute to make it stand out even more. You can add a caption to this table with the `<caption>` element and make the point of the table even clearer.

```
<table>
<caption>Things Are Not Always
What They Seem</caption>
<tr>
   <th>Fruits</th>
   <th>Vegetables</th>
   <th>Flowers</th>
</tr>
<tr>
   <td>Apples</td>
   <td>Carrots</td>
   <td>Daisies</td>
</tr>
<tr>
   <td>Oranges</td>
   <td>Potatoes</td>
   <td>Orchids</td>
</tr>
 <tr>
   <td>Tomatoes</td>
   <td>Squash</td>
   <td>Strawberries</td>
</tr>
</table>
```

CAUTION

If you elect to use the `<caption>` element, it must be the first element that appears within the `<table>` element.

You will notice that the length of the caption's text is determined by the width of the table itself and that the text of the caption is not given any special attributes. You can correct this latter situation with inline elements.

```
<table>
<caption><strong><em>Things
Are Not Always What They
Seem</em></strong></caption>
...
</table>
```

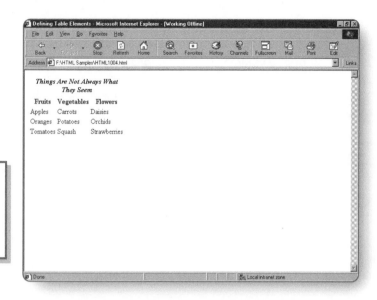

CAUTION

Only inline elements can be used in the `<caption>` element.

The basics of table design in XHTML are all right here with this handful of elements. As the need for tables grew, the XHTML toolset was expanded to meet the needs of XHTML documents.

Spanning and Borders

When you look at the tables in the previous examples, what do you see? A nice, even set of boxes all lined up in neat little rows and columns. There's not a lot wrong with this. After all, this is a table, not the Chrysler Building. Still, there are times when you need to be flexible with your data presentation. Luckily, your table can be flexible, too.

Table cells in XHTML can use a process known as *spanning* to better present data. In a nutshell, spanning allows a single cell to take up more space than just one row or one column. This is demonstrated in the next example.

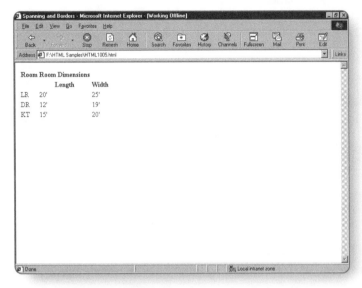

```
<table>
<tr>
    <th>Room</th>
    <th>Room Dimensions</th>
</tr>
<tr>
    <th></th>
    <th>Length</th>
    <th>Width</th>
</tr>
<tr>
    <td>LR</td>
    <td>20'</td>
    <td>25'</td>
</tr>
<tr>
    <td>DR</td>
    <td>12'</td>
    <td>19'</td>
</tr>
<tr>
    <td>KT</td>
    <td>15'</td>
    <td>20'</td>
</tr>
</table>
```

Things aren't really lined up well here, are they? The problem becomes even more apparent when borders are added to the table using the `border` attribute. With this attribute, you only have to assign a numeric value. The higher the number, the thicker the lines of the table cells will be.

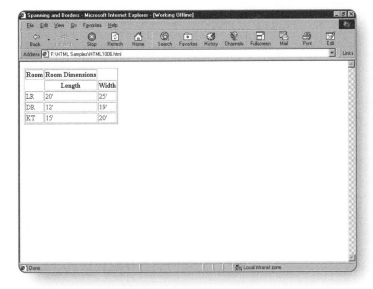

```
<table border="1">
<tr>
    <th>Room</th>
    <th>Room Dimensions</th>
</tr>
<tr>
    <th></th>
    <th>Length</th>
    <th>Width</th>
</tr>
<tr>
    <td>LR</td>
    <td>20'</td>
    <td>25'</td>
</tr>
<tr>
    <td>DR</td>
    <td>12'</td>
    <td>19'</td>
</tr>
<tr>
    <td>KT</td>
    <td>15'</td>
    <td>20'</td>
</tr>
</table>
```

Using the spanning attributes, we can correct the look of this table. First, look at the heading cell with Room within it. It could be adjusted to span over two rows using the rowspan attribute. This attribute also uses numeric values, which are now equal to the number of rows you want the data to span.

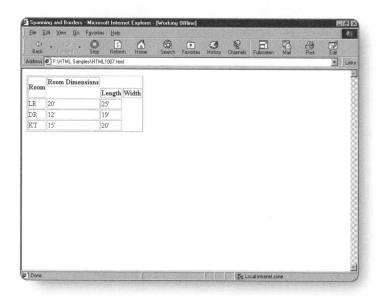

```
<tr>
   <th rowspan="2">Room</th>
   <th>Room Dimensions</th>
</tr>
<tr>
   <th></th>
   <th>Length</th>
   <th>Width</th>
</tr>
```

Well, that didn't quite do it, did it? That's because we forgot to take out the empty `<th>` cell we'd originally placed at the start of the second row to make sure Length and Width were in the correct columns. If we remove that empty cell, we have something better.

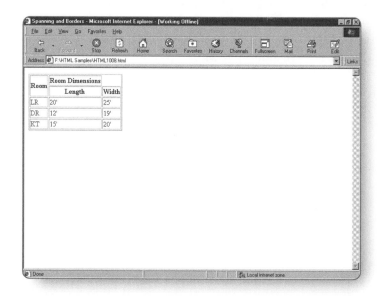

```
<tr>
   <th rowspan="2">Room</th>
   <th>Room Dimensions</th>
</tr>
<tr>
   <th>Length</th>
   <th>Width</th>
</tr>
```

Much better, don't you agree? The Room Dimensions header cell can be spanned across the Length and Width columns using the (what else?) `colspan` attribute, which is used in the same manner as `rowspan`.

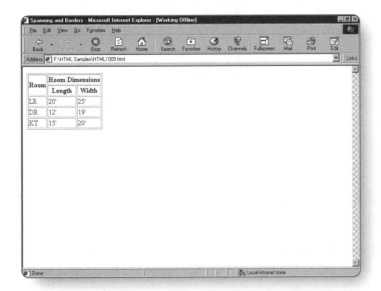

```
<tr>
   <th rowspan="2">Room</th>
   <th colspan="2">Room
Dimensions</th>
</tr>
<tr>
   <th>Length</th>
   <th>Width</th>
</tr>
```

You can see that, with careful editing, you can achieve some nice layout effects with spanning cells. When we used it to illustrate the cells within this example table, you saw the `border` attribute in action as well. This attribute's value is the thickness in pixels of a border you want to place around the table and its component cells. You want to be careful here, because it is very easy to make these lines too thick to look good.

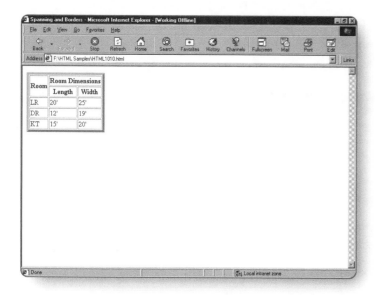

```
<table border="5">
<tr>
    <th rowspan="2">Room</th>
    <th colspan="2">Room
Dimensions</th>
</tr>
<tr>
    <th>Length</th>
    <th>Width</th>
</tr>
```

If you do not specify the `border` attribute, or if you set its value to `0`, no border will be visible in browsers.

Besides the border attribute, two other attributes control the lines in and around a table. The first one we will examine is the `frame` attribute, which controls the appearance of just the outer lines of the table. You can use nine values for this attribute, which are detailed in Table 10-1.

Table 10-1 `frame` Attribute Values

Value	Description
box	Four sides visible
border	Four sides visible
above	Top side visible
below	Bottom side visible
hsides	Top and bottom sides visible
vsides	Right and left sides visible
lhs	Left side visible
rhs	Right side visible
void	No sides visible

With these values in mind, we can create interesting effects with `frame`.

```
<table frame="hsides">
<tr>
   <th rowspan="2">Room</th>
   <th colspan="2">Room
Dimensions</th>
</tr>
<tr>
   <th>Length</th>
   <th>Width</th>
</tr>
```

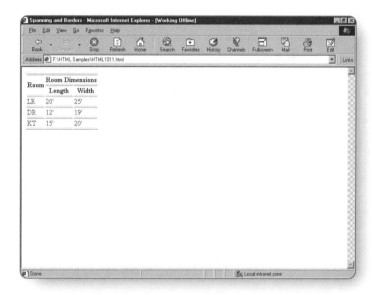

The other attribute that controls lines in tables is the `rules` attribute. This attribute, as you may have deduced, controls the appearance of lines between cells—in other words, *within* the table.

The `rules` attribute has fewer values than the `frame` attribute, as you can see in the listing within Table 10-2.

> **CAUTION**
>
> Don't confuse the `<table>` element's `frame` attribute with Web document frames! We'll discuss those more in Chapter 11, "You've Been Framed."

Table 10-2 `rules` Attribute Values

Value	Description
rows	Rules will only appear between rows
cols	Rules will only appear between columns
groups	Rules will appear only between row and column groups
all	Rules will appear between all rows and columns
none	No rules will appear

An example of how this would look can be easily demonstrated.

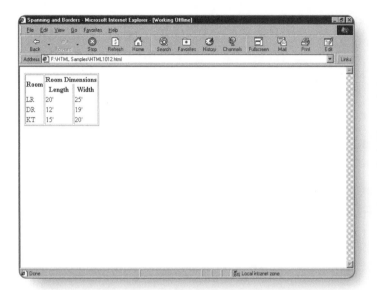

```
<table rules="cols">
<tr>
    <th rowspan="2">Room</th>
    <th colspan="2">Room
Dimensions</th>
</tr>
<tr>
    <th>Length</th>
    <th>Width</th>
</tr>
```

You can control the width of these lines by using these attributes in conjunction with the border attribute. When you use border first, it sets the size for the remainder of the attributes in the <table> element.

```
<table border="3"
frames="hsides" rules="rows">
<tr>
    <th rowspan="2">Room</th>
    <th colspan="2">Room
Dimensions</th>
</tr>
<tr>
    <th>Length</th>
    <th>Width</th>
</tr>
```

As you start to create larger tables, your formatting needs will grow by leaps and bounds unless you can keep all of these table elements in check. XHTML provides some nifty ways of accomplishing just that, as you will read in the "Row and Column Groups" section later in this chapter.

Now that you have reviewed the basics of table construction, it's time to move on to the advanced level of table sizing, grouping, and layout.

Tables 431: On to the Hard Stuff

By now, your head may be spinning with all of the table elements with which you have to contend. This is perfectly understandable, as is any reluctance to add more knowledge to this realm of tables. Don't worry; your head won't explode. The thing to remember is you can take as little or as much away from this discussion to get things done. Many of the XHTML editor programs take care of this stuff for you, so you won't be building a table from scratch. As good as those editors can be, though, you with your keen human brain can assuredly do better, so knowing this stuff is great for the inevitable tweaking you will find yourself doing.

Keep this in mind as you read through the next sections and learn about the many ways to improve your tables.

Absolute and Relative Widths

What size do you keep your browser? Full screen for maximum effect? Or as a smaller window, just for reference purposes? You might think this is a silly concern, but as a Web author, you need to be aware of the fact that different people have their different browser windows sized in different ways.

In Chapter 4, "Block Tags and You," you learned one of the ways XHTML could handle this problem: absolute and relative widths. The `<hr>` element, you'll recall, could have either a length designated in pixels or in percentage of the screen it spanned.

The same principle can be applied to the width of a table using, appropriately enough, the `width` attribute of the `<table>` element. Like the `<hr>` element, this attribute can have an absolute value in pixels or a relative value of percentage of screen spanned.

Absolute values are certainly the easiest to understand, but they can backfire. Look at this table in a narrow browser window.

```
<table border="1"
width="300">
<tr>
   <th rowspan="2">Room</th>
   <th colspan="2">Room
Dimensions</th>
</tr>
<tr>
   <th>Length</th>
   <th>Width</th>
</tr>
```

Watch what happens within the same browser window when relative size of 75 percent is used.

```
<table border="1"
width="75%">
<tr>
   <th rowspan="2">Room</th>
   <th colspan="2">Room
Dimensions</th>
</tr>
<tr>
   <th>Length</th>
   <th>Width</th>
</tr>
```

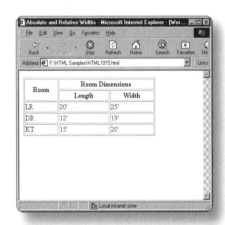

No matter how thin the browser window, the entirety of the table will be displayed—perhaps a bit scrunched, but there nonetheless. Unless you have a great reason for maintaining absolute values, you should try to use relative values as much as possible when setting table width.

Row and Column Groups

As reviewed earlier, all XHTML documents have a <head> and a <body> element. This division of elements helps to keep certain parts of the document organized so browsers can read them more efficiently.

The same holds true for XHTML tables, particularly large ones. Having all of those elements appearing in one place can be quite maddening to the eyes and the brain when you're trying to edit the source code.

Column Groups

When you first try to apply grouping to table columns, it is easy to get confused. Tables, after all, are primarily oriented around rows. Columns are sort of a by-product of all of those <td> elements lined up side by side.

Because of this row orientation in tables, the elements consigned to handling columns, <colgroup> and <col>, are actually empty elements. They don't contain anything at all. To make this work, these elements must appear early in the <table> element—only a <caption> element can appear first.

```
<table border="1">
<colgroup />
<colgroup span="2" />
    <col />
    <col />
<tr>
    <th rowspan=2>Room</th>
    <th colspan=2>Room Dimensions</th>
</tr>
```

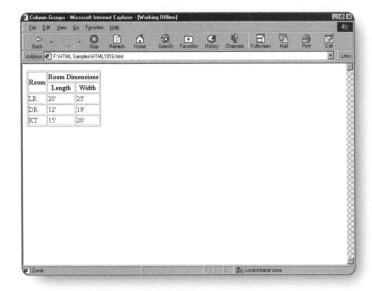

```
<tr>
   <th>Length</th>
   <th>Width</th>
</tr>
<tr>
   <td>LR</td>
   <td>20'</td>
   <td>25'</td>
</tr>
<tr>
   <td>DR</td>
   <td>12'</td>
   <td>19'</td>
</tr>
<tr>
   <td>KT</td>
   <td>15'</td>
   <td>20'</td>
</tr>
</table>
```

Not exactly dramatic, is it? But with the presence of these new elements, you can very quickly define new presentation styles by column.

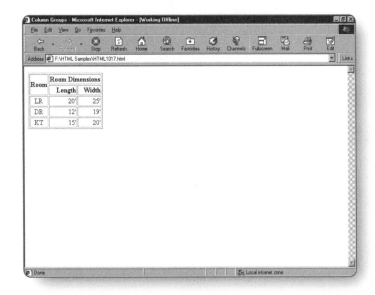

```
<table border="1">
<colgroup align="center" />
<colgroup span="2" />
   <col align="right" />
   <col align="right" />
<tr>
   <th rowspan=2>Room</th>
   <th colspan=2>Room
Dimensions</th>
</tr>
```

Now you can see a difference. The trick to this is to understand that each `<colgroup>` and `<col>` element stands for one column, unless it has been defined to have a higher span of columns. This example has two `<colgroup>` elements, but one has a `span` value of 2, so the number of columns represented by these elements is equal to three. This is right, because this is a three-column table. The two `<col>` elements are not added to the total, because in this example, they are nested within the second `<colgroup>` element.

Using `<colgroup>` elements in conjunction with `<col>` elements can render some nice effects. For instance, instead of setting the `align` attribute in the `<col>` elements, we could have more easily defined it in the `<colgroup>`. To make this clearer, suppose we want the width of each column to be fixed at 80 pixels. This shorthand use of attributes between `<colgroup>` and `<col>` is demonstrated in this example:

```
<table border="1">
<colgroup align="center"
width="80" />
<colgroup span="2" />
   <col align="right"
width="80" />
   <col align="right"
width="80" />
<tr>
   <th rowspan=2>Room</th>
   <th colspan=2>Room
Dimensions</th>
</tr>
```

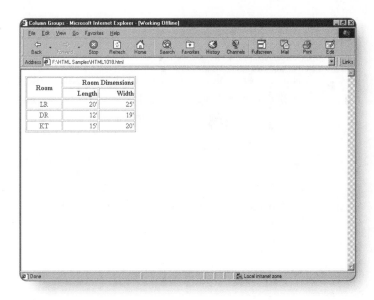

The exact same effect is achieved by trimming the code to this:

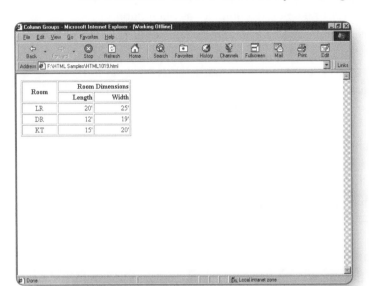

```
<table border="1">
<colgroup align="center"
width="80" />
<colgroup span="2"
align="right" width="80" />
<tr>
    <th rowspan=2>Room</th>
    <th colspan=2>Room
Dimensions</th>
</tr>
```

That covers column groups for now. Keep in mind that when you use style sheets in your document, you can assign whole styles to a column. You'll learn more about styles in Chapter 15, "Designing with Style (Sheets)."

Netscape Navigator does not handle style declarations within tables very well. Internet Explorer can manage table styles very well.

Table Head, Body, Foot

To help organize table rows, three elements in XHTML can be of use: `<thead>`, `<tbody>`, and `<tfoot>`. A table can have one `<thead>` element and one `<tfoot>` element only. It can have as many `<tbody>` elements as you see fit, which is a good idea considering this element is responsible for the grouping of rows. The only other stipulation is that each of these elements must contain at least one table row (using the `<tr>` element).

The <thead> and <tfoot> elements should contain all the elements and content that will appear within those sections of the table, such as in this example:

```
<table border="1">
<thead>
<tr>
   <th rowspan=2>Room</th>
   <th colspan=2>Room Dimensions</th>
</tr>
<tr>
   <th>Length</th>
   <th>Width</th>
</tr>
</thead>
<tfoot>
<tr>
   <td colspan="3">(Measurements in feet)</td>
</tr>
</tfoot>
<tr>
   <td>LR</td>
   <td>20'</td>
   <td>25'</td>
</tr>
<tr>
   <td>DR</td>
   <td>12'</td>
   <td>19'</td>
</tr>
<tr>
   <td>KT</td>
   <td>15'</td>
   <td>20'</td>
</tr>
</table>
```

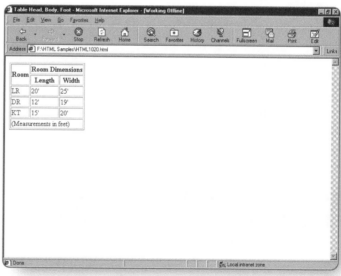

When you looked at the code and then the figure, did the positioning of the <tfoot> element immediately after the <thead> element confuse you? Actually, it's a requirement when using these elements. In <table>, <thead> and <tfoot> must appear first within the element (or after the <caption>, <colgroup>, or <col> elements, if present).

BROWSER
vs
BROWSER

The unusual positioning of the `<tfoot>` element may cause it to be unread or incorrectly read by browsers that do not support this element. In fact, it is recognized that Netscape Navigator does not read groups within tables. Internet Explorer browsers do recognize table groups, however.

These two elements are table row groups. The third element that is a row group container is `<tbody>`. `<tbody>` is the element that contains the rest of the table; should you need more row groups, additional `<tbody>` elements can take care of that.

```
<table border="1">
<thead>
<tr>
    <th rowspan=2>Room</th>
    <th colspan=2>Room Dimensions</th>
</tr>
<tr>
    <th>Length</th>
    <th>Width</th>
</tr>
</thead>
<tfoot>
<tr>
    <td colspan="3">(Measurements in feet)</td>
</tr>
</tfoot>
<tbody>
<tr>
    <td>LR</td>
    <td>20'</td>
    <td>25'</td>
</tr>
<tr>
    <td>DR</td>
    <td>12'</td>
    <td>19'</td>
</tr>
<tr>
    <td>KT</td>
    <td>15'</td>
    <td>20'</td>
</tr>
</tbody>
</table>
```

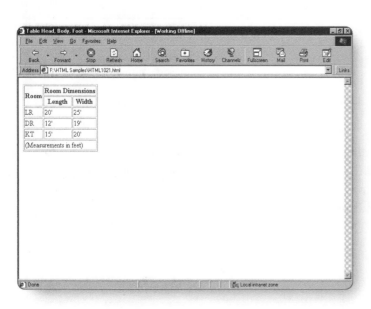

Using Tables for Layout

Perhaps the best way to demonstrate all the capabilities of tables is to show you some of the cool things a table can do. In Chapter 9, "Making a List and Checking It Twice," we mentioned that tables were a great tool to use for creating a bulleted list with graphical bullets. This is a good place to start.

Creating Bulleted Lists

When an XHTML bulleted list is presented, the bullet is well off to the side and the list item's content is well off to the side, never wrapping under the bullet itself. Unfortunately, when the list item is lengthy, this effect is not automatically achieved.

```
<dl>
<dd>
<img src="rd_paw_bullet.gif"
height="16" width="16" />The
largest of the spaniels, the
Irish Water Spaniel, is a
solid brown (leaning to
purple), crisp-textured,
curly-coated dog with a
hairless, rat-like tail and
smooth short-coated face. It
has a rather large head with
an arched skull. The curly
outer coat is lined with a
dense undercoat, which helps
insulate the dog in even the
coldest water.
</dd>
<dd>
<img src="rd_paw_bullet.gif"
height="16" width="16" />A
massive, muscular dog, the Irish
Wolfhound is one of the tallest breeds in the world. This gentle giant can
reach the size of a small pony. Standing on his hind legs the Irish Wolfhound
can reach up to 7 feet tall! He has a rough, shaggy coat and wiry bushy
eyebrows. Colors include gray, brindle, red, black or white. Gray is the most
common color.
</dd>
<dd>
<img src="rd_paw_bullet.gif" height="16" width="16" />The Italian Greyhound is
an elegant, miniature fine-boned Greyhound with a long head thinning gradually
to a pointed muzzle. It has a dark nose, thin lips and a healthy scissors
bite. Like his larger cousins, the brisket is deep, the abdomen tucked-in, and
the back arched.
</dd>
</dl>
```

If you place the contents of this list within a table, you can get much better results!

```
<table width="80%">
<col width="5%" align="center" valign="top" />
<col width="95%" align="left" valign="top" />
<tr>
<td><img src="rd_paw_bullet.gif" height="16" width="16" /></td>
<td>The largest of the spaniels, the Irish Water Spaniel, is a solid brown
(leaning to purple), crisp-textured, curly-coated dog with a hairless, rat-
like tail and smooth short-coated face. It has a rather large head with an
arched skull. The curly outer coat is lined with a dense undercoat, which
helps insulate the dog in even the coldest water.</td>
</tr>
<tr>
<td><img src="rd_paw_bullet.gif" height="16" width="16" /></td>
<td>A massive, muscular dog, the Irish Wolfhound is one of the tallest breeds
in the world. This gentle giant can reach the size of a small pony. Standing
on his hind legs the Irish Wolfhound can reach up to 7 feet tall! He has a
rough, shaggy coat and wiry bushy eyebrows. Colors include gray, brindle, red,
black or white. Gray is the most common color.</td>
</tr>
<tr>
<td><img src="rd_paw_bullet.gif" height="16" width="16" /></td>
<td>The Italian Greyhound is an elegant, miniature fine-boned Greyhound with a
long head thinning gradually to a pointed muzzle. It has a dark nose, thin
lips and a healthy scissors bite. Like his larger cousins, the brisket is
deep, the abdomen tucked-in, and the back arched.</td>
</tr>
</table>
```

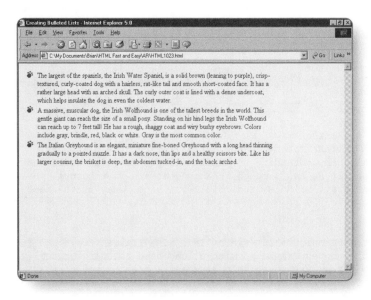

In this table-turned-list, you can see we restricted the width of the overall table to 80 percent of the screen so the text would not flow past the right edge of the window. We also held the column containing the bullet images to just 5 percent of the table's total width and the text column to 95 percent. Finally, we used the available `valign` attribute in `<col>` to make sure the bullets and text were all lined up at the top of their respective cells.

The effect achieved here is much better looking, and, because the borders are not visible, the casual observer will not know it's a table.

Creating a Photo Page

You can use unbordered tables to assist you in page layout. If you build your table well, you can place textual and graphical elements exactly where you want them on the page. Recall this example from Chapter 8:

```
<html>
<head>
<title>Ursa and Brie</title>
</head>
<body text="#9966FF" bgcolor="#FFFFFF">
<h1><font face="Comic Sans MS" color="#800080">Dogs!</font></h1>
<hr align="center"
width="75%" />
<h3 align="center"><font
face="Comic Sans MS"
color="#800080">Brie's first
conformation show is
coming!<br />
Her second show is next
weekend. We hope you can all
be there!</font></h3>
<p>
<font color="#9966FF"
face="Comic Sans MS">At 6
months, Brie is now around
85 lbs. She's getting so
big! Take a look at these
great pictures taken around
Christmas.</font>
</p>
<p align="center">
```

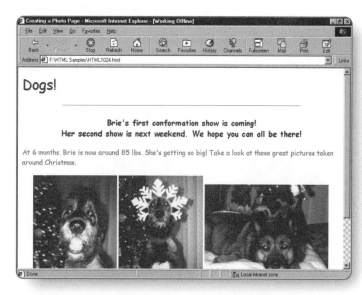

```
<img src="BrieXmas99.jpg" alt="How can you resist me?" align="top"
height="341" width="200" /> <img src="BrieFlakeXmas99.jpg" alt="I'm having a
bad hair day!" height="217" width="200" /> <img src="UrsaPuffBedXmas99.jpg"
alt="The illusion of gentility..." align = "bottom" height="197" width="300"
/>
</p>
</body>
</html>
```

Now, watch what happens to the page when we use a table to position the images!

```
<html>
<head>
<title>Ursa and Brie</title>
</head>
<body text="#9966FF" bgcolor="#FFFFFF">
<h1><font face="Comic Sans MS" color="#800080">Dogs!</font></h1>
<hr align="center" width="75%" />
<h3 align="center"><font face="Comic Sans MS" color="#800080">Brie's first
conformation show is coming!<br />
Her second show is next weekend. We hope you can all be there!</font></h3>
<p>
<font color="#9966FF" face="Comic Sans MS">At 6 months, Brie is now around 85
lbs. She's getting so big! Take a look at these great pictures taken around
Christmas.</font>
</p>
<table width="100%">
<tr>
<td width="33%" align="center" rowspan="2"><img border="0"
```

```
                                        src="BrieXmas99.jpg" alt="How
                                        can you resist me?"
                                        width="200" height="341"></td>
                                        <td width="33%"
                                        align="center"><img border="0"
                                        src="BrieFlakeXmas99.jpg"
                                        alt="You can't hide from a
                                        sight hound!" width="200"
                                        height="217"></td>
                                        </tr>
                                        <tr>
                                        <td width="33%"
                                        align="center"><img border="0"
                                        src="UrsaPuffBedXmas99.jpg"
                                        alt="The illusion of
                                        gentility..." width="300"
                                        height="197"></td>
                                        </tr>
                                        </table>
                                        </body>
                                        </html>
```

With tables, you can see how easy it is to experiment with table sizes to make your page look how you want it. You can even use tables to enhance standard sections of your document, not just photo albums.

```
<html>
<head>
<title>Ursa and Brie</title>
</head>
<body text="#9966FF" bgcolor="#FFFFFF">
<table width="100%">
<tr>
<td width="25%"><img border="0" src="lgdogs.gif" width="185"
height="115"></td>
<td width="75%"><img border="0" src="dog_tine_lg_wht.gif" width="110"
height="180"></td>
</tr>
</table>
<p align="center"><img border="0" src="bar.gif" width="436"
height="15"></p><h3 align="center"><font face="Comic Sans MS"
color="#800080">Brie's first conformation show is coming!<br />
Her second show is next weekend. We hope you can all be there!</font></h3>
<p>
<font color="#9966FF" face="Comic Sans MS">At 6 months, Brie is now around 85
lbs. She's getting so big! Take a look at these great pictures taken around
Christmas.</font>
</p>
<table width="100%">
<tr>
<td width="33%" align="center" rowspan="2"><img border="0"
src="BrieXmas99.jpg" alt="How
can you resist me?"
width="200" height="341"></td>
<td width="33%"
align="center"><img border="0"
src="BrieFlakeXmas99.jpg"
alt="You can't hide from a
sight hound!" width="200"
height="217"></td>
</tr>
<tr>
<td width="33%"
align="center"><img border="0"
src="UrsaPuffBedXmas99.jpg"
alt="The illusion of
gentility..." width="300"
height="197"></td>
</tr>
</table>
</body>
</html>
```

Conclusion

This chapter took a good look at some of the tools XHTML provides for tables. There is actually still more to learn, if you can believe it! You are encouraged to check out Appendix A, "XHTML Element and Entity List," to review a complete list of table elements and attributes. With this reference and the basic knowledge acquired in this chapter, you should be well on your way to table creation.

This chapter also brings us to the end of Part II of the book. Part III, "Mouse and Keyboard," will begin to explore the really advanced XHTML material, beginning with Chapter 11, "You've Been Framed," which examines one of the more complicated and controversial aspects of XHTML today: framed documents.

PART III

Mouse and Keyboard

11

You've Been Framed

Using frames in your Web document is sort of like opening up a beehive. If you do it right, all is good. If you do it wrong, be prepared for the angry buzzing of visitors to your site.

In this chapter, you'll learn how to do the following:

- Create simple frame pages
- Manage your frames professionally
- Make sure browsers that can't read frames can still read your pages
- Build special inline frames

When surfing on the Internet, every once in a while you will notice pages that seem to be carved into sections. Each section is apparently independent of the others, even though you have only visited a single XHTML file—or so you think.

What you have stumbled onto are frames, an innovative and sometimes annoying way to convey information on the World Wide Web. They are innovative because when used properly, they can add a lot of panache to your Web pages. If abused, they can become an annoying detriment to your document. To make matters worse, as with the Force, it is very easy to walk on the dark side of frames.

Dividing Your Document into Multiple Parts

It needs to be said up front that frames should be used with discretion on your Web pages. The issue here is one of time. When a framed page is loaded, you are not loading just one page, but multiple pages. For someone with a dial-up Internet connection, that can be a huge pain because a page with frames takes longer to load.

That said, frames can be used in moderation to pull off some nice effects. Before we get to those, let's start with the basics.

Using Simple Frames

Frames are created with the combination of two elements: `<frameset>` and `<frame>`. The `<frameset>` element is to framed documents what `<body>` is to non-framed documents. This is a literal statement. If you have a framed document, you must use the `<frameset>` element instead of the `<body>` element and position it just after the `<head>` element. The `<frameset>` element's primary responsibility is to build the spaces for the framed material to "pour" into.

Within the `<frameset>` element, the `<frame>` element is the one that actually calls the content for a frame. The `<frame>` element is an empty element that calls up the source material for a frame, much like the `<img>` element calls an image file for display. In fact, the `<frame>` element uses the `src` attribute to specify the URL (absolute or relative) of the file to display.

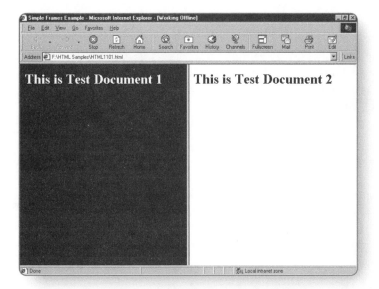

A visual example will certainly help you to see the relationship of these elements:

```
<html>
<head>
<title>Simple Frames
Example</title>
</head>
<frameset cols="50%,50%">
    <frame src="test1.html" />
    <frame src="test2.html" />
</frameset>
</html>
```

Breaking down this code, you can see the `cols` attribute within the `<frameset>` element. This attribute uses absolute and *two* sets of relative values to dictate the size of the frames: relational and percentage.

First, the absolute values are expressed in pixels with just a plain integer. If you wanted to specify the width of the left frame to 100 pixels, you would use these values:

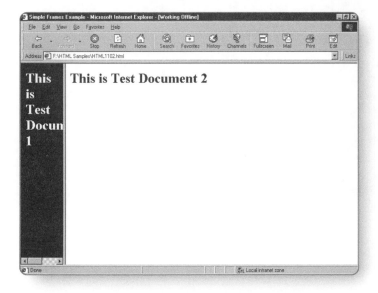

```
<html>
<head>
<title>Simple Frames
Example</title>
</head>
<frameset cols="100,*">
    <frame src="test1.html" />
    <frame src="test2.html" />
</frameset>
</html>
```

> **NOTE**
>
> When you use absolute values, there's a catch. You cannot specify the absolute size of all the frames in the frameset. If you were to try, the browser reading this code would (incorrectly) presume you were setting up a relational set of values and display accordingly. You must leave one of the frame's sizes open (using the * value) to use absolute values, whether you are creating two frames or 20.

Notice that we did absolutely nothing to the `<frame>` elements. Their job—calling up other files—is unaffected by these proceedings.

Unlike other aspects of XHTML, there are times when absolute values come in very handy, most notably when you are using a navigational row or column of buttons in a frame. You'll want that particular frame's size to be exact.

In many cases, you will want to use relative values to indicate frame size. The most familiar ones to you would be the percentage values used here.

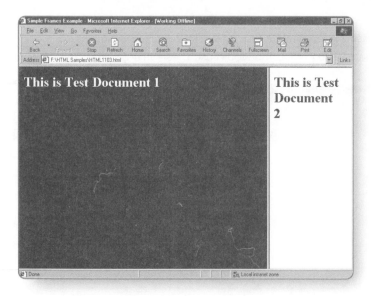

```
<html>
<head>
<title>Simple Frames
Example</title>
</head>
<frameset cols="75%,25%">
    <frame src="test1.html" />
    <frame src="test2.html" />
</frameset>
</html>
```

This percentage ratio is maintained no matter what size the browser window is.

Relational values are pretty interesting when dealing with frame size. These are concerned with relative lengths and denoted by an integer value immediately followed by an * (n*). If, for instance, you wanted the right column to be five times the size of the left, you would use the following:

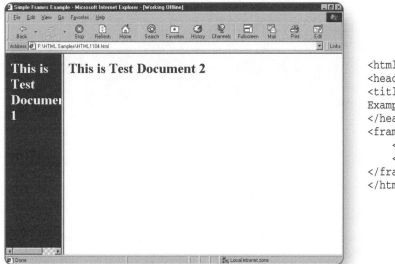

```
<html>
<head>
<title>Simple Frames
Example</title>
</head>
<frameset cols="1*,5*">
    <frame src="test1.html" />
    <frame src="test2.html" />
</frameset>
</html>
```

As with percentage values, this relational condition remains the same regardless of browser size. You might see this as being the same as percentages. You would be correct, too. But sometimes, relational values are easier to calculate than percentage values. (In this situation, the percentage value would have been 16.67 percent to 83.33 percent, which is certainly not as intuitive as 1 to 5!)

All of these value types are valid for the rows attribute as well.

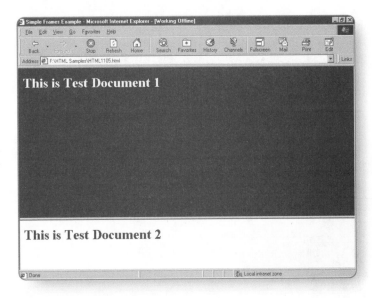

```
<html>
<head>
<title>Simple Frames
Example</title>
</head>
<frameset rows="75%,25%">
    <frame src="test1.html" />
    <frame src="test2.html" />
</frameset>
</html>
```

You can also work with both attributes together if you use nested `<frameset>` elements. Using a variation of the previous examples, first build the following:

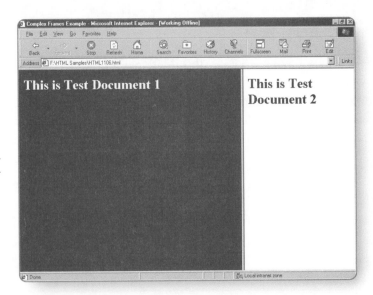

```
<html>
<head>
<title>Complex Frames
Example</title>
</head>
<frameset cols="2*,1*">
    <frame src="test1.html" />
    <frame src="test2.html" />
</frameset>
</html>
```

By enclosing this all within another `<frameset>` element, we can get a great effect:

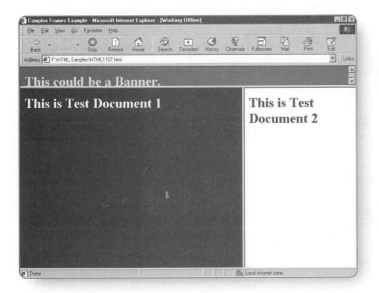

```
<html>
<head>
<title>Complex Frames
Example</title>
</head>
<frameset rows="10%,*">
   <frame src="banner.html" />
<frameset cols="2*,1*">
   <frame src="test1.html" />
   <frame src="test2.html" />
</frameset>
</frameset>
</html>
```

Special Frame Effects

You can do a couple of interesting things with frames to enhance their look. One of the most common questions people have is how to get rid of that gray border between frames. This is simply a matter of using the `frameborder` attribute in the `<frame>` element. This attribute has two values: `0` and `1`, which will hide or show the frame's border, respectively.

```
<html>
<head>
<title>Borderless Frames Example</title>
</head>
<frameset rows="10%,*" >
   <frame src="banner.html" frameborder="0" />
<frameset cols="2*,1*">
   <frame src="test1.html" frameborder="0" />
   <frame src="test2.html" frameborder="0" />
</frameset>
</frameset>
</html>
```

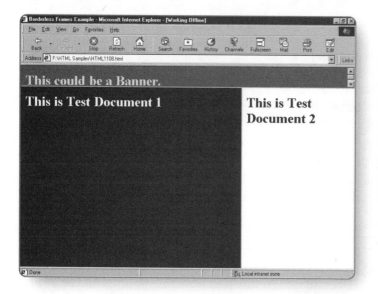

In the Internet Explorer browser, there still seems to be a gap between the frames. What gives? The sidebar below gives the answer. As the sidebar suggests, use the XHTML *and* browser-specific attributes for borderless frames.

BROWSER
BROWSER

Browsers handle borderless frames in disparate ways. In Internet Explorer, not only do you have to indicate the `frameborder` attribute, you must also set the value of the browser-specific attribute `framespacing` to 0. Netscape only requires its `border` attribute be equal to 0. To make sure you accommodate all visiting browsers, use the `border` and `frameborder` attributes in the `<frame>` element and the `framespacing` attribute in the `<frameset>` element.

```
<html>
<head>
<title>Borderless Frames Example</title>
</head>
<frameset rows="10%,*" framespacing="0" >
    <frame src="banner.html" frameborder="0" border="0" />
<frameset cols="2*,1*" framespacing="0">
    <frame src="test1.html" frameborder="0" border="0" />
    <frame src="test2.html" frameborder="0" border="0" />
</frameset>
</frameset>
</html>
```

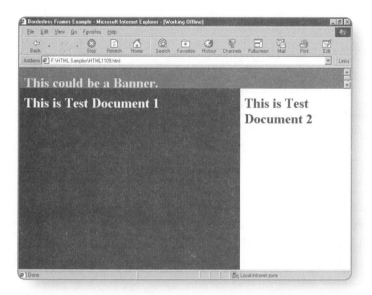

Another thing you might want to do is control the appearance of the scrollbar within each frame. This is done with the `scrolling` attribute of the `<frame>` element. Scrolling has three possible values: `yes`, `no`, and `auto`, which is the default value. Specifying `yes` always places the scrollbar in the frame, and `auto` does so only if the frame's content overflows from the frame. The `no` value always hides the scrollbars.

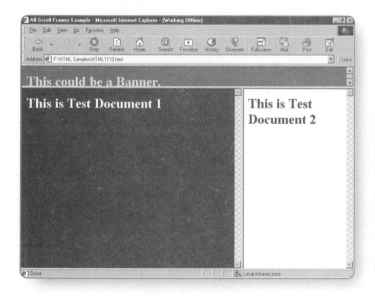

The following illustrates how the `yes` value of the `scrolling` attribute works with your browser.

CAUTION

You should rarely, if ever, specify no scrollbars. If you do this, you could potentially leave your site's visitors unable to view portions of the content.

```
<html>
<head>
<title>All-Scroll Frames Example</title>
</head>
<frameset rows="10%,*">
    <frame src="banner.html" scrolling="yes" />
<frameset cols="2*,1*">
    <frame src="test1.html" scrolling="yes" />
    <frame src="test2.html" scrolling="yes" />
</frameset>
</frameset>
</html>
```

If you visit framed Web pages, you may have noticed that you can resize the frames yourself by simply clicking and dragging the frame border (if it's there). As a Web page author, you might not want people to do this. For all of you control freaks out there, there's the `noresize` attribute. When you use this attribute in the `<frame>` element, your frame is "locked" into position.

Because `noresize` is valueless, in HTML it can appear as is within the `<frame>` element. In XHTML, it must appear as `noresize="noresize"` to be valid.

```
<html>
<head>
<title>All-Scroll Frames Example</title>
</head>
<frameset rows="10%,*">
    <frame src="banner.html" noresize="noresize" />
<frameset cols="2*,1*">
    <frame src="test1.html" noresize="noresize" />
    <frame src="test2.html" noresize="noresize" />
</frameset>
</frameset>
</html>
```

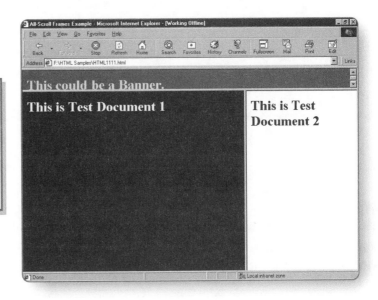

NOTE
If you have removed the borders from your frames, many browsers will not let users resize the frame.

Trafficking Frames

You've set up your frames just the way you want them. You have links in one frame, such as a navigation bar that leads to the rest of your fabulous site. You click on a link...and the whole page is replaced by the destination page, without frames. That wasn't supposed to happen! Where did the navigation frame go?

Fear not, loyal reader, we're here to help.

Linking to Other Frames

First, we will use this set of pages for our example:

```
<html>
<head>
<title>Navigating Frames</title>
</head>
<frameset cols="165,*">
    <frame src="navbar.html" scrolling="no" />
    <frame src="home.html" scrolling="no" />
</frameset>
</html>
```

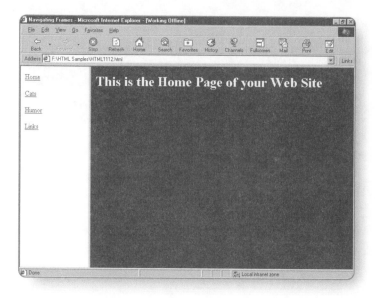

Okay, aesthetically, it leaves something to be desired. But all we're interested in now is the mechanics of the pages. The first thing you need to do to prepare for frame navigation is to give all of the frames in your document a name using (big surprise) the name attribute.

```html
<html>
<head>
<title>Navigating Frames</title>
</head>
<frameset cols="165,*">
    <frame src="navbar.html" scrolling="no" name="Navigation" />
    <frame src="home.html" scrolling="no" name="Content" />
</frameset>
</html>
```

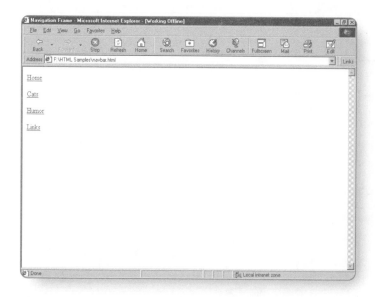

Though these names aren't visible, they are important nonetheless. These names enable your browser to know in which frame to open a linked file. To use these names, we must first open the navbar.html file that fills the left frame.

```
<html>
<head>
<title>Navigation Frame</title>
</head>
<body>
<p><a href="home.html">Home</a></p>
<p><a href="cats.html">Cats</a></p>
<p><a href="funny.html">Humor</a></p>
<p><a href="links.html">Links</a></p>
</body>
</html>
```

Again, not much to write home about. But here's where things get interesting. You know that the name of the right-side frame is `"Content"` and you want to have all of your site's pages open in that frame. Now you must declare this intent with the `target` attribute of `<a>`. If you set the value of `target` equal to the `name` of the frame in which you want the linked file to open, you will get the desired effect.

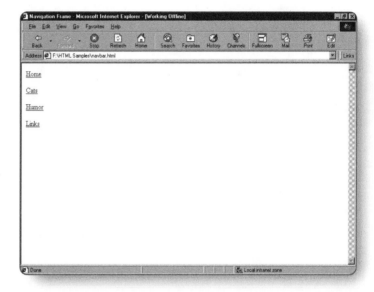

```
<html>
<head>
<title>Navigation Frame</title>
</head>
<body>
<p><a href="home.html" target="Content">Home</a></p>
<p><a href="cats.html" target="Content">Cats</a></p>
<p><a href="funny.html" target="Content">Humor</a></p>
<p><a href="links.html" target="Content">Home</a></p>
</body>
</html>
```

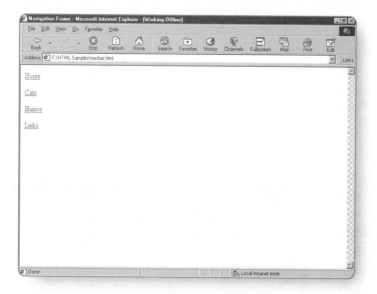

Now when you click using the main page's code, the linked page will open in the target frame.

TIP

If all the links in your site need to open in the same frame, you can use `<base target="name of target frame" />` in your component documents instead of using the `target` attribute in every instance of the `<a>` element.

```html
<html>
<head>
<title>Navigating Frames</title>
</head>
<frameset cols="165,*">
    <frame src="navbar.html" scrolling="no" name="Navigation" />
    <frame src="home.html" scrolling="no" name="Content" />
</frameset>
</html>
```

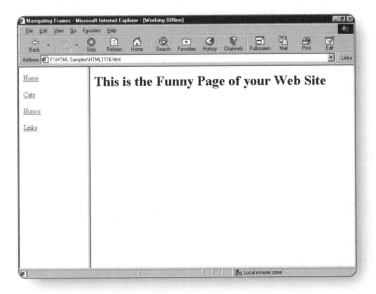

Opening New Windows

Many people have pet peeves: drivers who cut you off in traffic, most politicians... you know the rest. Here is one of our pet peeves: frames from one site that stay with you even after you have clicked a link to a completely different Web site! That burns us up, because it is so easy to fix!

Besides the names of frames, the target attribute of <a> has four special values. These special values are denoted by a preceding underline character (_) and serve as "reset" controls for frames.

Table 11-1 lists these special target values and their effect on framed documents.

You should be careful using these values, because it is easy to trip up clear navigation of your Web site. Be particularly careful with the _blank value. Although opening new browser windows is cool, too much of this drains your visitor's PC resources, not to mention annoys the user.

> **TIP**
>
> Always, always use the _top value when linking anywhere outside of your framed site! Don't let your frames cling to visitors' browsers like a leech!

Table 11-1 Special `target` Values

Value	Description
_blank	Opens the file in a brand-new browser window
_self	Opens the file in the current frame
_parent	Replaces the current frameset file with the new file
_top	Clears all of the frames and loads the file in the current browser

Dealing with the Frames-Challenged

The title of this section is meant to be humorous, but you should have two big concerns when creating frames on your site:

- What do you do about browsers that cannot read frames?

- What do you do about users who hate frames?

The answer to both of these questions is the same: you need to provide your site's readers with a non-frames option. The first way can be done on your framed entrance page using the <noframes> element. Confused? Don't be; all will become clear. With the <noframes> element, you can create an entire Web page visible only to those whose browsers do not see frames.

```
<html>
<head>
<title>Frames? What Frames?</title>
</head>
<frameset cols="165,*">
    <frame src="navbar.html" scrolling="no" name="Navigation" />
    <frame src="home.html" scrolling="no" name="Content" />
</frameset>
<noframes>
<body>
<h1>Whoops!</h1>
<p>You have come through the front door of the site, only to find that it uses
frames! Have no fear, friends! A non-frame version of this site is <a
href="nfhome.html">available</a>.</p>
</body>
</noframes>
</html>
```

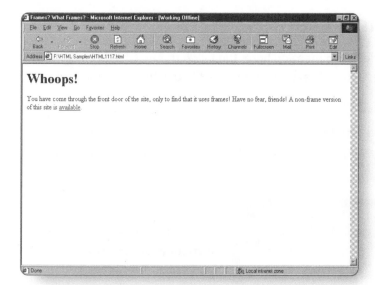

When non-frame browsers surf into your site, they should see a nice message pointing them to a home page for your non-framed pages.

TIP

Groaning at the prospect of maintaining another set of Web pages? No need, really. If you were using frames for navigation, which is common, just place a set of navigation links at the bottom of your "regular" set of Web pages. They will be slightly redundant when they appear within frames, but that's a small price to pay to avoid keeping track of multiple versions of the same files.

TIP

You should even put a link to the non-framed version of your site on your framed pages. Just because someone's browser can see frames does not mean that someone wants to contend with frames.

Inserting Inline Frames

Another type of frame deserves mention here: the inline frame, which can be used to create actual floating boxes of text on your page, filled with any content you want.

This feat is accomplished with the `<iframe>` element, which cleverly creates a rectangular area on your page that an entire XHTML document (or any other kind of file) could fit into.

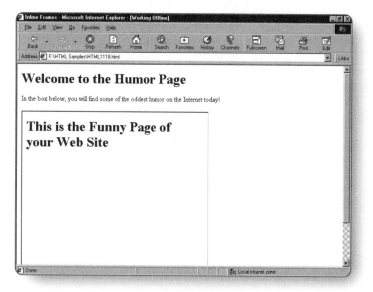

Two of the three most important attributes of `<iframe>` are `height` and `width`. The values of these attributes specify in pixels how big of an area you want the inline frame to be. The other important attribute is `src`, which, like its counterpart in the `<img>` and `<frames>` element, calls up the file to display in the inline frame.

```
<html>
<head>
<title>Inline Frames</title>
</head>
<body>
<h1>Welcome to the Humor Page</h1>
<p>In the box below, you will find some of the oddest humor on the Internet
today!</p>
<iframe src="funny.html" height="450" width="450">
</iframe>
</body>
</html>
```

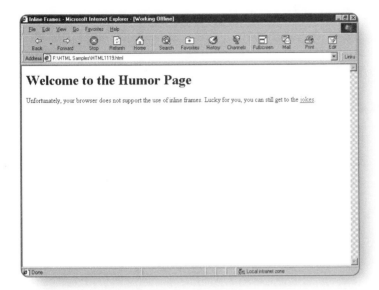

As with regular frames, not all browsers can see inline frames. Therefore, you should have a backup presentation ready. In `<iframe>`, you can insert as much alternate text as you want within the element—up to and including the entire original target document.

```
<html>
<head>
<title>Inline Frames</title>
</head>
<body>
<h1>Welcome to the Humor Page</h1>
<p>In the box below, you will find some of the oddest humor on the Internet
today!</p>
<iframe src="funny.html" height="450" width="450">
<p>Unfortunately, your browser does not support the use of inline frames.
Lucky for you, you can still get to the <a href="funny.html">jokes</a>.</p>
</iframe>
</body>
</html>
```

Conclusion

You have come a long way in learning some advanced XHTML techniques in this chapter. Though frames may still seem daunting, just build your pages slowly and carefully, checking your intra-site links and extra-site links very carefully. Links are the part that usually gets missed when a framed site is put together.

In Chapter 12, "Filling Out Forms," you will learn how to create the one awful thing that made the transition from paper to electronic format: the unstoppable form.

12

Filling Out Forms

It is estimated that over 70 percent of all business paperwork involves filling out forms. That's a lot of paper; not to mention the amount of time it takes to process each of those forms. There has to be a better way!

In this chapter, you'll learn how to do the following:

- Create simple forms
- Create complex forms for sophisticated data gathering
- Use the data you collect

The creators of XHTML have thoughtfully provided a solution to this paperwork mess by enabling us to create custom forms within our Web pages. The advantages of this are immediately obvious: a person could surf into the form page, provide the requested information, and send it directly to the data gatherer in electronic form! Compare this to filling out a paper form and delivering it to the right person, who then has to type in all the data from the paper form to the computer. Then add all the time it takes to file the form when it's finished, and you can see there's some real time and money to be saved by setting up electronic forms.

Of course, anything this useful is going to take some time to put together, but the XHTML involved in creating forms is not difficult, as you will soon see.

Creating a Simple Form

Before we start, let us explain a couple of things. There are essentially two parts to making a form with XHTML on your Web page: the XHTML part and the CGI part. When you create a form with XHTML, you will need to send the data collected in the form to somewhere else. This is handled by a Common Gateway Interface (CGI) script, which is a little application that typically takes data from a form, packages it, and then sends it to the appropriate user or file.

We will discuss CGI scripts in the "Collecting Form Data" section later in this chapter. For now, let's focus on building the front end to a form using the `<form>` element.

The `<form>` element has a number of attributes it uses to function properly, but none are as important as the `action` attribute. This attribute, which is mandatory for a working form, contains the URL of the aforementioned CGI script that will handle the form. Without this attribute, nothing in the form will work.

When a form is used, it must be submitted eventually. This is usually done with some kind of Submit button. The `method` attribute of the `<form>` element determines how the form's data is sent to the CGI script for handling. There are two values of `method`: `get` and `post`.

When the `method` is `get`, the input data is sent as a Get request to the Web server. Get requests are nothing more than your browser telling the Web server, "Excuse me, I would like to see this Web page. Would you be so kind as to send it to me?" Browsers do this every time they surf to a new Web page. What the `get` method does is append the typical Get request with all the data from your form, which your CGI script translates into a specific file request.

`get` is the default, but it is not always the best to use. Many browsers, for example, have a limit on just how many characters can be sent in a URL. Also, you can't send any special (non-ASCII) characters using `get`.

When the `method` is `post`, the form data is sent in the body of a request, not in the URL. This lets you send any number and type of characters to the server through the CGI script. For this reason, we recommend you use the `post` method whenever possible.

`<form>` has another attribute that will dictate how information is packaged and sent to the server. However, the `enctype` attribute always defaults to the value `application/x-www-form-urlencoded`—which is where it needs to be a vast majority of the time. Because the default is the norm, you can usually leave out this attribute.

There are additional attributes in `<form>`, but we'll cover them later. The important ones you need to remember now are `action` and `method`.

We need to mention one more element before starting the examples. The areas on the screen where you enter data are varied—text fields, check boxes, radio buttons. Despite this diversity, however, they are all products of the `<input>` element.

The way you can control these input areas is by defining the `type` attribute of the `<input>` element. The 10 values of `type` are listed in Table 12-1.

> **TIP**
>
> The only time the `enctype` attribute should be used is when you want users to upload whole files in a form's `<input>` element. Then `enctype` should equal `multipart/form-data` and `method` must equal `post`.

Table 12-1 The type Attribute Values

Value	Description
text	Creates a text box where characters can be typed
password	Creates a text box where characters can be typed but the input is masked as asterisks
checkbox	Generates a single check box control
radio	Generates a single radio button. Only one radio button in a group can be activated at a time
submit	Makes a special button type that submits all the data in the form to the CGI script
reset	Makes a special button type that resets all the data in the form to the original values
file	Displays a field where files can be inserted for upload
hidden	A non-displayed field that contains data the Web page author wants to include in the overall form data
image	Creates a graphical submit button
button	Creates a push button, which is usually used for client-side scripting

With these values in hand, let's begin by making a simple text field in a form.

```
<form action="dummy.cgi"
method="post">
<p>Please enter your favorite
fruit:</p>
<input type="text" />
</form>
```

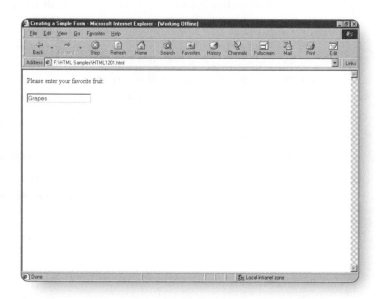

The default length of a text field is usually enough for your users. If you need something smaller or larger, you can use the `size` attribute to control the field size. If you want to further limit the amount of text a user can input in a text field, you can use the `maxlength` attribute. A great example of this is a field to enter the two-letter postal abbreviations for U.S. states and territories.

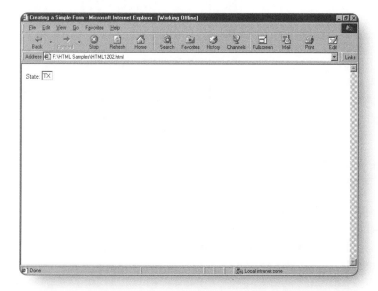

```
<form action="dummy.cgi"
method="post">
<p>State: <input type="text"
size="2" maxlength="2" /></p>
</form>
```

You can, for the record, use an `<input>` element outside of a `<form>` element in some browsers. However, Netscape Navigator will not allow this separation.

If you want to have a password entry field on your Web site, just use the `password` value of the `type` attribute.

```
<form action="dummy.cgi" method="post">
<p>Please enter your password: <input type="password" size="10" /></p>
</form>
```

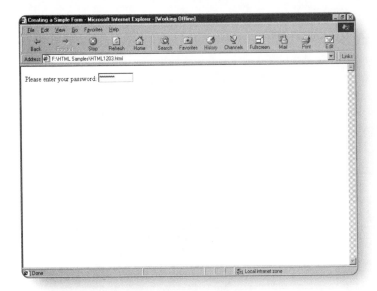

Though it looks like a text field, note how entered data appears only as asterisks.

With us so far? Great! Let's throw a new element into the mix to really get things going. Have you noticed the text that has been provided next to each field? When we first did it, we just used text adjacent to the fields. You can also use the <label> element—an element that describes the field and helps users navigate to it.

There are two ways to use the <label> element: implicitly and explicitly. Implicit use is the most straightforward method—you simply surround an <input> element with <label>.

```
<form action="dummy.cgi" method="post">
<h3>Please supply the following information.</h3>
<p>
<label>First name: <input type="text" size="12" /></label>
</p>
<p>
<label>Last name: <input type="text" size="20" /></label>
</p>
<p>
<label>E-mail: <input type="text" size="30" /></label>
</p>
</form>
```

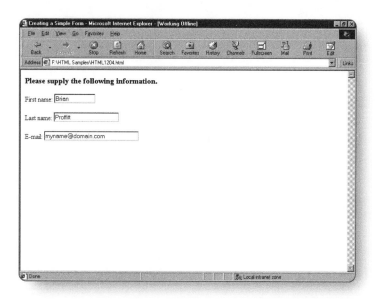

The difference between this and plain old ordinary text is subtle. When you click on the `<label>` text, the adjacent field is immediately brought into focus. In other words, the cursor appears in a text field.

You can improve this navigational ability by using the `accesskey` attribute. This, you may recall, creates a shortcut key that brings the given element (or, in this case, its field) into focus.

```
<form action="dummy.cgi" method="post">
<h3>Please supply the following information.</h3>
<p>
<label accesskey="f"><u>F</u>irst name: <input type="text" size="12"
/></label>
</p>
<p>
<label accesskey="l"><u>L</u>ast name: <input type="text" size="20" /></label>
</p>
<p>
<label accesskey="e"><u>E</u>-mail: <input type="text" size="30" /></label>
</p>
</form>
```

TIP

When using `accesskey`, be sure there is some kind of notation on your Web page to indicate this feature. In the previous example, we underlined the character that matched the `accesskey` value.

Now, when a user presses Alt+E simultaneously, the cursor is instantly placed in the E-mail text field.

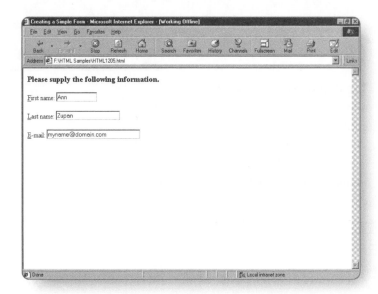

When you use `<label>` explicitly, you can actually separate the label from its field and still achieve the same effect. This is more of an advanced technique so it will be discussed in the "Making an Advanced Form" section later in this chapter.

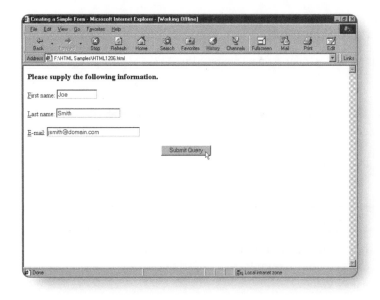

All our form examples have been missing a Submit button, which every good form should have. This special push button has one job: to submit the data in the form to the CGI script. It is easily created as another variant of the `<input>` element.

```
<form action="dummy.cgi" method="post">
<h3>Please supply the following information.</h3>
<p>
<label accesskey="f"><u>F</u>irst name: <input type="text" size="12"
/></label>
</p>
<p>
<label accesskey="l"><u>L</u>ast name: <input type="text" size="20" /></label>
</p>
<p>
<label accesskey="e"><u>E</u>-mail: <input type="text" size="30" /></label>
</p>
<center><input type="submit" /></center>
</form>
```

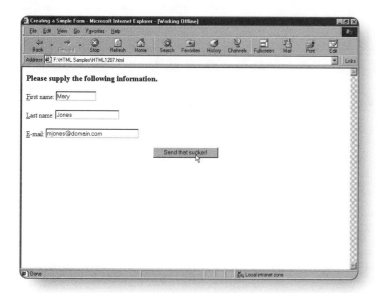

If you don't like the default text XHTML provides, you can create your own by using the `value` attribute.

```
<form action="dummy.cgi" method="post">
<h3>Please supply the following information.</h3>
<p>
<label accesskey="f"><u>F</u>irst name: <input type="text" size="12"
/></label>
</p>
<p>
<label accesskey="l"><u>L</u>ast name: <input type="text" size="20" /></label>
</p>
<p>
<label accesskey="e"><u>E</u>-mail: <input type="text" size="30" /></label>
</p>
<center><input type="submit" value="Send that sucker!" /></center>
</form>
```

You can also create a Reset
button in the same manner.

```
<form action="dummy.cgi" method="post">
<h3>Please supply the following information.</h3>
<p>
<label accesskey="f"><u>F</u>irst name: <input type="text" size="12"
/></label>
</p>
<p>
<label accesskey="l"><u>L</u>ast name: <input type="text" size="20" /></label>
</p>
<p>
<label accesskey="e"><u>E</u>-mail: <input type="text" size="30" /></label>
</p>
<center><input type="submit" value="Send that sucker!" />   <input
type="reset" value="I goofed! Do Over!" /></center>
</form>
```

Text fields and a submit/reset combination of buttons will likely be all you will need
in your forms. For the more adventurous among you, keep reading to discover how
to build even more form controls and how you can lay them out like a professional.

Making an Advanced Form

If your form needs go beyond that of a bunch of text fields, there are other controls you can use to make your form more efficient. Two of these form controls are radio buttons and check boxes.

For those of you unfamiliar with the term, radio buttons are those little round buttons that get filled in with a dark circle when selected. The rule about radio buttons is that only one in a group can be selected one at a time, just like the old car radio buttons (go ask your parents). Check boxes are just what they sound like: square boxes that get a little check mark in them when selected. The user can select as many check boxes as he or she wishes.

Creating these elements is easy. However, there are two additional steps you must take to get them to work. First, let's add radio buttons to our form:

```
<form action="dummy.cgi" method="post">
<h3>Please supply the following information.</h3>
<p>
<label accesskey="f"><u>F</u>irst name: <input type="text" size="12"
/></label>
</p>
<p>
<label accesskey="l"><u>L</u>ast name: <input type="text" size="20" /></label>
</p>
<p>
<label>Male  <input type="radio" /></label>
<br />
<label>Female  <input type="radio" /></label>
</p>
<p>
<label accesskey="e"><u>E</u>-mail: <input type="text" size="30" /></label>
</p>
<center><input type="submit" value="Send that sucker!" />   <input
type="reset" value="I goofed! Do Over!" /></center>
</form>
```

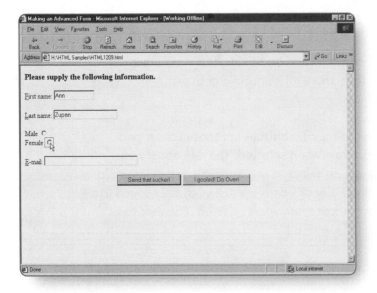

If we click on these radio buttons, we are surprised to find that they don't seem to function. The two buttons are not connected, so neither will work. We need to connect them using the name attribute. By giving each of these buttons the exact same name value, they will be connected.

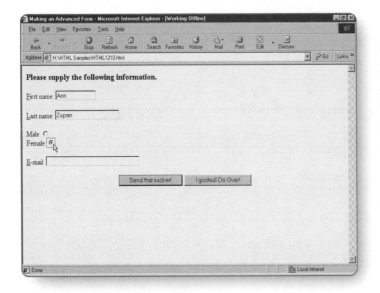

The other additional step we must take is to give each of these fields a value attribute. The value of value is sent to the CGI script when the form is submitted. You do not use this in a text field, because the value is whatever someone types into the field. value can be the same as the label for the field but it doesn't have to be.

```
<p>
<label>Male  <input type="radio" name="gender" value="Male" /></label>
<br />
<label>Female  <input type="radio" name="gender" value="Female" /></label>
</p>
```

NOTE

Now that we've brought up the `name` attribute, we can let you in on something very important: *all* fields and form controls (except buttons, where the value is implied) must have a `name` attribute with a valid value so that a form's data can be submitted.

With these additional attributes, the radio buttons will function both for the user and for the CGI script. A similar treatment must be given to check boxes.

```
<form action="dummy.cgi" method="post">
<h3>Please supply the following information.</h3>
<p>
<label accesskey="f"><u>F</u>irst name: <input name="first_name" type="text"
size="12" /></label>
</p>
<p>
<label accesskey="l"><u>L</u>ast name: <input name="last_name" type="text"
size="20" /></label>
</p>
<p>
<label>Male  <input type="radio" name="gender" value="Male" /></label>
<br />
<label>Female  <input type="radio" name="gender" value="Female" /></label>
</p>
<p>
<label accesskey="e"><u>E</u>-mail: <input name="email" type="text" size="30"
/></label>
</p>
<p>
<h3>Hobbies (Check all that apply)</h3>
<label>Cow tipping <input type="checkbox" name="hobbies" value="Cow"
/></label>
<br />
<label>Web page authoring <input type="checkbox" name="hobbies" value="Web"
/></label>
<br />
<label>Gambling <input type="checkbox" name="hobbies" value="vegas" /></label>
<br />
<label>Computers <input type="checkbox" name="hobbies" value="geek" /></label>
<br />
<label>Cooking <input type="checkbox" name="hobbies" value="Emeril" /></label>
</p>
<center><input type="submit" value="Send that sucker!" />   <input
type="reset" value="I goofed! Do Over!" /></center>
</form>
```

Once the form is submitted, the values of the selected check boxes and radio buttons are passed to the CGI script. Because you have named these form controls, you can have multiple sets of them anywhere in your Web document—they won't interfere with each other.

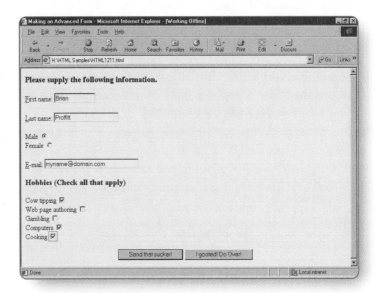

TIP

You can also apply `name` and `value` attributes to your form's button controls. This allows different actions to take place depending on which button is pushed.

Another nifty form control is the `<button>` element. This element may seem redundant with the `<input>` element at first, but you will soon see it's clearly not. For one thing, unlike the `<input>` element, `<button>` is not an empty element, so you can put all manner of things inside it.

The `<button>` element has three different values of its `type` attribute: `submit` (the default), `reset`, and `button`, a generic push button. These are completely synonymous with the same values of the `<input>` `type` attribute. You can do more creative things with the `<button>` element, even with just the text. By converting the buttons in our form from `<input>` to `<button>`, you can see what we mean.

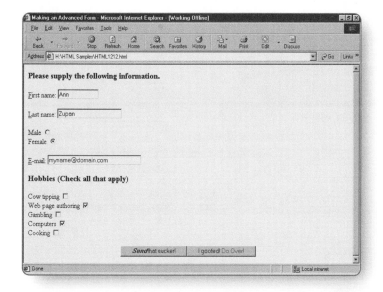

```
<center><button><b><i>Send</i>
</b>  that sucker!</button>
<button type="reset">I goofed!
<font color="red">Do
Over!</font></button></center>
```

We did not have to declare the first button as `type="submit"` because submit is the default. Not only can you play with the text of the button, you can also add images!

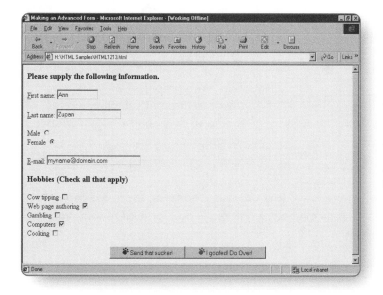

```
<center><button><img
src="bl_paw_bullet.gif" />
Send that sucker!</button>
<button type="reset"><img
src="rd_paw_bullet.gif" /> I
goofed! Do
Over!</button></center>
```

Inline graphics can be added to a button for a stylistic accent. For a really cool look, you can have the image *become* the button!

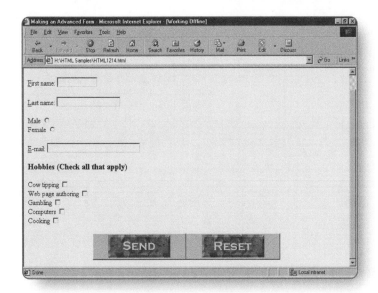

```
<center><button><img
src="../images/send.gif"
/></button>    <button
type="reset"><img
src="../images/reset.gif"
/></button></center>
```

TIP

If you use images alone to convey a button's meaning, be sure to include an `alt` attribute and value in the `<img>` element for those browsers that are not reading images; otherwise, your buttons will be useless.

TIP

There are hundreds of excellent sources out on the Web for button graphics. Simply search for "Web graphics" on your favorite Internet search engine to find and download a huge variety of graphics.

If you want your users to enter a lot of text on your Web form, say in a comments field, the text type of the `<input>` element won't really do. For a lot of text, you will need the `<textarea>` element.

The `<textarea>` element is not tricky to set up; it has two mandatory elements, `rows` and `cols`. The attributes determine the number of rows and character columns in the text area field. Adding this to our form, we get the following:

```
<form action="dummy.cgi" method="post">
<h3>Please supply the following information.</h3>
<p>
<label accesskey="f"><u>F</u>irst name: <input name="first_name" type="text"
size="12" /></label>
</p>
<p>
<label accesskey="l"><u>L</u>ast name: <input name="last_name" type="text"
size="20" /></label>
</p>
<p>
<label>Male  <input type="radio" name="gender" value="Male" /></label>
<br />
<label>Female  <input type="radio" name="gender" value="Female" /></label>
</p>
<p>
<label accesskey="e"><u>E</u>-mail: <input name="email" type="text" size="30"
/></label>
</p>
<p>
<h3>Hobbies (Check all that apply)</h3>
<label>Cow tipping <input type="checkbox" name="hobbies" value="Cow"
/></label>
<br />
<label>Web page authoring <input type="checkbox" name="hobbies" value="Web"
/></label>
<br />
<label>Gambling <input type="checkbox" name="hobbies" value="vegas" /></label>
<br />
<label>Computers <input type="checkbox" name="hobbies" value="geek" /></label>
<br />
<label>Cooking <input type="checkbox" name="hobbies" value="Emeril" /></label>
</p>
<p>
<textarea name="story" rows="10" cols="75 ">Please type your story
here.</textarea>
</p>
<center><button><img src="../images/send.gif" /></button>    <button
type="reset"><img src="../images/reset.gif" /></button></center>
</form>
```

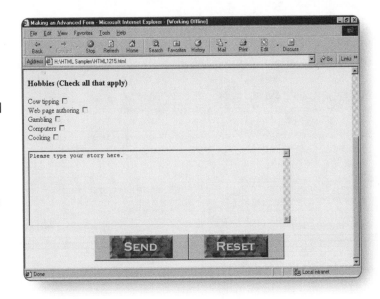

Looking at the output of the latest example, you can see that it is not the best-organized form in the world. The fields and labels seem to just fall on the page, with no clear organization. What's the best way to organize a form? With a table, of course!

As you learned in Chapter 10, "Building Tables," you can create invisible tables that can produce sharp layouts for your Web pages. The following code gives but one example of a layout for our form:

```
<h3>Please supply the following information.</h3>
<form action="dummy.cgi" method="post">
<table border="0" align="left" cellspacing="2" cellpadding="2">
<tr>
<td align="left"><label accesskey="f"><u>F</u>irst name: <input
name="first_name" type="text" size="12" /></label></td>
<td align="left" rowspan="5"><b>What is your Weirdest Story?</b><br><textarea
name="story" rows="15" cols="50 ">Please type your story here.</textarea></td>
</tr>
<tr>
<td><label accesskey="l"><u>L</u>ast name: <input name="last_name" type="text"
size="20" /></label></td>
</tr>
<tr>
<td><label accesskey="e"><u>E</u>-mail: <input name="email" type="text"
size="30" /></label></td>
</tr>
<tr>
<td><label>Male  <input type="radio" name="gender" value="Male" /></label>
<label>Female  <input type="radio" name="gender" value="Female"
/></label></td>
</tr>
<tr>
<td><b>Hobbies (Check all that apply)</b>
```

```
<label>Cow tipping <input type="checkbox" name="hobbies" value="Cow"
/></label>
<br />
<label>Web page authoring <input type="checkbox" name="hobbies" value="Web"
/></label>
<br />
<label>Gambling <input type="checkbox" name="hobbies" value="vegas" /></label>
<br />
<label>Computers <input type="checkbox" name="hobbies" value="geek" /></label>
<br />
<label>Cooking <input type="checkbox" name="hobbies" value="Emeril"
/></label></td>
</tr>
<tr>
<td align="center" colspan="2"><button><img src="../images/send.gif"
/></button>   <button type="reset"><img src="../images/reset.gif"
/></button></td>
</tr>
</table>
</form>
```

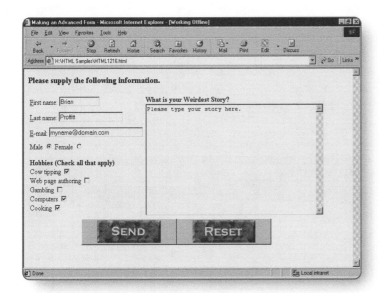

Not bad, but we can do a bit better.

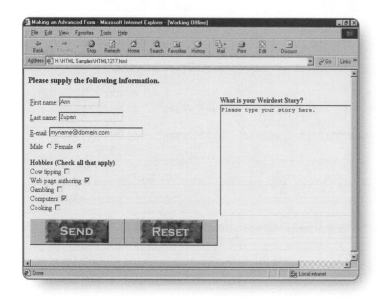

Remember when we mentioned earlier in this chapter that you could use the `<label>` element explicitly? Now's when this will come in handy. By adding another column in the middle of the table, we have the following:

```
<tr>
<td align="left"><label accesskey="f"><u>F</u>irst name: <input
name="first_name" type="text" size="12" /></label></td>
<td></td>
<td align="left" rowspan="5"><b>What is your Weirdest Story?</b><br><textarea
rows="15" cols="50 ">Please type your story here.</textarea></td>
</tr>
```

We can then place the `<label>` element in one column, and `<input>` element in the next one.

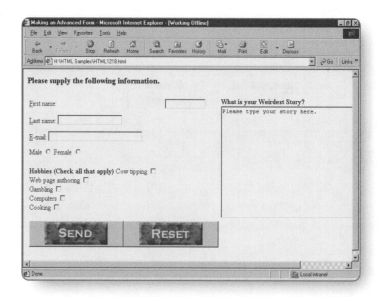

```
<tr>
<td align="left"><label accesskey="f"><u>F</u>irst name: </label></td>
<td><input name="first_name" type="text" size="12" /></td>
<td align="left" rowspan="5"><b>What is your Weirdest Story?</b><br><textarea
rows="15" cols="50 ">Please type your story here.</textarea></td>
</tr>
```

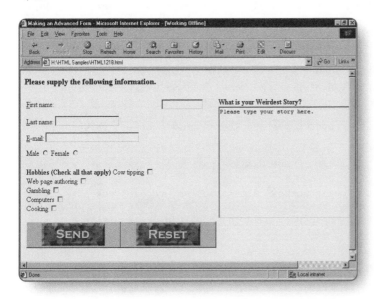

While this looks all right, there is still one more thing we need to do. In order to explicitly connect the label with the input field, we must use the `for` attribute in `<label>` to link to the `name` attribute in `<input>`. Giving these attributes the same value will link them no matter where they are on the page. After doing this and making some adjustments to the table, we will have this:

```
<h3>Please supply the following information.</h3>
<form action="dummy.cgi" method="post">
<table border="0" align="left" cellspacing="2" cellpadding="2">
<tr>
<tr>
<td align="left"><label for="first_name" accesskey="f"><u>F</u>irst name:
</label></td>
<td><input name="first_name" type="text" size="12" /></td>
<td align="left" rowspan="5"><b>What is your Weirdest Story?</b><br><textarea
rows="15" cols="50 ">Please type your story here.</textarea></td>
</tr>
</tr>
<tr>
<td align="left"><label for="last_name" accesskey="l"><u>L</u>ast name:
</label></td>
<td><input name="last_name" type="text" size="20" /></td>
```

```
</tr>
<tr>
<td align="left"><label for="email" accesskey="e"><u>E</u>-mail: </label></td>
<td><input name="email" type="text" size="30" /></td>
</tr>
<tr>
<td colspan="2" align="center"><label>Male  <input type="radio" name="gender"
value="Male" /></label>  <label>Female  <input type="radio" name="gender"
value="Female" /></label></td>
</tr>
<tr>
<td colspan="2"><b>Hobbies (Check all that apply)</b><br />
<label>Cow tipping <input type="checkbox" name="hobbies" value="Cow"
/></label>
<br />
<label>Web page authoring <input type="checkbox" name="hobbies" value="Web"
/></label>
<br />
<label>Gambling <input type="checkbox" name="hobbies" value="vegas" /></label>
<br />
<label>Computers <input type="checkbox" name="hobbies" value="geek" /></label>
<br />
<label>Cooking <input type="checkbox" name="hobbies" value="Emeril"
/></label></td>
</tr>
<tr>
<td align="center" colspan="3"><button><img src="../images/send.gif"
/></button>   <button type="reset"><img src="../images/reset.gif"
/></button></td>
</tr>
</table>
</form>
```

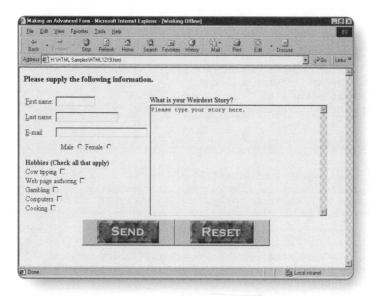

Collecting Form Data

Once you have your form built, you will need to do something with it. You have two options—only one of them acceptable. You could have the data e-mailed somewhere by placing a `mailto` value in the `action` attribute of `<form>`. We strongly discourage you from doing this, for two reasons. First, a lot of older browsers do not support this action. Second, anytime you put an e-mail address on a Web page, even in the code, a search engine is going to pick it up and you are going to get a lot of junk e-mail (spam) in the account in which you are trying to collect data. Stay away from this option and go with the better one: a CGI script.

If you have been reading this chapter, you have seen a little bit about how forms work, but in order for a form to truly function, one thing must be made clear: *all form fields and controls must have a* `name` *attribute with a valid value.* This is so that when data is passed to the CGI script for processing, it can have clear value assignments (name1=value1, name2=value2, and so on).

The trick of using CGI is, if you are not a programmer, how are you going to use it? And there is another problem with CGI for everyone: not all Web hosts allow CGI to run on their systems, because they don't want to open themselves up to the potential security problems a badly written piece of CGI code could cause.

There are answers. First, for all you programmers, we strongly recommend you pick up a good book on Perl. Learning how to write CGI scripts is not too difficult if you already have a programming skill set.

For you non-programmers, there are great Web sites out there that will provide free CGI scripts for your pages. Check out the CGI Resource Index at **http://www.cgi-resources.com/Programs_and_Scripts/** for these freebies.

If your service provider is unwilling to let you use CGI locally, remember that you can always use a remote URL in the `action` attribute of `<form>`. There are even sites that will host your CGI script remotely for free. Visit **http://www.cgi-resources.com/Programs_and_Scripts/Remotely_Hosted/Form_Processing/** to learn more.

Once you have your CGI script in place, you can then sit back and watch the data roll in!

Conclusion

Building a form is not complicated, provided you stick to some basic rules of the road. Remember, if you see a form technique out on the Web that you really admire, take a look at the source code and see what the author did to accomplish the effect.

Some of the most interesting effects achieved on the Internet involve the use of images as navigation tools. In Chapter 13, we'll show you just how easy it is to build your own interactive navigation images—otherwise known as image maps.

13

Navigating with Images

On many occasions, you will find yourself clicking on images to move around a Web site. For those of you who ever wanted to learn how to do this on your own site, you've turned to the right page!

In this chapter, you'll learn how to do the following:

- Use thumbnail images to enhance your site's navigation
- Select the right kind of image for an image map
- Create an image map

Sailors used to navigate with clocks. By taking a measurement of the sun at its highest point in the sky, they knew when local noon was. They compared that to the time on their clocks, which was always set to keep the time at home. Once they knew how far apart local noon and home noon were, they had a pretty good idea of how far east or west of home they were—which is pretty amazing if you think about it. Just a little simple math told them so much.

When dealing with images, a lot of what you have to implement is really just simple math. So dig up those old geometry memories; you're going to use them.

Surfing with Thumbnail Images

When your Web site has a lot of images, it is colorful, attractive, and usually appealing to readers. At the same time, a lot of images cause readers a lot of headaches. Images take time to download, particularly large images.

You can, however, improve the download speed of your pages while preserving the whole reason for having images.

In this example, the Web page shows photos taken at the Grand Canyon.

```
<center><h1>Grand Canyon: A Painting in Real Life</h1></center>
<p>These pictures were taken on a family vacation in 1998. They are slightly
hazy, due to smoke from the brush fires occurring that month on the North Rim
of the Canyon. Pictures alone cannot convey the incredible majesty of seeing
the Canyon for yourself--go now!</p>
<p><img src="../images/13.jpg" height="400" width="600" border="0" /></p>
<p><img src="../images/16.jpg" height="400" width="600" border="0" /></p>
<p><img src="../images/17.jpg" height="400" width="600" border="0" /></p>
<p><img src="../images/29.jpg" height="400" width="600" border="0" /></p>
<p><img src="../images/30.jpg" height="400" width="600" border="0" /></p>
<p><img src="../images/31.jpg" height="400" width="600" border="0" /></p>
<p><img src="../images/32.jpg" height="600" width="400" border="0" /></p>
<p><img src="../images/33.jpg" height="400" width="600" border="0" /></p>
<p><img src="../images/34.jpg" height="400" width="600" border="0" /></p>
<p><img src="../images/35.jpg" height="400" width="600" border="0" /></p>
<p><img src="../images/38.jpg" height="400" width="600" border="0" /></p>
<p><img src="../images/39.jpg" height="600" width="400" border="0" /></p>
<p><img src="../images/40.jpg" height="600" width="400" border="0" /></p>
<p><img src="../images/41.jpg" height="400" width="600" border="0" /></p>
<p><img src="../images/42.jpg" height="400" width="600" border="0" /></p>
<p><img src="../images/43.jpg" height="400" width="600" border="0" /></p>
<p><img src="../images/44.jpg" height="400" width="600" border="0" /></p>
```

Visually, this is a simple page with 17 images. You find these kinds of pages all over the Internet. At second glance, this page has some problems. First, it's a long scrolling page, which is not always a good thing. People want to see as much information on a single pane as possible. Scrolling is an extra step. Secondly, and this is the insidious part, the images are 668 KB, which means even on a fast modem, they would take more than a minute to download. That may not seem

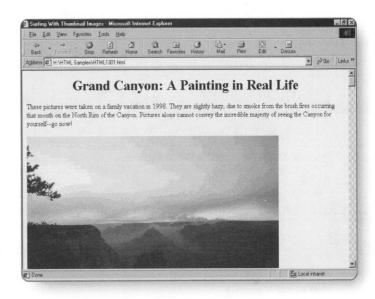

like a big deal, but these minutes add up. And, your visitors might not want to see every image you have.

The way to get around this is to use a graphics program to create thumbnail images and display them instead of the originals. Thumbnail images are miniature versions of your images that are designed to convey the gist of the original image.

Once you make the thumbnails, you can use a table to lay them out on your page. You should then include a link from the thumbnail image to the original image. In this example, we have done that and included a text link from the original image's file name.

> **NOTE**
>
> Graphic programs such as Adobe Photoshop (**http://www.adobe.com/**), ThumbsPlus (**http://www.cerious.com/**), and ACDSee (**http://www.acdsee.com/**) are very capable of creating thumbnail images.

```
<center><h1>Grand Canyon: A Painting in Real Life</h1></center>
<p>These pictures were taken on a family vacation in 1998. They are slightly
hazy, due to smoke from the brush fires occurring that month on the North Rim
of the Canyon. Pictures alone cannot convey the incredible majesty of seeing
the Canyon for yourself--go now!</p>
<p>Click on any of these thumbnail images to see a full size version of the
image!</p>
<center>
```

```
<table>
<tr>
<td align="center" valign="bottom"><font size="-2"><a
href="../images/13.jpg"><img src="../images/tn_13.jpg" alt="13.jpg" border="0"
/><br />13.jpg</a></font></td>
<td align="center" valign="bottom"><font size="-2"><a
href="../images/16.jpg"><img src="../images/tn_16.jpg" alt="16.jpg" border="0"
/><br />16.jpg</a></font></td>
<td align="center" valign="bottom"><font size="-2"><a
href="../images/17.jpg"><img src="../images/tn_17.jpg" alt="17.jpg" border="0"
/><br />17.jpg</a></font></td>
<td align="center" valign="bottom"><font size="-2"><a
href="../images/29.jpg"><img src="../images/tn_29.jpg" alt="29.jpg" border="0"
/><br />29.jpg</a></font></td>
<td align="center" valign="bottom"><font size="-2"><a
href="../images/30.jpg"><img src="../images/tn_30.jpg" alt="30.jpg" border="0"
/><br />30.jpg</a></font></td>
<td align="center" valign="bottom"><font size="-2"><a
href="../images/31.jpg"><img src="../images/tn_31.jpg" alt="31.jpg" border="0"
/><br />31.jpg</a></font></td>
</tr>
<tr>
<td align="center" valign="bottom"><font size="-2"><a
href="../images/32.jpg"><img src="../images/tn_32.jpg" alt="32.jpg" border="0"
/><br />32.jpg</a></font></td>
<td align="center" valign="bottom"><font size="-2"><a
href="../images/33.jpg"><img src="../images/tn_33.jpg" alt="33.jpg" border="0"
/><br />33.jpg</a></font></td>
<td align="center" valign="bottom"><font size="-2"><a
href="../images/34.jpg"><img src="../images/tn_34.jpg" alt="34.jpg" border="0"
/><br />34.jpg</a></font></td>
<td align="center" valign="bottom"><font size="-2"><a
href="../images/35.jpg"><img src="../images/tn_35.jpg" alt="35.jpg" border="0"
/><br />35.jpg</a></font></td>
<td align="center" valign="bottom"><font size="-2"><a
href="../images/38.jpg"><img src="../images/tn_38.jpg" alt="38.jpg" border="0"
/><br />38.jpg</a></font></td>
<td align="center" valign="bottom"><font size="-2"><a
href="../images/39.jpg"><img src="../images/tn_39.jpg" alt="39.jpg" border="0"
/><br />39.jpg</a></font></td>
</tr>
<tr>
<td align="center" valign="bottom"><font size="-2"><a
href="../images/40.jpg"><img src="../images/tn_40.jpg" alt="40.jpg" border="0"
/><br />40.jpg</a></font></td>
<td align="center" valign="bottom"><font size="-2"><a
href="../images/41.jpg"><img src="../images/tn_41.jpg" alt="41.jpg" border="0"
/><br />41.jpg</a></font></td>
<td align="center" valign="bottom"><font size="-2"><a
href="../images/42.jpg"><img src="../images/tn_42.jpg" alt="42.jpg" border="0"
/><br />42.jpg</a></font></td>
<td align="center" valign="bottom"><font size="-2"><a
href="../images/43.jpg"><img src="../images/tn_43.jpg" alt="43.jpg" border="0"
/><br />43.jpg</a></font></td>
```

```
<td align="center" valign="bottom"><font size="-2"><a
href="../images/44.jpg"><img src="../images/tn_44.jpg" alt="44.jpg" border="0"
/><br />44.jpg</a></font></td>
</tr>
</table>
</center>
```

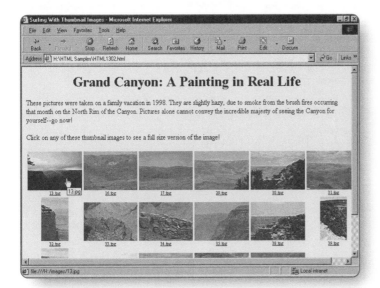

Granted, this is a lot of extra XHTML code, but the benefits are worth it. Readers of this page can now see all of the images and choose to view the full-size images they want. The total memory used by these thumbnails is now just 44 KB, which should load quickly using even the slowest of modems.

Thumbnails are not right for every situation. If the image is an integral part of the page's content, a thumbnail is definitely not a good idea. Only use thumbnails in "picture-album" situations or when you have a lot of image links on a page.

Choosing the Right Image

Before you can use image maps, you must use the appropriate image for the task. Not just any image will do. Most successful image maps have these traits in common:

- They are not too large
- They have distinct areas
- Each area of the image is easily recognized

If, for example, you want to provide your users with a clickable image map of the United States, you could present it in this manner:

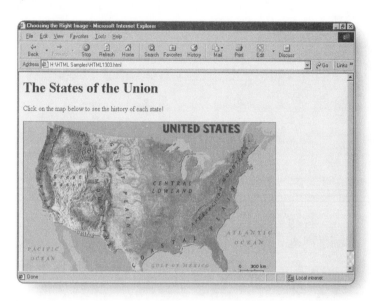

```
<h1>The States of the
Union</h1>
<p>
Click on the map below to see
the history of each state!
</p>
<img src="usap.gif">
```

This is a pretty map, but not a good one to use for an image map. Even if we could figure out where the state areas would be, it would be difficult for many users to click on the right state. Here is a better image:

```
<h1>The States of the
Union</h1>
<p>
Click on the map below to see
the history of each state!
</p>
<img src="usa.gif">
```

This is a better graphic to use because each state is outlined and labeled. This kind of distinctiveness is what your image map should have. With this in mind, you can create a basic image map.

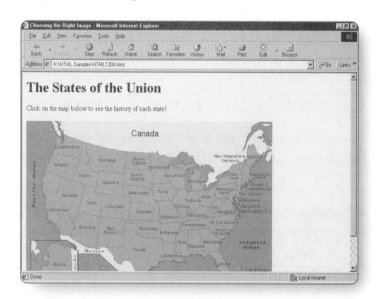

Building a Client-Side Image Map

In the world of image maps, you can use two kinds. The older type is the *server-side* image map. This method accesses a separate map file on the Web server that tells the browser reading it the coordinates of each clickable area ("hot spot"). This first way of doing image maps was cumbersome and confusing.

Today, there's a new way, called *client-side* image maps. Client-side image maps have all the hot-spot information inside the XHTML document. The client (otherwise known as the browser) can then interpret the information without needing to access the server. Given the convenience and ease of client-side image maps, we focus on them in this chapter.

A client-side image map uses three elements in tandem to function. One you already know: `<img>`. The other two are new to you: `<map>` and `<area>`.

The `<map>` element is the XHTML element that contains the `<area>` elements of an image map. The `<area>` element in turn is where the coordinates of each hot spot are registered and the link to a new file is created. In fact, it may help you to think of `<area>` as the image equivalent to the `<a>` element. You can have as many hot spots in an image map as you want, and different hot spots can be linked to the same XHTML document.

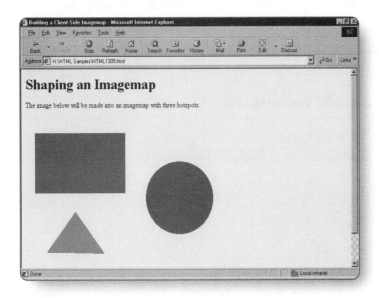

To illustrate, we'll begin with a very simple (and very classic) demonstration of image map creation.

```
<h1>Shaping an Imagemap</h1>
<p>The image below will be
made into an imagemap with
three hotspots.</p>
<img src="shapes.gif"
border="0">
```

First, you must create the `<map>` element that will house all of the image map's `<area>` elements. The `<map>` element is assigned a `name` value, which is used by the `<img>` element's `usemap` attribute.

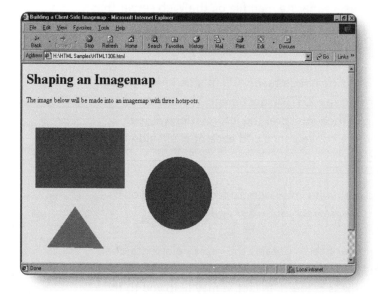

```
<h1>Shaping an Imagemap</h1>
<p>The image below will be
made into an imagemap with
three hotspots.</p>
<map name="shape"></map>
<img
src="../images/shapes.gif"
usemap="#shape" border="0">
```

Notice that the `usemap` value is the `name` of the `<map>` element with a pound sign in front of it. This combination links the image with the `<map>` element and lends image map functionality to the graphic.

The first hot spot will be on the rectangle. Add an `<area>` element within `<map>` and set the `shape` value of `<area>` to be `rect`. `shape` has three values: `rect` (for rectangles), `circle` (for circles), and `poly` (for polygonal and irregular shapes).

```
<h1>Shaping an Imagemap</h1>
<p>The image below will be made into an imagemap with three hotspots.</p>
<map name="shape">
<area shape="rect">
</map>
<img src="../images/shapes.gif" usemap="#shape" border="0">
```

There is no real change yet on the screen. Now you must provide the coordinates of the rectangle hot spot. When the shape value is rect, the coords value is the coordinates of the upper-left corner and the lower-right corner of the rectangle, in pixels.

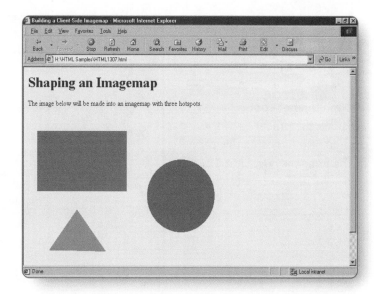

Using a graphics program, we determined that the upper-left corner of the rectangle is 22 pixels to the right of the origin point and 32 pixels down, making the first set of coordinates 22,32. The lower-right corner coordinates are 235,166, which makes the value of coords equal to 22,32,235,166. Adding the href attribute to link a file to the hot spot and the alt attribute for those browsers that cannot use images results in the following:

<table>
<tr><td>

NOTE

In any of these images, the coordinates start at the top left corner of the image, which is 0,0 or origin point.

</td></tr>
</table>

```
<h1>Shaping an Imagemap</h1>
<p>The image below will be made into an imagemap with three hotspots.</p>
<map name="shape">
<area shape="rect" alt="Rectangle" coords="22,32,235,166"
href="rectangle.html">
</map>
<img src="..images/shapes.gif" usemap="#shape" border="0">
```

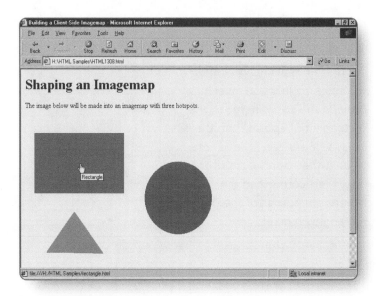

Though the hot spot is invisible, the presence of the pop-up text indicates this part of the image is now "hot."

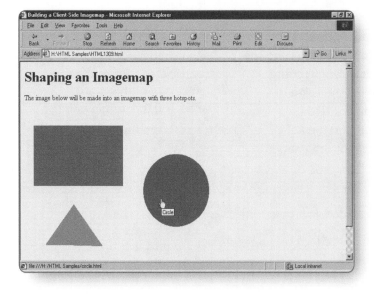

Circular hot spots use a different set of coordinates. A circle uses the coordinates of the center of the circle and the length of the radius (the distance from the center to the edge of the circle). After determining these coordinates, this `<area>` element can be added.

```
<h1>Shaping an Imagemap</h1>
<p>The image below will be made into an imagemap with three hotspots.</p>
<map name="shape">
<area shape="rect" alt="Rectangle" coords="22,32,235,166"
href="rectangle.html" />
<area shape="circle" alt="Circle" coords="363,177,81" href="circle.html" />
</map>
<img src="..images/shapes.gif" usemap="#shape" border="0">
```

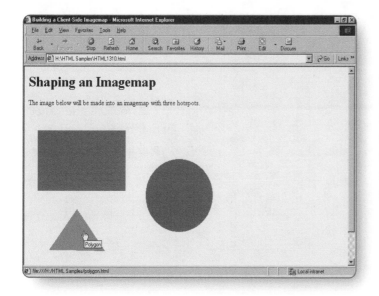

The final shape is the triangle, also known as a polygon. Polygon coordinates are the coordinates of every vertex (corner) of the shape. In this example, those coordinates are as follows:

```
<h1>Shaping an Imagemap</h1>
<p>The image below will be made into an imagemap with three hotspots.</p>
<map name="shape">
<area shape="rect" alt="Rectangle" coords="22,32,235,166"
href="rectangle.html" />
<area shape="circle" alt="Circle" coords="363,177,81" href="circle.html" />
<area shape="poly" alt="Polygon" coords="116,207,186,299,49,296"
href="polygon.html" />
</map>
<img src="../images/shapes.gif" usemap="#shape" border="0">
```

For accuracy's sake, another <area> element needs to be added to the <map> element. This <area> element provides instructions for what the browser should do if anything but the hot spots on the image are clicked. The shape value in this case is default.

```
<h1>Shaping an Imagemap</h1>
<p>The image below will be made into an imagemap with three hotspots.</p>
<map name="shape">
<area shape="rect" alt="Rectangle" coords="22,32,235,166"
href="rectangle.html" />
<area shape="circle" alt="Circle" coords="363,177,81" href="circle.html" />
<area shape="poly" alt="Polygon" coords="116,207,186,299,49,296"
href="polygon.html" />
<area shape="default" href="clickagain.html" />
</map>
<img src="../images/shapes.gif" usemap="#shape" border="0">
```

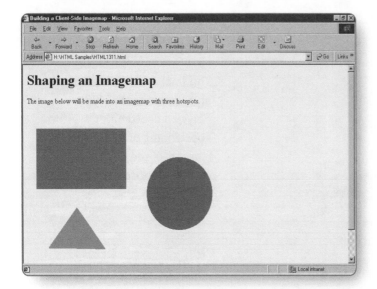

And that's it! You can add other `<map>` elements to a page, as long as you keep their `name` values unique to each other.

NOTE

Though you can certainly code image maps by hand, wonderful tools are available to assist you in automatically generating the proper code. One such tool is Mapedit, which can be found at **http://www.boutell.com/mapedit/**.

NOTE

The CD-ROM has hot spots for all 50 states in the source code.

Image maps can be as simple or as complicated as you need them to be. With the right tool, you can create some great image maps in minutes. Remember that map of the United States? Here's what an image map with just the 13 original colonies might look like.

```
<map name="usa">
<area shape="poly" alt="New Hampshire"
coords="518,83,522,82,531,107,530,111,517,115,515,106,517,98,519,94"
href="newhampshire.html" />
<area shape="poly" alt="New York"
coords="501,91,518,86,517,96,514,109,517,116,510,117,507,103"
href="newyork.html" />
<area shape="poly" alt="New York"
coords="452,138,459,129,455,129,455,125,469,119,470,121,482,115,480,110,479,10
7,483,100,490,94,495,94,502,91,507,105,511,118,510,126,514,137,510,141,519,139
,526,135,527,137,512,145,509,146,509,141,501,139,497,136,493,133,454,141"
href="newyork.html" />
```

```
<area shape="poly" alt="Pennsylvania"
coords="446,142,452,138,454,139,494,133,500,138,499,143,499,148,503,153,499,16
0,453,170" href="pennsylvania.html" />
<area shape="poly" alt="Maryland"
coords="460,167,498,160,501,176,507,176,502,190,498,178,494,174,492,168,490,17
5,486,175,476,166,465,171,458,169" href="maryland.html" />
<area shape="poly" alt="Massachusetts"
coords="522,82,524,78,521,77,525,75,523,67,528,50,530,53,536,51,537,48,543,56,
543,64,549,69,553,72,557,73,559,77,546,88,544,91,533,99,531,107"
href="massachusets.html" >
<area shape="poly" alt="Massachusetts"
coords="509,117,530,111,530,120,537,120,538,124,543,123,538,129,533,129,528,12
0,511,125" href="massachusetts.html" />
<area shape="poly" alt="Rhode Island"
coords="526,121,530,120,531,127,529,126,530,130,528,132,526,128"
href="rhodeisland.html" />
<area shape="poly" alt="Connecticut"
coords="511,126,527,122,530,131,516,136,513,140,513,135,512,131"
href="connecticut.html" />
<area shape="poly" alt="New Jersey"
coords="502,139,509,141,508,148,511,153,507,169,504,166,500,166,499,162,502,15
4,503,152,500,148,499,142" href="newjersey.html" />
<area shape="poly" alt="Delaware" coords="500,164,505,176,499,176,498,165"
href="delaware.html" />
<area shape="poly" alt="Virginia"
coords="448,170,449,159,453,168,459,169,463,173,469,168,475,166,480,170,475,17
0,470,176,468,178,464,183,461,186,457,194,447,200,443,200,434,190,437,184,442,
180,446,173" href="virginia.html" />
<area shape="poly" alt="Virginia"
coords="474,167,487,175,484,178,489,182,491,179,493,186,498,191,498,194,503,19
9,457,208,429,210,440,198,446,203,455,199,467,180,474,172"
href="virginia.html" />
<area shape="poly" alt="North Carolina"
coords="446,208,494,202,496,208,501,207,503,202,506,199,508,210,504,216,501,21
6,500,218,503,220,502,224,492,227,490,234,487,236,483,237,471,228,460,229,456,
226,441,227,435,232,422,233,434,223,446,216" href="ncarolina.html" />
<area shape="poly" alt="South Carolina"
coords="436,234,442,228,456,227,460,229,471,229,483,237,482,240,479,243,477,24
7,469,259,463,265,458,260,455,254,438,237,433,236" href="scarolina.html" >
<area shape="poly" alt="Georgia"
coords="409,236,435,234,453,252,460,262,460,281,455,283,456,286,454,286,451,28
5,424,288,422,283,423,274,414,247" href="georgia.html" />
<area shape="default" href="notcolony.html" />
</map><h1>The Thirteen Original Colonies</h1>
<p>
Click on the map below to see the history of each colony!
</p>
<img src="../images/usa.gif" usemap="#usa" border="0">
```

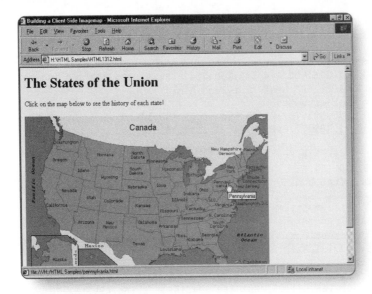

Conclusion

Using an image as a navigation tool (or two or three) is an easy way to really bump up the coolness factor of your Web documents. Just remember not to overdo images anywhere on your site, or you'll limit the accessibility of your Web pages!

In recent years, more Web pages have gone beyond HTML and XHTML and are using miniature software programs called scripts to present documents in stunning ways. In Chapter 14, you will learn how to get some of these scripts on your Web site—without having to write a single line of code!

14

Adding Applets to Your Web Site

Imagine, if you can, an Internet without Amazon.com. Or eBay, MSNBC, Yahoo!, or any of those sites you like that make visiting the Internet a unique experience. This was the Internet back in 1991—a plain, stark house of mostly academic information. It was useful; don't get us wrong. But in terms of exciting stuff, we've seen better shows on C-Span. My, have things changed.

In this chapter, you'll learn how to do the following:

● Find and use pre-made scripts for your Web page

● Start creating your own scripted applets

Today, the Internet is no longer just a collection of informative documents, though that remains a big part of this worldwide network. Today the Internet is active, responsive, and ever-changing. This shift from static to mobile information is the direct result of the introduction of client-side applications embedded within formerly ordinary Web pages. Like the server-side CGI scripts you've read about, these programs can adjust the Web page instantly to the commands of the reader. And, unlike CGI, these scripts go out to the client's browser—greatly increasing the responsiveness of the application.

After reading this and the title of the chapter, some of you might be breaking out in a cold sweat and thinking, "They want me to write a program?" Well, if you know how, you are certainly welcome to try. But one of the great things about the Internet is that it makes available a vast wealth of information—including scripts you can cut and paste into your pages for your own use, sometimes for free!

Using Pre-Made Applets

Scripts, when sent to the client, are called *applets*, which is a cutesy name for these miniature applications. The neat thing about applets is that they are actually running on the PCs of your site's visitors and not tying up your Web server's resources. They can do this with minimal download time because the scripts are kept small.

The secret of how applets work is within the browsers themselves. Right now, there are two big formats under which an applet's script can be run: JavaScript and VBScript. There are significant differences in how these two programming languages make up their scripts, and both bring some interesting features to the table. Both share at least one trait; most of the code needed to run an applet is already installed on the two leading browsers: Netscape Navigator and Internet Explorer. The script that comes along on the Web page simply fills in the unique information about the applet that distinguishes it from other applets.

Netscape Navigator cannot run VBScript applets without the ScriptActive plug-in application. Although this plug-in can be downloaded from Netscape, it is a consideration for you as a Web author. Do you want to exclude or, at best, delay certain users from fully experiencing your site?

This book is not intended to teach programming. But there are ways to add scripting functionality to your pages without writing code. Sneaky? Hardly. It's just an efficient use of the tools that are out there.

Obtaining an Applet

If you are not a programmer, no one seriously should expect you to learn how to code your own scripts. That is, not without some time to learn and practice. You have better things to do!

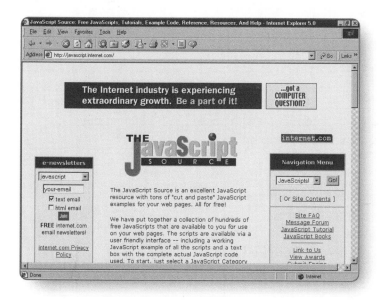

To keep our examples universal, we are going to stay with the one scripting language most browsers can read unassisted: JavaScript. One of the best places to find examples of JavaScript is **http://javascript.internet.com**.

When you visit this site, you can select from over 500 free scripts that you are welcome to place on your own Web pages. All that is asked is that you leave the original author information embedded within the script so that visitors to your site know where the script came from.

After browsing around, we have located a script that is a great addition to any Web page: a pull-down menu that takes your readers anywhere you want them to go.

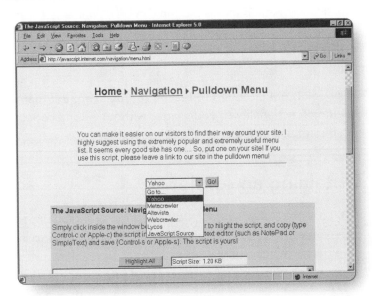

Putting the Applet on Your Page

When you acquire an applet for your site, there are typically two things you need to do: place the `<script>` element information within the `<head>` element of your document and the code the script is acting on in the `<body>` element of the page.

The pull-down menu is a great tool to add to our 13 colonies Web page from the last chapter. Using the menu, the reader can progress through the expansion of the United States through major territorial advances and purchases.

NOTE

If there are images that are used by a script, then a third step of loading the images into the correct location on your Web server should be performed.

The first thing we need to do is select the code in the sample to place within the <head> element. After pressing Ctrl + C, the script code is held in the operating system's clipboard until it is pasted somewhere else.

The somewhere else in this case is within the 13 colonies' Web page. Pressing Ctrl + V at the desired insertion point is the usual method of pasting text back into a document.

NOTE

To save space, the contents of the <map> element in this example are abridged. The addition of the <script> element in no way affects the image map functions of this page.

```
<html>
<head>
<title>Territorial History of the United States</title>
<script language="JavaScript">
<!-- Original: Alex Tu <boudha1@hotmail.com> -->
<!-- Web Site:  http://www.geocities.com/MadisonAvenue/4368 -->
<!-- This script and many more are available free online at -->
<!-- The JavaScript Source!! http://javascript.internet.com -->
<!-- Begin
function formHandler(form){
var URL = document.form.site.options[document.form.site.selectedIndex].value;
window.location.href = URL;
}
// End -->
</script>
</head>
<body>
<map name="usa">...</map>
<h1>The Thirteen Original Colonies</h1>
<p>
Click on the map below to see the history of each colony!
</p>
<img src="../images/usa.gif" usemap="#usa" border="0" />
</body>
</html>
```

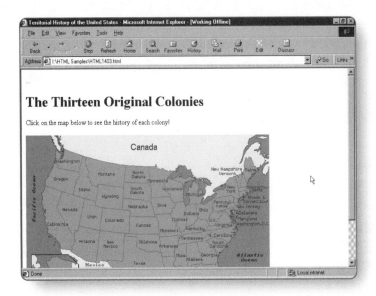

Next, we cut and paste the actual tools that the script uses. In this case, it is within a single `<form>` element.

```
<body>
<map name="usa">...</map>
<h1>The Thirteen Original Colonies</h1>
<center>
<form name="form">
<select name="site" size=1>
<option value="">Go to....
<option value="http://www.yahoo.com">Yahoo
<option value="http://www.metacrawler.com">Metacrawler
<option value="http://www.altavista.digital.com">Altavista
<option value="http://www.webcrawler.com">Webcrawler
<option value="http://www.lycos.com">Lycos
<option value="http://javascript.internet.com">JavaScript Source
</select>
<input type=button value="Go!" onClick="javascript:formHandler()">
</form>
</center>
<p>
Click on the map below to see the history of each colony!
</p>
<img src="../images/usa.gif" usemap="#usa" border="0" />
</body>
</html>
```

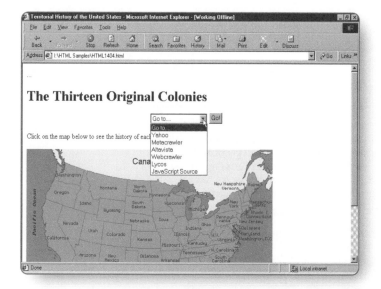

That's it—you have a fully functional script within your Web page! Of course, it's not quite ready for prime time, but it is a simple matter to get this corrected.

Putting the Finishing Touches on the Applet

In our example, the default values the script's author used to connect to other Web sites are still here. For our purposes, we want the pull-down menu to link to local pages. This is really no big deal; the URL value the script needs can be absolute, like the ones here, or relative, like the ones we need.

The pull-down menu is displayed with the <select> element, which in turn contains <option> elements. Each <option> element is a choice on the pull-down menu and has a value attribute equal to the URL of the listed Web sites. All we need to do is change the values to what we want, add additional <option> elements as needed, and we are set.

If you look at the <option> element carefully, you notice the lack of a closing tag. The original script, in a manner consistent with HTML 4.0, did not include this tag. To make the example consistent with XHTML, we add the </option> tag in the next step. A closing delimiter also is added to the <input> element.

```
<body>
<map name="usa">...</map>
<h1>The Thirteen Original Colonies</h1>
<center>
<form name="form">
<select name="site" size=1>
<option value="">Go to.... </option>
<option value="nw.html">Northwest Territory</option>
<option value="lapurch.html">Louisiana Purchase</option>
<option value="ntp.html">Northern Title Purchase</option>
<option value="florida.html">Treaty of 1819</option>
<option value="txannex.html">Texas Annexation</option>
<option value="oregon.html">Oregon Territory</option>
<option value="mexico.html">Mexican West</option>
<option value="gadsden.html">Gadsden Purchase</option>
<option value="alaska.html">Alaska Purchase</option>
<option value="hawaii.html">Hawaii Annexation</option>
</select>
<input type=button value="Go!" onClick="javascript:formHandler()" />
</form>
</center>
<p>
Click on the map below to see the history of each colony!
</p>
<img src="../images/usa.gif" usemap="#usa" border="0" />
</body>
</html>
```

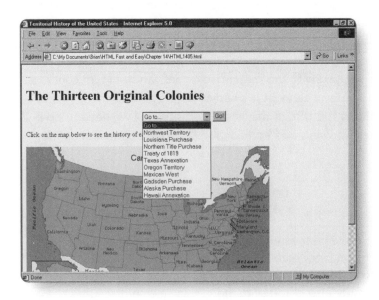

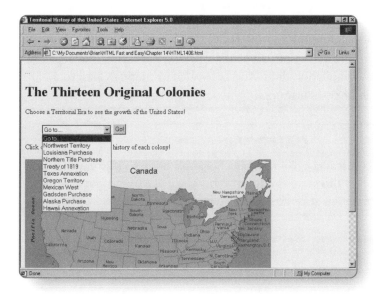

In the interest of clarity, a bit of explanatory text should be added to this new control.

```
<body>
<map name="usa">...</map>
<h1>The Thirteen Original Colonies</h1>
<p>
Choose a Territorial Era to see the growth of the United States!
</p>
<center>
<form name="form">
<select name="site" size=1>
<option value="">Go to.... </option>
<option value="nw.html">Northwest Territory</option>
<option value="lapurch.html">Louisiana Purchase</option>
<option value="ntp.html">Northern Title Purchase</option>
<option value="florida.html">Treaty of 1819</option>
<option value="txannex.html">Texas Annexation</option>
<option value="oregon.html">Oregon Territory</option>
<option value="mexico.html">Mexican West</option>
<option value="gadsden.html">Gadsden Purchase</option>
<option value="alaska.html">Alaska Purchase</option>
<option value="hawaii.html">Hawaii Annexation</option>
</select>
<input type=button value="Go!" onClick="javascript:formHandler()" />
</form>
</center>
<p>
Click on the map below to see the history of each colony!
</p>
<img src="../images/usa.gif" usemap="#usa" border="0" />
</body>
</html>
```

Applets come in all sizes. One thing to note, however, is that larger applets, although they do not take a long time to download, take a while to *compile*—what the computer does to turn the script into an actual working program. The larger the script, the longer the compilation time. And too much of that can lead to a premature departure of your site's visitors.

CAUTION

Do not, under any circumstances, borrow another Web page's scripts without the express permission of the script's author. Whereas it is okay to get scripts from designated repositories, it is most assuredly not cool to do so from a private Web site.

NOTE

As with images and tables, a fair balance must be achieved when using applets. This is clearly a case where less is more and more can be a big heap of trouble.

Building Applets from Scratch

If you want to build your own scripts, who are we to stop you? Unlike XHTML, scripts use a true programming language that is nicely contained in the `<script>` element. The mindset for scripting, therefore, is a bit different.

Still, nothing is as rewarding as doing something yourself, so here is a list of good sources to get you started:

- Microsoft Scripting Technologies (VBScript)
  http://msdn.microsoft.com/scripting/default.htm?/scripting/vbscript

- The JavaScript Source
  http://javascript.internet.com/

- eScriptZone
  http://www.escriptzone.com/

- *Hands On Visual InterDev* (Prima, 1998)

- *Hands On Visual C++ 6 for Web Development* (Prima, 1998)

- *Hands On Visual Basic 6 for Web Development* (Prima, 1998)

Conclusion

This chapter took a brief look at adding interactivity to your Web pages through scripting. So much work has been done in scripting; it is really easy to add wonderful tools to your Web site without a lot of hassle. This is one area where you should capitalize on the generosity of others!

A newer technology to the science of creating a Web page is cascading style sheets. CSS give your pages the exact look and feel you want with minimal additional XHTML code. In the long-awaited Chapter 15, "Designing with Style (Sheets)," you learn how to apply this technology to your own Web site and make your pages shine!

15

Designing with Style (Sheets)

So far, you have worked on using elements and their attributes in strictly defined ways. Using cascading style sheets, you can change how all elements are presented with just a little extra information.

In this chapter, you'll learn how to do the following:

- Understand the fundamentals of creating style rules and style sheets
- Combine styles and manage their inherited properties
- Build great-looking effects for text, links, images, and lists
- Link your document to internal styles or external style sheets

Throughout this book, you have seen references to elements and attributes in XHTML that are *deprecated*. The term deprecated is applied to those elements and attributes that the World Wide Web Consortium (or W3C—the standards body for markup languages) has decided will be phased out of future versions of the language. The `<blink>` element was deprecated very early in HTML history, for example.

When an element is deprecated, it is usually replaced by something functionally equivalent. The `<s>` and `<strike>` elements, for example, are deprecated, but something is needed to create strikethrough text.

Enter styles and the technology to deliver them: the cascading style sheet. CSS has been around as a W3C recommendation since 1996 and has been in its second level iteration (CSS2) since late 1998. Despite this availability, it has received neither a lot of use in the Web authoring community nor unconditional browser support, even from Internet Explorer and Netscape Navigator. This is a real loss because CSS functionality is very easy to use—once you get the hang of it.

Ultimately, the deprecation of various HTML and XHTML elements will cause a wider adoption of CSS. And after reading this chapter, you will certainly find yourself ahead of the curve.

Examining Style Sheets

If you have followed the syntax of XHTML throughout this book, you will notice that the syntax of CSS is different, but not enough to really confuse you. CSS enables you to apply global styles *based on content*. It's easy to forget this because most of the results are visually oriented. But the underlying goal of using CSS is not to display unrelated passages of text in different styles; you have XHTML elements for doing that.

CSS is used to display related passages of text in related presentational ways. If you have a special element in your document, you might like it to be styled in a manner different from the rest of your text. For example, you want the Sections of the Constitution to appear in bold and italic. Right now, you can go about this three ways.

First, you can apply presentational elements to each instance of special elements.

```
<head>
<title>The Constitution of the United States of America</title>
</head>
<p>
We the people of the United States, in order to form a more perfect union,
establish justice, insure domestic tranquility, provide for the common
defense, promote the general welfare, and secure the blessings of liberty to
ourselves and our posterity, do ordain and establish this Constitution for the
United States of America.
</p>
<h2>Article I</h2>
<p>
<b><i>Section 1. All legislative powers herein granted shall be vested in a
Congress of the United States, which shall consist of a Senate and House of
Representatives.</i></b>
</p>
<p>
<b><i>Section 2. The House of Representatives shall be composed of members
chosen every second year by the people of the several states, and the electors
in each state shall have the qualifications requisite for electors of the most
numerous branch of the state legislature. </i></b>
</p>
```

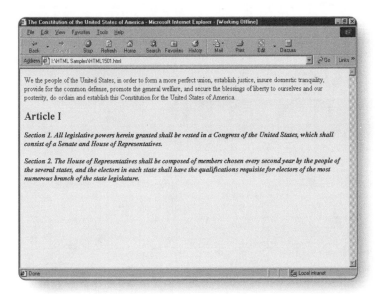

You can use the second method to assign a style to the <p> elements that contain Sections.

```
<head>
<style type="text/css">
.section {font-style: italic; font-weight: bold}
<title>The Constitution of the United States of America</title>
</style>
</head>
<body>
<p>
We the people of the United States, in order to form a more perfect union,
establish justice, insure domestic tranquility, provide for the common
defense, promote the general welfare, and secure the blessings of liberty to
ourselves and our posterity, do ordain and establish this Constitution for the
United States of America.
</p>
<h2>Article I</h2>
<p class="section">
Section 1. All legislative powers herein granted shall be vested in a Congress
of the United States, which shall consist of a Senate and House of
Representatives.
</p>
<p class="section">
Section 2. The House of Representatives shall be composed of members chosen
every second year by the people of the several states, and the electors in
each state shall have the qualifications requisite for electors of the most
numerous branch of the state legislature.
</p>
</body>
```

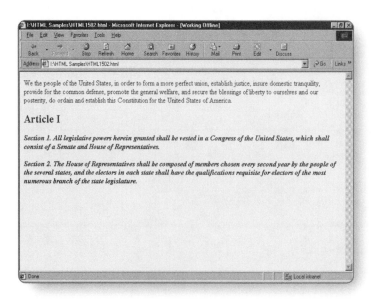

We can hear your objections about the extra typing now, but they'll have to wait a while until we begin to review the mechanics of style sheets.

The third option would be to take advantage of XHTML's new features and declare an XML namespace that contains a `<section>` element to accomplish the same thing. (`<section>`'s default presentation would be bold italic.)

```
<!DOCTYPE html PUBLIC "-//W3C//DTD XHTML 1.0 Transitional//EN" "DTD/xhtml1-
transitional.dtd">
<html xmlns="http://www.proffitt.org/xhtml">
<head>
<title>The Constitution of the United States of America</title>
</head>
<body>
<p>
We the people of the United States, in order to form a more perfect union,
establish justice, insure domestic tranquility, provide for the common
defense, promote the general welfare, and secure the blessings of liberty to
ourselves and our posterity, do ordain and establish this Constitution for the
United States of America.
</p>
<h2>Article I</h2>
<section>
Section 1. All legislative
powers herein granted shall be
vested in a Congress of the
United States, which shall
consist of a Senate and House
of Representatives.
</section>
<section>
Section 2. The House of
Representatives shall be
composed of members chosen
every second year by the
people of the several states,
and the electors in each
state shall have the
qualifications requisite for
electors of the most numerous
branch of the state
legislature.
</section>
</body>
```

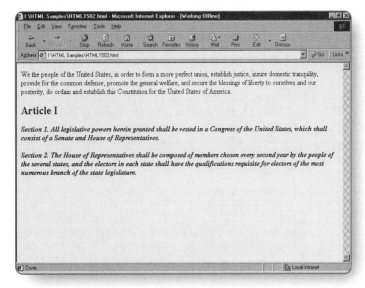

This last method is a perfect XHTML solution to the problem. But XHTML is a new tool out on the World Wide Web, and its acceptance among browsers is even lower than CSS. For now, the compromise should be CSS, which has a greater acceptance.

Rules and Style Sheets

It is no accident that the principles of CSS are remarkably similar to those of XHTML. As markup languages mature, they are moving away from presentation-oriented elements to content-oriented elements. XHTML lets you do this with a "pure" XML element, and CSS uses the class or id attributes on existing HTML and XHTML elements. The result is the same, although CSS is less efficient.

Styles are defined within rules. If you put a whole bunch of rules together, you get a style sheet. When you make a rule, it has two parts: a selector and a declaration.

```
<head>
<title>The Constitution of the United States of America</title>
<style type="text/css">
h2 {color: red}
.section {font-style: italic; font-weight: bold}
</style>
</head>
<body>
<p>
We the people of the United States, in order to form a more perfect union,
establish justice, insure domestic tranquility, provide for the common
defense, promote the general welfare, and secure the blessings of liberty to
ourselves and our posterity, do ordain and establish this Constitution for the
United States of America.
</p>
<h2>Article I</h2>
<p class="section">
Section 1. All legislative powers herein granted shall be vested in a Congress
of the United States, which shall consist of a Senate and House of
Representatives.
</p>
```

NOTE

In these initial examples, all style rules are held within the `<style>` element. For other ways of delivering style to a document, see "Using Styles," later in this chapter.

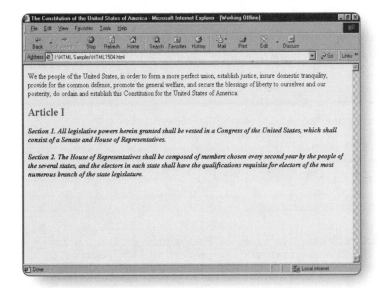

Within the `<style>` element in the preceding example, h2 was the selector and `{color: red}` was the declaration. With this rule in place, all the content of the `<h2>` elements in this document will appear red.

If this looks easy, that's because it is! There is more to selectors and rules than just existing XHTML elements, as you will see in the next section.

Selectors, Properties, and Values

Using the h2 selector in the previous example was an instance of using a type selector. Four main selector types can be used in a style rule:

- Type
- Attribute
- Descendant
- External

You have already seen a type selector in action and unbeknownst to you, you have seen an attribute selector as well. An attribute selector is keyed to apply styles to all elements that contain the appropriate class or id value. In earlier examples, .section was the class attribute selector. Any element with the class="section" combination will have that rule's style applied. A class attribute selector, which may appear multiple times within a document, is denoted in a style rule with a dot (.).

Similarly, an `id` attribute selector is denoted by a pound sign (#). It is functionally identical to a `class` selector, with the exception that an `id` selector may appear only *once* in the document. Using this to mark one-time-only passages is the best use of an `id` selector.

```
<head>
<title>The Constitution of the United States of America</title>
<style type="text/css">
h2 {color: red}
#preamble {color: blue; font-weight: bold}
.section {font-style: italic; font-weight: bold}
</style>
</head>
<body>
<p id="preamble">
We the people of the United States, in order to form a more perfect union,
establish justice, insure domestic tranquility, provide for the common
defense, promote the general welfare, and secure the blessings of liberty to
ourselves and our posterity, do ordain and establish this Constitution for the
United States of America.
</p>
<h2>Article I</h2>
<p class="section">
Section 1. All legislative powers herein granted shall be vested in a Congress
of the United States, which shall consist of a Senate and House of
Representatives.
</p>
```

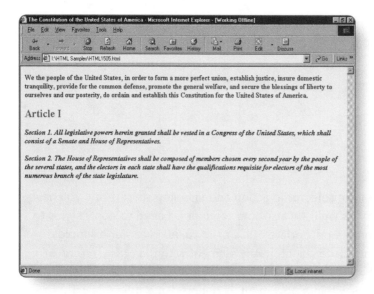

A descendant selector is a unique selector created by the combination of other selectors. You do this when you finish creating style rules that give certain selectors the same attributes. In this example, the `<h2>` element and the `<strong>` element have both been declared to have the color red. When these elements are used together, the `<strong>` element's color will be overrun by the `<h2>` element's. A descendant selector enables you to declare what happens when these two elements are used together.

```
<head>
<title>The Constitution of the United States of America</title>
<style type="text/css">
h2 {color: red}
strong {color: red}
h2 strong {background: aqua}
#preamble {color: blue; font-weight: bold}
.section {font-style: italic; font-weight: bold}
</style>
</head>
<body>
<p id="preamble">
We the people of the United States, in order to form a more perfect union,
establish justice, insure domestic tranquility, provide for the common
defense, promote the general welfare, and secure the blessings of liberty to
ourselves and our posterity, do ordain and establish this Constitution for the
United States of America.
</p>
<h2><strong>Article</strong>
I</h2>
<p class="section">
Section 1. All legislative
powers herein granted shall
be vested in a Congress of
the United States, which
shall consist of a Senate and
House of Representatives.
</p>
```

This particular example looks weird, but you get the point.

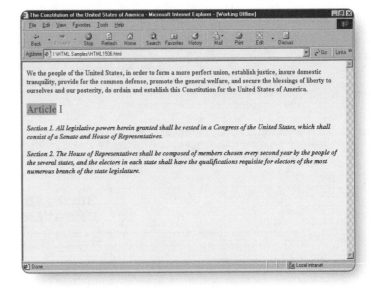

The last type of selector is the least supported of them all: the external selector. External selectors come in two categories: pseudo-classes and pseudo-elements. A pseudo-class is an entirely fictitious selector that is used to deliver some great results that XHTML can't. Right now, only the <a> element uses pseudo-classes, which you can review in the "Creative Links" section, later in this chapter.

Pseudo-elements are elements designed to apply to parts of a document that normally do not get *context* elements. If you wanted to make the first letter of the preamble very large without CSS, you could apply the presentational <font> element around the "W." If you apply the pseudo-element :first-letter to the passage, you might get something like this:

```
<head>
<title>The Constitution of the United States of America</title>
<style type="text/css">
P:first-letter {font-size: 200%; font-weight: bold}
h2 {color: red}
strong {color: red}
h2 strong {background: aqua}
#preamble {color: blue; font-weight: bold}
.section {font-style: italic; font-weight: bold}
</style>
</head>
<body>
<p id="preamble">
<p:first-letter>W</p:first-letter>e the people of the United States, in order
to form a more perfect union, establish justice, insure domestic tranquility,
provide for the common defense, promote the general welfare, and secure the
blessings of liberty to ourselves and our posterity, do ordain and establish
this Constitution for the United States of America.
</p>
<h2><strong>Article</strong> I</h2>
<p class="section">
Section 1. All legislative powers herein granted shall be vested in a Congress
of the United States, which shall consist of a Senate and House of
Representatives.
</p>
```

BROWSER
~~**BROWSER**~~

The reason there is no illustration of this example is that it works only in a very limited amount of browsers. Opera, which can read much of CSS2's selectors, is one. Until adoption of pseudo-elements is more widespread, you can get around this issue by using the generic XHTML elements <span> (for inline work) and <div> (for block-level applications).

Because pseudo-elements get so little support, here's how to work around the issue using the `<span>` element, which is a fair substitute for inline style applications:

```
<head>
<title>The Constitution of the United States of America</title>
<style type="text/css">
span {font-size: 200%; font-weight: bold}
h2 {color: red}
strong {color: red}
h2 strong {background: aqua}
#preamble {color: blue; font-weight: bold}
.section {font-style: italic; font-weight: bold}
</style>
</head>
<body>
<p id="preamble">
<span>W</span>e the people of the United States, in order to form a more
perfect union, establish justice, insure domestic tranquility, provide for the
common defense, promote the general welfare, and secure the blessings of
liberty to ourselves and our posterity, do ordain and establish this
Constitution for the United States of America.
</p>
<h2><strong>Article</strong> I</h2>
<p class="section">
Section 1. All legislative powers herein granted shall be vested in a Congress
of the United States, which shall consist of a Senate and House of
Representatives.
</p>
```

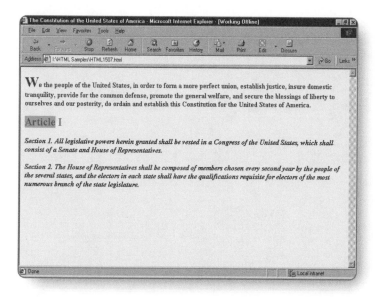

Style Inheritance

Before you start getting into the fun stuff and building some style examples, we need to briefly explain the concept of *inheritance.* Inheritance plays a big factor in how style applications work, especially in nested elements where one style can override another.

The big rule of inheritance in style sheets is that any style declarations made for a parent element are the default styles—unless a more specific declaration is made in a child element. Here's what we mean:

```
<head>
<title>How a Bill Becomes a Canadian Law</title>
<style type="text/css">
body {color: white; background: black}
ol {color: red; background: yellow}
</style>
</head>
<body>
<ol type="I">
<li>DEFINITIONS</li>
<ul>
<li>Public Bills<br />
These are proposals for laws that will affect the public in general. Most
public bills are introduced by Government Ministers. Bills sponsored by the
Government are numbered from C-1 to C-200 in order of presentation. If they
are introduced first in the Senate, they are numbered starting S-1.</li>
<li>Private Bills<br />
These are limited in scope: they concern an individual or group of individuals
only. They confer a right on some person or group, or relieve them of a
responsibility.</li>
</ul>
<li>POLICY PROPOSAL<br />
Most legislation originates with the Government. Policy proposal requiring
legislation is submitted to Cabinet by Minster(s).</li>
</ol>
</body>
```

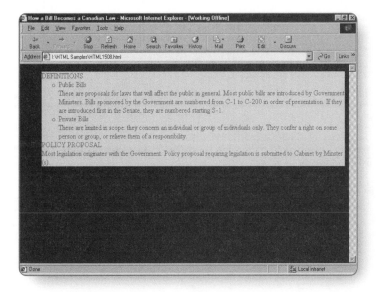

While it is not clear in a grayscale image, the text of the ordered list in the <ol> element is red and its background is yellow. So is the text within the <ul> element that the <ol> element contains! This is because, in this case, the <ul> element is the child of the parent <ol> element and, therefore, has to take on the attributes of the parent. If you leave the style rules alone and make the <ul> element the parent of <ol>, you see a different page.

```html
<head>
<title>How a Bill Becomes a Canadian Law</title>
<style type="text/css">
body {color: white; background: black}
ol {color: red; background: yellow}
</style>
</head>
<body>
<ul>
<li>DEFINITIONS</li>
<ol type="I">
<li>Public Bills<br />
These are proposals for laws that will affect the public in general. Most
public bills are introduced by Government Ministers. Bills sponsored by the
Government are numbered from C-1 to C-200 in order of presentation. If they
are introduced first in the Senate, they are numbered starting S-1.</li>
<li>Private Bills<br />
These are limited in scope: they concern an individual or group of individuals
only. They confer a right on some person or group, or relieve them of a
responsibility.</li>
</ol>
<li>POLICY PROPOSAL<br />
Most legislation originates with the Government. Policy proposal requiring
legislation is submitted to Cabinet by Minster(s).</li>
</ul>
</body>
```

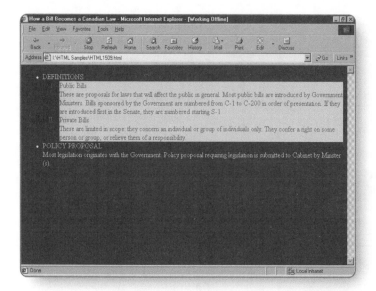

Here you see that the `<ul>` element takes on the attributes of *its* immediate parent (`<body>`) and the `<ol>` element is assigned its style based on the rule in the `<style>` element.

TIP

To avoid any glaring errors, always test your pages' output before publishing them on the Internet. Test, test, test!

This is how inheritance works with CSS. If you pay attention to the parent-child relationships of elements in your documents, you should have little trouble.

These are the basic rules of using CSS. You can use them now to create some examples to dazzle the browsers coming into your site!

Creating a Style Sheet

You have the style rules of CSS pretty well figured out, and thanks to Appendix B, "CSS2 Resource Guide," you have a solid list of all the properties you can manipulate. Now it's just a question of playing around and figuring out what looks good. And that's really the important thing here: you are the Webmaster, and you can decide how you want your pages to look. The only word of caution we might proscribe is this: "Keep your design simple." The more cluttered the look, the less legible your pages.

Customized Text

The majority of your CSS work will be applying styles to blocks of text. With CSS, you can get some stunning text work done that in the past you might have had to use an image to achieve.

Consider the following passage of text:

```
<p>
"Strength does not come from
physical capacity. It comes
from an indomitable will."
<br />
-M. Gandhi
</p>
```

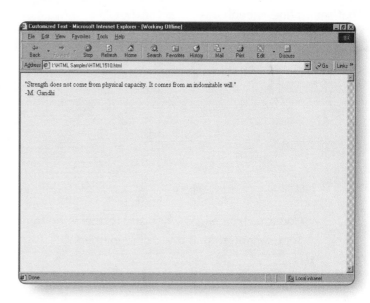

Nothing fancy, just a good quote. Ordinarily, you would place this passage in a `<blockquote>` element and be done with it. With CSS, the possibilities are endless. Why don't you place this quote in its own text box—without using a single image?

In the `<head>` element of the document, you begin by creating a class for the special text box. The first thing you could do is give this styled element a new background, such as brown.

```
<head>
<title>The Strength of Nonviolence</title>
<style>
.textbox {background: brown}
</style>
<body text="FFFFFF">
<p class="textbox">
"Strength does not come from physical capacity. It comes from an indomitable
will." <br />
-M. Gandhi
</p>
</body>
```

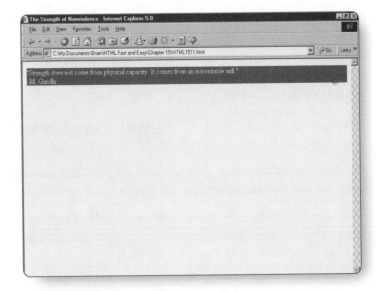

That seems fine, though the text is lost in the dark background.

You can change it to white and increase the font size to 150 percent of the base font, inherited from the `<body>` element.

```
<head>
<title>The Strength of Nonviolence</title>
<style>
.textbox {background: brown; color: #FFFFFF; font-size: 150%}
</style>
<body>
<p class="textbox">
"Strength does not come from physical capacity. It comes from an indomitable
will." <br />
-M. Gandhi
</p>
</body>
```

NOTE

You can specify colors in either plain English or hexadecimal color equivalents.

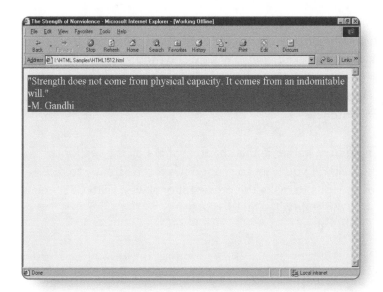

This action makes the text much easier read. It does not look like much of a box, however—more like highlighted text.

You can create the box effect by indenting the margins on each side and adding a border.

```
<head>
<title>The Strength of
Nonviolence</title>
<style>
.textbox {background: brown;
color: #FFFFFF; font-size:
150%; margin-left: 15%;
margin-right: 15%; border:
black solid}
</style>
<body>
<p class="textbox">
"Strength does not come from
physical capacity. It comes
from an indomitable will."
<br />
-M. Gandhi
</p>
</body>
```

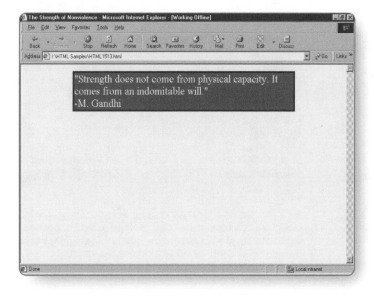

Now you have a good-looking text box, which can be used again and again in this document, if needed. That is the beauty of using CSS. Because presentational elements can accomplish the same thing, you may be wondering whether all this extra typing is worth the trouble. Here's the catch to those presentation elements: you have to apply them (and change them if need be) every instance they appear in order to maintain style consistency.

Remember the CSS example from earlier in this chapter, where all the section paragraphs were bold and italic? If you want to change them consistently to red text, you will have a lot of changes to make the presentational way. With CSS, you can make just one change in the style rule and be done!

```
<head>
<style type="text/css">
.section {color: red}
<title>The Constitution of the United States of America</title>
</style>
</head>
<body>
<p>
We the people of the United States, in order to form a more perfect union,
establish justice, insure domestic tranquility, provide for the common
defense, promote the general welfare, and secure the blessings of liberty to
ourselves and our posterity, do ordain and establish this Constitution for the
United States of America.
</p>
<h2>Article I</h2>
<p class="section">
Section 1. All legislative powers herein granted shall be vested in a Congress
of the United States, which shall consist of a Senate and House of
Representatives.
</p>
<p class="section">
Section 2. The House of Representatives shall be composed of members chosen
every second year by the people of the several states, and the electors in
each state shall have the qualifications requisite for electors of the most
numerous branch of the state legislature.
</p>
</body>
```

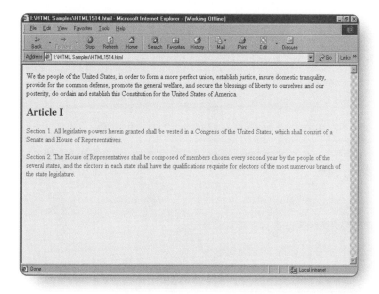

Creative Links

In a fit of honesty, we will admit that links are a rather dull part of XHTML. Mostly blue and always underlined, they don't lend a lot of pizzazz to your documents.

Until now.

CSS can make use of a special tool called pseudo-class to make the contents of the <a> element come alive with color.

Unfortunately, the pseudo-classes of the <a> element do not work in the current version of Netscape Navigator.

There are four pseudo-classes of the <a> element, which may seem familiar to you: :link, :hover, :visited, and :active. When declared in the style sheet, each pseudo-class can receive its own look. Start with the following example.

```
<head>
<title>Recommended Sites</title>
<style>
body {font-size: large; font-family: Arial}
</style>
</head>
<body>
<p>
If you want to visit a really great site for auctions, try <a
href="http://www.ebay.com">eBay</a> or <a
href="http://www.amazon.com">Amazon.com</a>. Wine collectors can have a blast
at <a href="http://www.wine.com">Wine.com</a>.
</p>
</body>
```

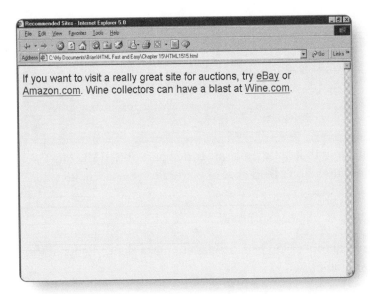

Now you can add the pseudo-class style rules.

```
<head>
<title>Recommended Sites</title>
<style>
body {font-size: large; font-family: Arial}
a:link {background: aqua; color: maroon; text-decoration: none}
a:hover {background: maroon; color: aqua; text-decoration: none}
a:visited {background: black; color: white; text-decoration: none}
a:active {background: blue; color: white; text-decoration: none}
</style>
</head>
<body>
<p>
```

```
If you want to visit a really great site for auctions, try <a
href="http://www.ebay.com">eBay</a> or <a
href="http://www.amazon.com">Amazon.com</a>. Wine collectors can have a blast
at <a href="http://www.wine.com">Wine.com</a>.
</p>
</body>
```

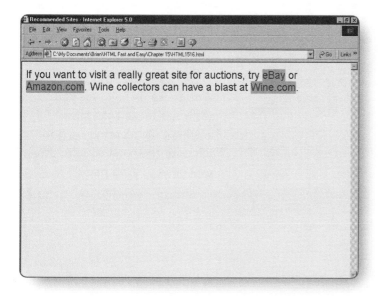

Did you notice the really cool change? By using the `text-decoration: none` declaration, you actually got rid of the ubiquitous underline! The color changes are a really noticeable and unique way to highlight links. You can even specify different colors for different link types using the *real* `class` attribute!

```
<head>
<title>Recommended Sites</title>
<style>
body {font-size: large; font-family: Arial}
a:link.retail {background: aqua; color: maroon; text-decoration: none}
a:link.auction {background: green; color: blue; text-decoration: none}
a:hover.retail {background: maroon; color: aqua; text-decoration: none}
a:hover.auction {background: blue; color: green; text-decoration: none}
a:visited {background: black; color: white; text-decoration: none}
a:active {background: blue; color: white; text-decoration: none}
</style>
</head>
<body>
<p>
```

```
If you want to visit a really great site for auctions, try <a
href="http://www.ebay.com" class="auction">eBay</a> or <a
href="http://www.amazon.com" class="retail">Amazon.com</a>. Wine collectors
can have a blast at <a href="http://www.wine.com" class="retail">Wine.com</a>.
</p>
</body>
```

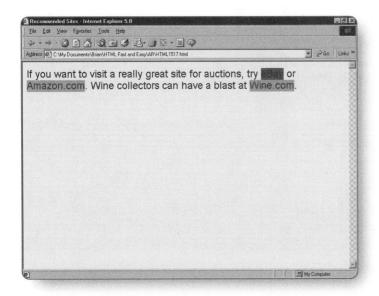

With these techniques, you really can make links more aesthetically pleasing—a good thing for the most sought after tool on your Web page!

Special Bulleted Lists

Remember how we created bulleted lists with special images as bullets? In Chapter 10, "Building Tables," you learned how to do this by using tables instead of an actual <ul> element. What if we could show you a way to get the same effect and still use <ul>? With CSS, it's easy.

Here is the basic list we created with the <table> element in Chapter 10:

```
<ul>
<li>The largest of the spaniels, the Irish Water Spaniel, is a solid brown
(leaning to purple), crisp-textured, curly-coated dog with a hairless, rat-
like tail and smooth short-coated face. It has a rather large head with an
arched skull. The curly outer coat is lined with a dense undercoat, which
helps insulate the dog in even the coldest water.</li>
```

```
<li>A massive, muscular dog, the Irish Wolfhound is one of the tallest breeds
in the world. This gentle giant can reach the size of a small pony. Standing
on his hind legs the Irish Wolfhound can reach up to 7 feet tall! He has a
rough, shaggy coat and wiry bushy eyebrows. Colors include gray, brindle, red,
black or white. Gray is the most common color.</li>
<li>The Italian Greyhound is an elegant, miniature fine-boned Greyhound with a
long head thinning gradually to a pointed muzzle. It has a dark nose, thin
lips and a healthy scissors bite. Like his larger cousins, the brisket is
deep, the abdomen tucked-in, and the back arched.</li>
</ul>
```

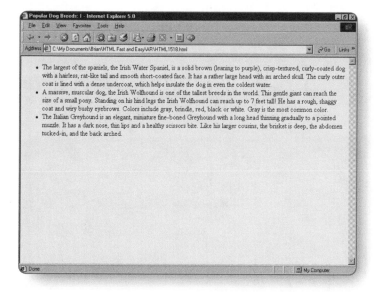

To give each of these first level `<li>` elements an image instead of the standard bullet, we just need to make a rule in the style sheet.

```
<head>
<title>Popular Dog Breeds: I</title>
<style>
li {list-style-image: url(../images/rd_paw_bullet.gif)}
</style>
<body>
<ul>
<li> The largest of the spaniels, the Irish Water Spaniel, is a solid brown
(leaning to purple), crisp-textured, curly-coated dog with a hairless, rat-
like tail and smooth short-coated face. It has a rather large head with an
arched skull. The curly outer coat is lined with a dense undercoat, which
helps insulate the dog in even the coldest water.</li>
```

```
<li> A massive, muscular dog, the Irish Wolfhound is one of the tallest breeds
in the world. This gentle giant can reach the size of a small pony. Standing
on his hind legs the Irish Wolfhound can reach up to 7 feet tall! He has a
rough, shaggy coat and wiry bushy eyebrows. Colors include gray, brindle, red,
black or white. Gray is the most common color.</li>
<li> The Italian Greyhound is an elegant, miniature fine-boned Greyhound with
a long head thinning gradually to a pointed muzzle. It has a dark nose, thin
lips and a healthy scissors bite. Like his larger cousins, the brisket is
deep, the abdomen tucked-in, and the back arched.</li>
</ul>
</body>
```

The `list-style-image: url(../images/rd_paw_bullet .gif)` declaration calls the appropriate image to use in the list. Because of the `url()` parameter, this one is a little different from the declarations that you've seen so far. This additional parameter enables any image file, be it with a relative or absolute URL, to be called up for use.

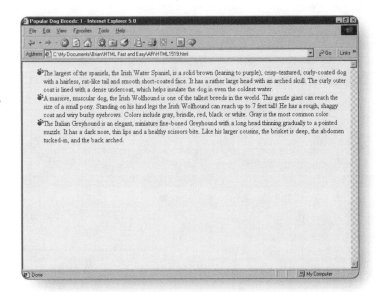

This is a handy way of using graphical bullets because it takes a little extra time for a browser to render tables as opposed to a styled list.

Using Styles

You can use styles in your document many ways. But how do you incorporate rules into your document? You have already seen one method—using the `<style>` element. You can use three additional methods to apply styles.

Internal Styles

For work with a single document where you don't need to duplicate the styles anywhere else, using the `<style>` element is really the best way to go. On rare occasions, you may want to add a style to only one element in the document. You can accomplish this by using any XHTML element's `style` attribute. Both of these methods are *embedding* styles.

If you just want to make the first letter of a document large and make no other style changes, here is a perfectly valid way of doing so:

```
<head>
<title>The Constitution of the United States of America</title>
</head>
<body>
<p>
<span style="font-size: 200%; font-weight: bold">W</span>e the people of the
United States, in order to form a more perfect union, establish justice,
insure domestic tranquility, provide for the common defense, promote the
general welfare, and secure the blessings of liberty to ourselves and our
posterity, do ordain and establish this Constitution for the United States of
America.
</p>
</body>
```

You will not want to do this too often, because this one-at-a-time style method can become inefficient very quickly. Still, it's a good trick for on-the-fly styling.

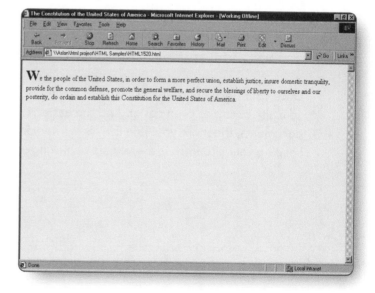

External Style Sheets

Embedding styles should not happen very often, since embedded styles affect only one document at a time. Most Web sites have more than one document, and you ideally should have all of a site's documents maintain similar styles for consistency's sake. You could, of course, copy the same `<style>` element content into all your documents. There is a faster way, however, which is called *linking.*

With linking, you simply link your document to a pre-made style sheet that is sitting somewhere else on the Internet. This style sheet is an actual separate document and will tell any documents how to behave.

In the `<head>` element of your documents, simply add the following `<link>` element:

```
<link rel="stylesheet" href="stylesheet.css" type="text/css" />
```

The `stylesheet.css` is the file name for your CSS document. There is nothing fancy about a CSS document, either. It's a plain-text document with all the rules listed and saved with a .css file extension.

> ### CAUTION
> Make sure that you have the `rel="stylesheet"` value in the `<link>` element or the link will not work.

Once your documents are all linked to a central style sheet, changing the look of your site becomes even easier. And the easier it is to change the look of your documents, the more you'll do it. This is a very important thing to do, because keeping your site fresh is a vital part of making sure that it continues to be visited.

Conclusion

You are now at the end of our discussions on cascading style sheets and XHTML.

As the Internet becomes a bigger and bigger part of our daily lives, the need to create low-bandwidth-impact pages with eye-popping designs becomes more important. With this new merging of HTML and XML, creating stylistic and truly content-oriented Web pages becomes that much easier.

This book has given you the basic markup language principles and what you need to start using XHTML 1.0. As time goes on and markup languages become more and more complex, these basics will help you learn even better and sharper Web authoring skills.

PART IV

Appendixes

A

XHTML Element and Entity List

Though this book has attempted to highlight as many XHTML elements as possible, the simple truth is there was no way to discuss every element. Nor could we fully discuss all the special inline characters that can be displayed using XHTML entities.

In this appendix, we list the complete XHTML element set, which covers all the HTML 4.0 elements. These elements are listed in alphabetical order and include descriptions of what they can do. All known attributes for the element are also listed. To create a more efficient list, three sets of common attributes are used: core, i18n, and event attributes.

Table A-1 lists the core attributes, as well as a brief description of the attribute. Table A-2 lists the i18n attributes and Table A-3 the event attributes.

Each element section contains information on the element's status, that is, whether it is a deprecated element. Finally, any element that can contain and be contained by the listed element is displayed.

Table A-1 Core Attributes

Attribute	Description
class	List of classes the element can lie within
id	Unique ID for the element
style	Style information for the element
title	Advisory title

Table A-2 i18n Attributes

Attribute	Description
dir	Direction of neutral text
lang	The document's language

Table A-3 Event Attributes

Attribute	Event Description
onclick	A pointer button was clicked
ondblclick	A pointer button was double-clicked
onkeydown	A key was pressed down
onkeypress	A key was pressed and released
onkeyup	A key was released
onmousedown	A pointer button was pressed down
onmousemove	A pointer was moved within
onmouseout	A pointer was moved away
onmouseover	A pointer was moved onto
onmouseup	A pointer button was released

XHTML Elements

<!--enter comment text here-->

Allows Web page author to insert comments within the source code for a page.

Attributes: None

Contains: n/a

Contained in: All elements

<!DOCTYPE>

Specifies the Document Type Definition for the document; HTML and XHTML have three document types each: Strict, Transitional (Loose), and Frameset

Attributes: None

Strict XHTML DTD: `<!DOCTYPE html public "-//W3C//DTD XHTML 1.0 Strict//EN" "http://www.w3.org/TR/xhtml1/DTD/strict.dtd">`

Transitional XHTML DTD: `<!DOCTYPE html public "-//W3C//DTD XHTML 1.0 Transitional//EN" "http://www.w3.org/TR/xhtml1/DTD/transitional.dtd">`

Frameset XHTML DTD: `<!DOCTYPE html public "-//W3C//DTD XHTML 1.0 Frameset//EN" "http://www.w3.org/TR/xhtml1/DTD/frameset.dtd">`

Strict HTML DTD: `<!DOCTYPE html public "-//W3C//DTD HTML 4.0//EN" "http://www.w3.org/TR/REC-html40/strict.dtd">`

Transitional HTML DTD: `<!DOCTYPE html public "-//W3C//DTD HTML 4.0//EN" "http://www.w3.org/TR/REC-html40/loose.dtd">`

Frameset HTML DTD: `<!DOCTYPE html public "-//W3C//DTD HTML 4.0//EN" "http://www.w3.org/TR/REC-html40/frameset.dtd">`

Contains: n/a

Contained in: n/a

<a>

Anchor element that creates hyperlinks

Attributes: Core, i18n, Events

Attribute	Description	Attribute	Description
accesskey	Shortcut key	onfocus	Element received focus
charset	Character encoding of link	rel	Relationship to link
coords	Client-side image map	rev	Relationship from link
href	Hypertext reference	shape	Client-side image map
hreflang	Language of link	tabindex	Position in tabbing order
name	Named link destination	target	Frame to render link in
onblur	Element lost focus	type	Content type of link

Contains: All inline elements except <a>
Contained in: All inline and block elements except <a>

<abbr>
Abbreviation element to mark up abbreviations
Attributes: Core, i18n, Events
Contains: All inline elements
Contained in: All inline and block elements

<acronym>
Acronym element to mark up acronyms
Attributes: Core, i18n, Events
Contains: All inline elements
Contained in: All inline and block elements

<address>
Address element that provides Web page author contact information
Attributes: Core, i18n, Events
Contains: All inline elements (Strict HTML); all inline elements and <p> (Transitional HTML)
Contained in: <applet>, <blockquote>, <body>, <button>, <center>, <dd>, <del>, <div>, <fieldset>, <form>, <iframe>, <ins>, <li>, <map>, <noframes>, <noscript>, <object>, <td>, <th>

<applet>
Java applet element used to embed Java mini programs called applets; deprecated in HTML 4.0 and XHTML 1.0
Attributes: Core

Attribute	Description	Attribute	Description
align	Applet alignment	hspace	Horizontal gutter
alt	Alternate text	name	Name for inter-applet communication
archive	Archive files		
code	Class file	object	Serialized applet
codebase	Base URL for class files	vspace	Vertical gutter
height	Applet height	width	Applet width

Contains: <param> followed by all inline and block elements
Contained in: All inline and block elements except <pre>

<area>

Client-side image-map element for defining hyperlinked region

Attributes: Core, i18n, Events

Attribute	Description	Attribute	Description
alt	Alternate text	onfocus	Region received focus
coords	Coordinates of region	shape	Shape of region
href	Hypertext reference	tabindex	Position in tabbing order
nohref	Inactive region	target	Frame to render link in
onblur	Region lost focus		

Contains: Empty element

Contained in: <map>

<b>

Bold text element

Attributes: Core, i18n, Events

Contains: Inline elements

Contained in: All inline and block elements

<base>

Document base URL element used to define the exact location of a Web page

Attribute	Description	Attribute	Description
href	Base URL reference	target	Frame to render link in

Contains: Empty element

Contained in: <head>

<basefont>

Font element that changes the base font setting for the entire Web page; deprecated in HTML 4.0 and XHTML 1.0

Attribute	Description	Attribute	Description
color	Font color adjustment	id	Unique ID for the element
face	Font face adjustment	size	Font size adjustment

Contains: Empty element

Contained in: All inline and block elements except <pre>

<bdo>

BiDi override element that enables text to flow from left to right or from right to left, as is done in Hebrew

Attributes: Core

Attribute	Description	Attribute	Description
dir	Directionality of text	lang	Language of text

Contains: All inline elements
Contained in: All inline and block elements

\<big\>

Element used to create large text characters
Attributes: Core, i18n, Events
Contains: All inline elements
Contained in: All inline and block elements

\<blockquote\>

Block quotation element that indents text on each side
Attributes: Core, i18n, Events

Attribute	Description
cite	URL source of quote

Contains: Block elements and \<script\> (Strict HTML); all inline and block elements (Transitional HTML)
Contained in: \<applet\>, \<body\>, \<button\>, \<center\>, \<dd\>, \<del\>, \<div\>, \<fieldset\>, \<form\>, \<iframe\>, \<ins\>, \<li\>, \<map\>, \<noframes\>, \<noscript\>, \<object\>, \<td\>, \<th\>

\<body\>

The document body element, required in all non-frame HTML documents
Attributes: Core, i18n, Events

Attribute	Description
alink	Active link color for document
background	Background image for document
bgcolor	Background color for document
link	Link color for document
onload	Document has been loaded
onunload	Document has been exited
text	Text color for document
vlink	Visited link color for document

Contains: Block elements, \<script\>, \<ins\>, \<del\> (Strict HTML); all inline and block elements, \<ins\>, \<del\> (Transitional HTML)
Contained in: \<html\> (Strict and Transitional HTML); \<noframes\> (Frameset HTML)

Line-break element

Attributes: Core

Attribute	Description
clear	Clear floating objects

Contains: Empty element

Contained in: All inline and block elements

<button>

Button element that defines a push button on a Web page

Attributes: Core, i18n, Events

Attribute	Description	Attribute	Description
accesskey	Shortcut key	onfocus	Button received focus
disabled	Disable button	tabindex	Position in tabbing order
name	Key in submitted form	type	Type of button
onblur	Button lost focus	value	Value in submitted form

Contains: Inline elements except <a>, <input>, <select>, <textarea>, <label>, <button>, <iframe>

Contained in: Block elements except <form>, <isindex>, <fieldset>

<caption>

Element that displays a caption over a table

Attributes: Core, i18n, Events

Attribute	Description
align	Caption alignment

Contains: All inline elements

Contained in: <table> (must be first element if used)

<center>

Element that centers content of elements on page; deprecated in HTML 4.0 and XHTML 1.0

Attributes: Core, i18n, Events

Contains: All inline and block elements

Contained in: <applet>, <blockquote>, <body>, <button>, <dd>, <del>, <div>, <fieldset>, <form>, <iframe>, <ins>, <li>, <map>, <noframes>, <noscript>, <object>, <td>, <th>

\<cite\>

Inline citation element
Attributes: Core, i18n, Events
Contains: Inline elements
Contained in: All inline and block elements

\<code\>

Computer code element that displays contents in monospaced type
Attributes: Core, i18n, Events
Contains: Inline elements
Contained in: All inline and block elements

\<col\>

Table-column element used to organize and style columns
Attributes: Core, i18n, Events

Attribute	Description	Attribute	Description
align	Horizontal alignment of cells	span	Number of columns
char	Alignment character for cells	valign	Vertical alignment of cells
charoff	Alignment character offset	width	Width of each column

Contains: Empty element
Contained in: \<table\>, \<colgroup\>

\<colgroup\>

Table-column group used to organize and style columns
Attributes: Core, i18n, Events

Attribute	Description	Attribute	Description
align	Horizontal alignment of cells	span	Number of columns
char	Alignment character for cells	valign	Vertical alignment of cells
charoff	Alignment character offset	width	Width of each column

Contains: \<col\>
Contained in: \<table\>

\<dd\>

Definition description element for definition lists
Attributes: Core, i18n, Events
Contains: All inline and block elements
Contained in: \<dl\>

<del>

Element that marks deleted text
Attributes: Core, i18n, Events

Attribute	Description	Attribute	Description
cite	URL for deletion reason	datetime	Deletion date and time

Contains: All inline and block elements
Contained in: All inline and block elements

<dfn>

Element that contains defining instance of marked term
Attributes: Core, i18n, Events
Contains: Inline elements
Contained in: All inline and block elements

<dir>

Directory list element; deprecated in HTML 4.0 and XHTML 1.0
Attributes: Core, i18n, Events

Attribute	Description
compact	Compact list item display

Contains: <li> (which cannot contain block elements)
Contained in: <applet>, <blockquote>, <body>, <button>, <center>, <dd>, <del>, <div>, <fieldset>, <form>, <iframe>, <ins>, <li>, <map>, <noframes>, <noscript>, <object>, <td>, <th>

<div>

A generic block-level element ideally suited for use with cascading style sheets
Attributes: Core, i18n, Events

Attribute	Description
align	Horizontal alignment

Contains: All inline and block elements
Contained in: <applet>, <blockquote>, <body>, <button>, <center>, <dd>, <del>, <fieldset>, <form>, <iframe>, <ins>, <li>, <map>, <noframes>, <noscript>, <object>, <td>, <th>

<dl>

Definition list element for creating unnumbered and unbulleted lists

Attributes: Core, i18n, Events

Attribute   *Description*

compact   Compact list item display

Contains: <dd> and <dt>

Contained in: <applet>, <blockquote>, <body>, <button>, <center>, <dd>, <del>, <div>, <fieldset>, <form>, <iframe>, <ins>, <li>, <map>, <noframes>, <noscript>, <object>, <td>, <th>

<dt>

Definition term element for definition lists

Attributes: Core, i18n, Events

Contains: All inline elements

Contained in: <dl>

<em>

Emphasis element that provides a content-oriented method of marking emphasized text

Attributes: Core, i18n, Events

Contains: All inline elements

Contained in: All inline and block elements

<fieldset>

Defines groups of controls with a form

Attributes: Core, i18n, Events

Contains: <legend> element and all inline and block elements

Contained in: <applet>, <blockquote>, <body>, <button>, <center>, <dd>, <del>, <div>, <form>, <iframe>, <ins>, <li>, <map>, <noframes>, <noscript>, <object>, <td>, <th>

<font>

Controls various attributes of a displayed font; deprecated in HTML 4.0 and XHTML 1.0

Attributes: Core, i18n

Attribute	*Description*	*Attribute*	*Description*
color	Font color	size	Font size
face	Font face		

Contains: All inline elements

Contained in: All inline and block elements except <pre>

<form>

Creates an interactive form on Web documents

Attributes: Core, i18n, Events

Attribute	Description
accept-charset	Supported input characters
action	URL to form-handling script
enctype	Content type of form
method	HTTP method for form submittal
onreset	Form was reset
onsubmit	Form was submitted
target	Frame to render form results

Contains: <script> or block-level elements except <form> (Strict HTML); all inline and block-level elements except <form> (Transitional HTML)

Contained in: <applet>, <blockquote>, <body>, <button>, <center>, <dd>, <del>, <div>, <fieldset>, <iframe>, <ins>, <li>, <map>, <noframes>, <noscript>, <object>, <td>, <th>

<frame>

Frame-container element

Attributes: Core

Attribute	Description
frameborder	Frame border
longdesc	URL pointing to description of frame
marginheight	Margin height
marginwidth	Margin width
name	Name of frame
noresize	Disable frame resizing
scrolling	Ability to scroll
src	URL pointing to content of frame

Contains: Empty element

Contained in: <frameset>

<frameset>

Frameset element, synonymous with <body> in an unframed document

Attributes: Core, i18n, Events

Attribute	Description	Attribute	Description
cols	Column lengths in pixels	onunload	Frames have been removed
onload	Frames have been loaded	rows	Row lengths in pixels

Contains: `<frame>`, `<frameset>`, `<noframe>`
Contained in: `<html>`

`<h1>—<h6>`

Headings used to indicate various outlined sections of the document
Attributes: Core, i18n, Events

Attribute	Description
`align`	Horizontal alignment

Contains: All inline elements
Contained in: `<applet>`, `<blockquote>`, `<body>`, `<button>`, `<center>`, `<dd>`, `<del>`, `<div>`, `<fieldset>`, `<form>`, `<iframe>`, `<ins>`, `<li>`, `<map>`, `<noframes>`, `<noscript>`, `<object>`, `<td>`, `<th>`

`<head>`

Delineates the document head section
Attributes: i18n

Attribute	Description
`profile`	URL pointing to meta information

Contains: One `<title>` element, `<base>`, `<isindex>`, `<link>`, `<meta>`, `<object>`, `<script>`, `<style>`
Contained in: `<html>`

`<hr>`

Horizontal-rule element
Attributes: Core, Events

Attribute	Description	Attribute	Description
`align`	Horizontal alignment	`size`	Line height
`noshade`	Disables line shading	`width`	Line width

Contains: Empty element
Contained in: `<applet>`, `<blockquote>`, `<body>`, `<button>`, `<center>`, `<dd>`, `<del>`, `<div>`, `<fieldset>`, `<form>`, `<iframe>`, `<ins>`, `<li>`, `<map>`, `<noframes>`, `<noscript>`, `<object>`, `<td>`, `<th>`

`<html>`

HTML document element—the element from which all other elements spring
Attributes: i18n

Attribute	Description
`version`	HTML version

Contains: `<head>` then `<body>` (Strict and Transitional HTML); `<head>` then `<frameset>` (Frameset HTML)

Contained in: n/a

`<i>`

Italic-text presentational element

Attributes: Core, i18n, Events

Contains: All inline elements

Contained in: All inline and block elements

`<iframe>`

Inline frame element that creates a floating frame, which in turn contains an entirely new document

Attributes: Core

Attribute	Description	Attribute	Description
`align`	Frame alignment	`marginwidth`	Margin width
`frameborder`	Frame border	`name`	Name of frame
`height`	Frame height	`scrolling`	Ability to scroll
`longdesc`	URL pointing to long description	`src`	URL pointing to content of frame
`marginheight`	Margin height	`width`	Frame width

Contains: All inline and block elements

Contained in: All inline and block elements

`<img>`

Inline image element that displays the contents of image files

Attributes: Core, i18n, Events

Attribute	Description	Attribute	Description
`align`	Image alignment	`longdesc`	URL pointing to long description
`alt`	Alternate text		
`border`	Link border width	`src`	URL pointing to image
`height`	Image height in pixels	`usemap`	Link to client-side image `<map>` element
`hspace`	Horizontal gutter in pixels		
`ismap`	URL to server-side image map file	`vspace`	Vertical gutter in pixels
		`width`	Image width in pixels

Contains: Empty element

Contained in: All inline and block elements except `<pre>`

\<input>

A form's input control element
Attributes: Core, i18n, Events

Attribute	Description
accept	Allowed media types for file upload
accesskey	Shortcut key
align	Alignment of image input
alt	Alternate text for image input
checked	Check radio button or check box
disabled	Disable element
maxlength	Maximum number of characters for text input
name	Key in submitted form
onblur	Control lost focus
onchange	Control value changed
onfocus	Control received focus
onselect	Control text selected
readonly	Prevent changes
size	Recommended number of characters for text input
src	Source for image
tabindex	Tab order position
type	Type of input control
usemap	Link to client-side image \<map> element
value	Value of input

Contains: Empty element
Contained in: All inline and block elements except \<button>

\<ins>

Inserted text element used to mark up edited text
Attributes: Core, i18n, Events

Attribute	Description
cite	Reason for insertion
datetime	Date and time of insertion

Contains: All inline and block elements
Contained in: All inline and block elements

\<isindex>

Single-line input prompt element; deprecated in HTML 4.0 and XHTML 1.0

Attributes: Core, i18n

Attribute	Description
prompt	Message for prompting

Contains: Empty element
Contained in: `<applet>`, `<blockquote>`, `<body>`, `<button>`, `<center>`, `<dd>`, `<del>`, `<div>`, `<fieldset>`, `<form>`, `<iframe>`, `<ins>`, `<li>`, `<map>`, `<noframes>`, `<noscript>`, `<object>`, `<td>`, `<th>`

<kbd>

Defines text to be input, usually in a monospaced font
Attributes: Core, i18n, Events
Contains: All inline elements
Contained in: All inline and block elements

<label>

A form's field label element
Attributes: Core, i18n, Events

Attribute	Description	Attribute	Description
accesskey	Shortcut key	onblur	Label lost focus
for	Associated input control	onfocus	Label received focus

Contains: All inline elements except `<label>`
Contained in: All inline and block elements except `<button>`

<legend>

A form's field group caption
Attributes: Core, i18n, Events

Attribute	Description	Attribute	Description
accesskey	Shortcut key	align	Alignment (relative to fieldset)

Contains: All inline elements
Contained in: `<fieldset>`

<li>

List item element
Attributes: Core, i18n, Events

Attribute	Description	Attribute	Description
type	Style of list item marker	value	Number in sequence

Contains: All inline and block elements; inline elements only in `<dir>` and `<menu>`
Contained in: `<dir>`, `<menu>`, `<ol>`, `<ul>`

<link>

Document-relationship element used to connect the document to various files, including style sheets

Attributes: Core, i18n, Events

Attribute	Description	Attribute	Description
charset	Character encoding of link	rel	Relationship to link
href	URL pointing to linked file	rev	Relationship from link
hreflang	Language of linked file	target	Frame to render link
media	Media appropriate for link	type	Content type of link

Contains: Empty element

Contained in: <head>

<map>

Image-map element for client-side image maps

Attributes: Core, i18n, Events

Attribute	Description
name	Name of map

Contains: All block elements and <area>

Contained in: All inline and block elements

<menu>

Menu list element; deprecated in HTML 4.0 and XHTML 1.0

Attributes: Core, i18n, Events

Attribute	Description
compact	Compact list item display

Contains: <li> (which cannot contain block elements)

Contained in: <applet>, <blockquote>, <body>, <button>, <center>, <dd>, <del>, <div>, <fieldset>, <form>, <iframe>, <ins>, <li>, <map>, <noframes>, <noscript>, <object>, <td>, <th>

<meta>

Metadata element used to specify internal information about a document

Attributes: i18n

Attribute	Description	Attribute	Description
content	Associated data	name	Property name
http-equiv	HTTP response header name	scheme	Form of data

Contains: Empty element

Contained in: <head>

<noframes>

Provides alternate content for non-frames-capable browsers

Attributes: Core, i18n, Events

Contains: All inline and block elements (Transitional HTML); one `<body>` element (Frameset HTML)

Contained in: `<applet>`, `<blockquote>`, `<body>`, `<button>`, `<center>`, `<dd>`, `<del>`, `<div>`, `<fieldset>`, `<form>`, `<iframe>`, `<ins>`, `<li>`, `<map>`, `<noscript>`, `<object>`, `<td>`, `<th>`

<noscript>

Provides alternate content for browsers unable to run script

Attributes: Core, i18n, Events

Contains: All inline and block elements

Contained in: `<applet>`, `<blockquote>`, `<body>`, `<button>`, `<center>`, `<dd>`, `<del>`, `<div>`, `<fieldset>`, `<form>`, `<iframe>`, `<ins>`, `<li>`, `<map>`, `<noframes>`, `<object>`, `<td>`, `<th>`

<object>

Enables various objects (Java scripts, images, multimedia) to be embedded in the document

Attributes: Core, i18n, Events

Attribute	Description	Attribute	Description
align	Object alignment	hspace	Horizontal gutter in pixels
archive	Archive files	name	Name for form submission
border	Link border width in pixels	standby	Message to show while loading
classid	URL pointing to location of implementation	tabindex	Position in tabbing order
codebase	Base URL for classid, data, archive	type	Content type of object
		usemap	Link to client-side image
codetype	Content type of code		`<map>` element
data	URL pointing to object data	vspace	Vertical gutter in pixels
declare	Do not instantiate object		
height	Object height	width	Object width

Contains: `<param>` then inline and block elements

Contained in: `<head>` and all inline and block elements except `<pre>`

`<ol>`

Ordered-list element to create numbered lists
Attributes: Core, i18n, Events

Attribute	Description	Attribute	Description
compact	Compact list item display	type	Numbering style
start	Starting number		

Contains: `<li>`
Contained in: `<applet>`, `<blockquote>`, `<body>`, `<button>`, `<center>`, `<dd>`, `<del>`, `<div>`, `<fieldset>`, `<form>`, `<iframe>`, `<ins>`, `<li>`, `<map>`, `<noframes>`, `<noscript>`, `<object>`, `<td>`, `<th>`

`<optgroup>`

Defines choice groups in the `<select>` element
Attributes: Core, i18n, Events

Attribute	Description	Attribute	Description
disabled	Disable group of choices	label	Group label

Contains: `<option>`
Contained in: `<select>`

`<option>`

Menu options in the `<select>` element
Attributes: Core, i18n, Events

Attribute	Description	Attribute	Description
disabled	Disable choice	selected	Default choice
label	Option label	value	Value of option

Contains: Plain text and entities
Contained in: `<optgroup>`, `<select>`

`<p>`

Paragraph element, the primary text-block container
Attributes: Core, i18n, Events

Attribute	Description
align	Horizontal alignment

Contains: All inline elements
Contained in: `<applet>`, `<blockquote>`, `<body>`, `<button>`, `<center>`, `<dd>`, `<del>`, `<div>`, `<fieldset>`, `<form>`, `<iframe>`, `<ins>`, `<li>`, `<map>`, `<noframes>`, `<noscript>`, `<object>`, `<td>`, `<th>`

<param>

Object-parameter element of `<applet>` and `<object>` elements

Attribute	Description	Attribute	Description
id	ID of element	value	Property value
name	Property name	valuetype	Type of value
type	Content type of value resource		

Contains: Empty element

Contained in: `<applet>`, `<object>`

<pre>

Preformatted text element for positioning text blocks

Attributes: Core, i18n, Events

Attribute	Description
width	Line width in characters

Contains: All inline elements except `<applet>`, `<basefont>`, `<big>`, `<font>`, `<img>`, `<object>`, `<small>`, `<sub>`, `<sup>`

Contained in: `<applet>`, `<blockquote>`, `<body>`, `<button>`, `<center>`, `<dd>`, `<del>`, `<div>`, `<fieldset>`, `<form>`, `<iframe>`, `<ins>`, `<li>`, `<map>`, `<noframes>`, `<noscript>`, `<object>`, `<td>`, `<th>`

<q>

Short quotation inline element

Attributes: Core, i18n, Events

Attribute	Description
cite	URL pointing to quote's source

Contains: All inline elements

Contained in: All inline and block elements

<s>

Strikethrough text element; deprecated in HTML 4.0 and XHTML 1.0

Attributes: Core, i18n, Events

Contains: All inline elements

Contained in: All inline and block elements

<samp>

Sample output content element, usually displayed in monospaced font

Attributes: Core, i18n, Events

Contains: All inline elements

Contained in: All inline and block elements

\<script>

Client-side script element to run interactive applets in a document

Attribute	Description
charset	Character encoding of external script
defer	Script execution may wait
language	Scripting language name
src	URL pointing to external script location
type	Content type of scripting language

Contains: Plain-text script

Contained in: \<head> and all inline and block elements

\<select>

Option selector control for forms

Attributes: Core, i18n, Events

Attribute	Description	Attribute	Description
disabled	Disable selector	onchange	Element value changed
multiple	Allow multiple selections	onfocus	Element received focus
name	Key in submitted form	size	Number of visible options
onblur	Element lost focus	tabindex	Tab order position

Contains: \<optgroup>, \<option>

Contained in: All inline and block elements except \<button>

\<small>

Small text element used to relatively size inline text

Attributes: Core, i18n, Events

Contains: All inline elements

Contained in: All inline and block elements except \<pre>

\<span>

A generic inline element ideally suited for use with cascading style sheets

Attributes: Core, i18n, Events

Contains: All inline elements

Contained in: All inline and block elements

\<strike>

Strikethrough text element; deprecated in HTML 4.0 and XHTML 1.0

Attributes: Core, i18n, Events

Contains: All inline elements

Contained in: All inline and block elements

<strong>

Strong emphasis content element
Attributes: Core, i18n, Events
Contains: All inline elements
Contained in: All inline and block elements

<style>

Embedded style-sheet element that contains style rules for a document
Attributes: i18n

Attribute	Description	Attribute	Description
media	Media to which to apply style	type	Content type of style language
title	Title of style sheet		

Contains: Plain-text style sheet
Contained in: <head>

<sub>

Subscript content element
Attributes: Core, i18n, Events
Contains: All inline elements
Contained in: All inline and block elements

<sup>

Superscript content element
Attributes: Core, i18n, Events
Contains: All inline elements
Contained in: All inline and block elements

<table>

Table element to organize text and images in rows and columns
Attributes: Core, i18n, Events

Attribute	Description	Attribute	Description
align	Table alignment	frame	Outer border
bgcolor	Table background color	rules	Inner borders
border	Border width	summary	Purpose/structure of table
cellpadding	Spacing within cells		
cellspacing	Spacing between cells	width	Table width

Contains: <caption>, <col>, <colgroup>, <tbody>, <tfoot>, <thead>
Contained in: <applet>, <blockquote>, <body>, <button>, <center>, <dd>, <del>, <div>, <fieldset>, <form>, <iframe>, <ins>, <li>, <map>, <noframes>, <noscript>, <object>, <td>, <th>

<tbody>

Table-body element that defines row groups in a table
Attributes: Core, i18n, Events

Attribute	Description
align	Horizontal alignment of grouped cells
char	Alignment character for cells
charoff	Alignment character offset (in characters)
valign	Vertical alignment of grouped cells

Contains: <tr>
Contained in: <table>

<td>

Table data cell element
Attributes: Core, i18n, Events

Attribute	Description
abbr	Abbreviation for header cell
align	Horizontal alignment
axis	Category of header cell
bgcolor	Cell background color
char	Alignment character
charoff	Alignment character offset (in characters)
colspan	Number of columns spanned by the cell
headers	Header cells for current cell
height	Cell height (relative or absolute)
nowrap	Disable word wrap
rowspan	Number of rows spanned by the cell
scope	Cells covered by header cell
valign	Vertical alignment
width	Cell width (relative or absolute)

Contains: All inline and block elements
Contained in: <tr>

<textarea>

Multi-line text input control for a form
Attributes: Core, i18n, Events

Attribute	Description	Attribute	Description
accesskey	Shortcut key	onfocus	Control received focus
cols	Number of columns	onselect	Control text selected
disabled	Disable control	readonly	Prevent changes
name	Key in submitted form	rows	Number of rows
onblur	Control lost focus	tabindex	Tab order position
onchange	Control value changed		

Contains: Plain text and entities

Contained in: All inline and block elements except `<button>`

`<tfoot>`

Table-footer element that defines row groups in a table

Attributes: Core, i18n, Events

Attribute	Description
align	Horizontal alignment of grouped cells
char	Alignment character for cells
charoff	Alignment character offset (in characters)
valign	Vertical alignment of grouped cells

Contains: `<tr>`

Contained in: `<table>`

`<th>`

Table-header cell element

Attributes: Core, i18n, Events

Attribute	Description
abbr	Abbreviation for header cell
align	Horizontal alignment
axis	Category of header cell
bgcolor	Cell background color
char	Alignment character
charoff	Alignment character offset (in characters)
colspan	Number of columns spanned by the cell
headers	Header cells for current cell
height	Cell height (relative or absolute)
nowrap	Disable word wrap
rowspan	Number of rows spanned by the cell
scope	Cells covered by header cell
valign	Vertical alignment
width	Cell width (relative or absolute)

Contains: All inline and block elements
Contained in: `<tr>`

`<thead>`

Table-header element that defines row groups in a table
Attributes: Core, i18n, Events

Attribute	Description
`align`	Horizontal alignment of grouped cells
`char`	Alignment character for cells
`charoff`	Alignment character offset (in characters)
`valign`	Vertical alignment of grouped cells

Contains: `<tr>`
Contained in: `<table>`

`<title>`

Document-title element that places text in the title bar of the browser
Attributes: i18n
Contains: Plain text and entities
Contained in: `<head>`

`<tr>`

Table-row element
Attributes: Core, i18n, Events

Attribute	Description
`align`	Horizontal alignment of grouped cells
`bgcolor`	Row background color
`char`	Alignment character for cells
`charoff`	Alignment character offset (in characters)
`valign`	Vertical alignment of grouped cells

Contains: `<th>`, `<td>`
Contained in: `<tbody>`, `<tfoot>`, `<tbody>`

`<tt>`

Teletype-text presentational element
Attributes: Core, i18n, Events
Contains: All inline elements
Contained in: All inline and block elements

\<u>

Underlined-text presentational element; deprecated in HTML 4.0 and XHTML 1.0
Attributes: Core, i18n, Events
Contains: All inline elements
Contained in: All inline and block elements

\<ul>

Unordered-list element for displaying bulleted lists
Attributes: Core, i18n, Events

Attribute	Description
compact	Compact list item display
type	Bullet style

Contains: `<li>`
Contained in: `<applet>`, `<blockquote>`, `<body>`, `<button>`, `<center>`, `<dd>`, `<del>`, `<div>`, `<fieldset>`, `<form>`, `<iframe>`, `<ins>`, `<li>`, `<map>`, `<noframes>`, `<noscript>`, `<object>`, `<td>`, `<th>`

\<var>

Variable-content element
Attributes: Core, i18n, Events
Contains: All inline elements
Contained in: All inline and block elements

XHTML Entities

To create special characters in XHTML—that is, characters not always shown on your keyboard—you have to make use of entities. Entities are always displayed using an ampersand (&) at the beginning of the entity and a semicolon (;) at the end. Entities can be in codeword or decimal number form.

For example, the cent sign(¢) is written in word form as `&cent;` and in decimal form as `&#162;`. The following table lists all the entity characters in XHTML to date, their word forms, and their decimal forms.

Special Character	*Word*	*Decimal*
acute accent	&acute;	&#180;
alef symbol	&alefsym;	&#8501;
almost equal to	&asymp;	&#8776;
ampersand	&amp;	&#38;
angle	&ang;	&#8736;
approximately equal to	&cong;	&#8773;
asterisk operator	&lowast;	&#8727;
black club suit	&clubs;	&#9827;
black diamond suit	&diams;	&#9830;
black heart suit	&hearts;	&#9829;
black spade suit	&spades;	&#9824;
blackletter capital I	&image;	&#8465;
blackletter capital R	&real;	&#8476;
broken vertical bar	&brvbar;	&#166;
bullet = black small circle	&bull;	&#8226;
capital letter A acute	&Aacute;	&#193;
capital letter A circumflex	&Acirc;	&#194;
capital letter A diaeresis	&Auml;	&#196;
capital letter A grave	&Agrave;	&#192;
capital letter A ring	&Aring;	&#197;
capital letter A tilde	&Atilde;	&#195;
capital letter alpha	&Alpha;	&#913;
capital letter beta	&Beta;	&#914;
capital letter C cedilla	&Ccedil;	&#199;
capital letter chi	&Chi;	&#935;
capital letter delta	&Delta;	&#916;
capital letter E acute	&Eacute;	&#201;
capital letter E circumflex	&Ecirc;	&#202;
capital letter E diaeresis	&Euml;	&#203;
capital letter E grave	&Egrave;	&#200;
capital letter epsilon	&Epsilon;	&#917;
capital letter eta	&Eta;	&#919;
capital letter ETH	&ETH;	&#208;
capital letter gamma	&Gamma;	&#915;
capital letter I acute	&Iacute;	&#205;
capital letter I circumflex	&Icirc;	&#206;
capital letter I diaeresis	&Iuml;	&#207;

Special Character	Word	Decimal
capital letter I grave	&Igrave;	&#204;
capital letter iota	&Iota;	&#921;
capital letter kappa	&Kappa;	&#922;
capital letter lambda	&Lambda;	&#923;
capital letter mu	&Mu;	&#924;
capital letter N tilde	&Ntilde;	&#209;
capital letter nu	&Nu;	&#925;
capital letter O acute	&Oacute;	&#211;
capital letter O circumflex	&Ocirc;	&#212;
capital letter O diaeresis	&Ouml;	&#214;
capital letter O grave	&Ograve;	&#210;
capital letter O slash	&Oslash;	&#216;
capital letter O tilde	&Otilde;	&#213;
capital letter omega	&Omega;	&#937;
capital letter omicron	&Omicron;	&#927;
capital letter phi	&Phi;	&#934;
capital letter pi	&Pi;	&#928;
capital letter psi	&Psi;	&#936;
capital letter rho	&Rho;	&#929;
capital letter S caron	&Scaron;	&#352;
capital letter sigma	&Sigma;	&#931;
capital letter tau	&Tau;	&#932;
capital letter theta	&Theta;	&#920;
capital letter THORN	&THORN;	&#222;
capital letter U acute	&Uacute;	&#218;
capital letter U circumflex	&Ucirc;	&#219;
capital letter U diaeresis	&Uuml;	&#220;
capital letter U grave	&Ugrave;	&#217;
capital letter upsilon	&Upsilon;	&#933;
capital letter xi	&Xi;	&#926;
capital letter Y acute	&Yacute;	&#221;
capital letter Y diaeresis	&Yuml;	&#376;
capital letter zeta	&Zeta;	&#918;
capital ligature AE	&AElig;	&#198;
capital ligature OE	&OElig;	&#338;
carriage return	&crarr;	&#8629;
cedilla	&cedil;	&#184;

Special Character	Word	Decimal
cent sign	`&cent;`	`&#162;`
contains as member	`&ni;`	`&#8715;`
copyright sign	`&copy;`	`&#169;`
cubed	`&sup3;`	`&#179;`
currency sign	`&curren;`	`&#164;`
dagger	`&dagger;`	`&#8224;`
degree sign	`&deg;`	`&#176;`
diaeresis	`&uml;`	`&#168;`
direct sum	`&oplus;`	`&#8853;`
discretionary hyphen	`&not;`	`&#172;`
division sign	`&divide;`	`&#247;`
dot operator	`&sdot;`	`&#8901;`
double dagger	`&Dagger;`	`&#8225;`
double low-9 quotation mark	`&bdquo;`	`&#8222;`
double prime	`&Prime;`	`&#8243;`
downward arrow	`&darr;`	`&#8595;`
downward double arrow	`&dArr;`	`&#8659;`
element of	`&isin;`	`&#8712;`
em dash	`&mdash;`	`&#8212;`
em space	` `	` `
empty set	`&empty;`	`&#8709;`
en dash	`&ndash;`	`&#8211;`
en space	` `	` `
euro sign	`&euro;`	`&#8364;`
feminine ordinal indicator	`&ordf;`	`&#170;`
for all	`&forall;`	`&#8704;`
fraction one-half	`&frac12;`	`&#189;`
fraction one-quarter	`&frac14;`	`&#188;`
fraction slash	`&frasl;`	`&#8260;`
fraction three-quarters	`&frac34;`	`&#190;`
greater than or equal to	`&ge;`	`&#8805;`
greater-than sign	`&gt;`	`&#62;`
horizontal ellipsis = three-dot leader	`&hellip;`	`&#8230;`
identical to	`&equiv;`	`&#8801;`
infinity	`&infin;`	`&#8734;`
integral	`&int;`	`&#8747;`
intersection	`&cap;`	`&#8745;`

Special Character	Word	Decimal
inverted exclamation mark	&iexcl;	&#161;
inverted question mark	&iquest;	&#191;
left ceiling	&lceil;	&#8968;
left double-quotation mark	&ldquo;	&#8220;
left floor	&lfloor;	&#8970;
left right arrow	&harr;	&#8596;
left right double arrow	&hArr;	&#8660;
left single-quotation mark	&lsquo;	&#8216;
left-pointing angle bracket	&lang;	&#9001;
left-pointing double angle quotation mark	&laquo;	&#171;
left-to-right mark	&lrm;	&#8206;
leftward arrow	&larr;	&#8592;
leftward double arrow	&lArr;	&#8656;
less than or equal to	&le;	&#8804;
less-than sign	&lt;	&#60;
logical and	&and;	&#8743;
logical or	&or;	&#8744;
lozenge	&loz;	&#9674;
masculine ordinal indicator	&ordm;	&#186;
micro sign	&micro;	&#181;
middle	&middot;	&#183;
minus sign	&minus;	&#8722;
modifier letter circumflex accent	&circ;	&#710;
multiplication sign	&times;	&#215;
nabla	&nabla;	&#8711;
n-ary summation	&sum;	&#8721;
non-breaking space		
not a subset of	&nsub;	&#8836;
not an element of	&notin;	&#8713;
not equal to	&ne;	&#8800;
overline	&macr;	&#175;
overline	&oline;	&#8254;
paragraph sign	&para;	&#182;
partial differential	&part;	&#8706;
per mille sign	&permil;	&#8240;
perpendicular	&perp;	&#8869;
pi symbol	&piv;	&#982;

Special Character	Word	Decimal
plus-or-minus sign	&plusmn;	&#177;
pound sign	&pound;	&#163;
Prime	&prime;	&#8242;
product sign	&prod;	&#8719;
proportional to	&prop;	&#8733;
quotation mark	&quot;	&#34;
registered trademark sign	&reg;	&#174;
right ceiling	&rceil;	&#8969;
right double-quotation mark	&rdquo;	&#8221;
right floor	&rfloor;	&#8971;
right single-quotation mark	&rsquo;	&#8217;
right-pointing angle bracket	&rang;	&#9002;
right-pointing double angle quotation	&raquo;	&#187;
right-to-left mark	&rlm;	&#8207;
rightward arrow	&rarr;	&#8594;
rightward double arrow	&rArr;	&#8658;
script capital P	&weierp;	&#8472;
section sign	&sect;	&#167;
single left-pointing angle quotation mark	&lsaquo;	&#8249;
single low-9 quotation mark	&sbquo;	&#8218;
single right-pointing angle quotation mark	&rsaquo;	&#8250;
small f with hook = function = florin	&fnof;	&#402;
small letter a acute	&aacute;	&#225;
small letter a circumflex	&acirc;	&#226;
small letter a diaeresis	&auml;	&#228;
small letter a grave	&agrave;	&#224;
small letter a ring	&aring;	&#229;
small letter a tilde	&atilde;	&#227;
small letter alpha	&alpha;	&#945;
small letter beta	&beta;	&#946;
small letter c cedilla	&ccedil;	&#231;
small letter chi	&chi;	&#967;
small letter delta	&delta;	&#948;
small letter e acute	&eacute;	&#233;
small letter e circumflex	&ecirc;	&#234;
small letter e diaeresis	&euml;	&#235;
small letter e grave	&egrave;	&#232;

Special Character	Word	Decimal
small letter epsilon	&epsilon;	&#949;
small letter eta	&eta;	&#951;
small letter eth	&eth;	&#240;
small letter final sigma	&sigmaf;	&#962;
small letter gamma	&gamma;	&#947;
small letter i acute	&iacute;	&#237;
small letter i circumflex	&icirc;	&#238;
small letter i diaeresis	&iuml;	&#239;
small letter i grave	&igrave;	&#236;
small letter iota	&iota;	&#953;
small letter kappa	&kappa;	&#954;
small letter lambda	&lambda;	&#955;
small letter mu	&mu;	&#956;
small letter n tilde	&ntilde;	&#241;
small letter nu	&nu;	&#957;
small letter o acute	&oacute;	&#243;
small letter o circumflex	&ocirc;	&#244;
small letter o diaeresis	&ouml;	&#246;
small letter o grave	&ograve;	&#242;
small letter o stroke = small letter o slash	&oslash;	&#248;
small letter o tilde	&otilde;	&#245;
small letter omega	&omega;	&#969;
small letter omicron	&omicron;	&#959;
small letter phi	&phi;	&#966;
small letter pi	&pi;	&#960;
small letter psi	&psi;	&#968;
small letter rho	&rho;	&#961;
small letter s caron	&scaron;	&#353;
small letter sharp s	&szlig;	&#223;
small letter sigma	&sigma;	&#963;
small letter tau	&tau;	&#964;
small letter theta	&theta;	&#952;
small letter theta symbol	&thetasym;	&#977;
small letter thorn	&thorn;	&#254;
small letter u acute	&uacute;	&#250;
small letter u circumflex	&ucirc;	&#251;
small letter u diaeresis	&uuml;	&#252;

Special Character	Word	Decimal
small letter u grave	&ugrave;	&#249;
small letter upsilon	&upsilon;	&#965;
small letter xi	&xi;	&#958;
small letter y acute	&yacute;	&#253;
small letter y diaeresis	&yuml;	&#255;
small letter zeta	&zeta;	&#950;
small ligature ae	&aelig;	&#230;
small ligature oe	&oelig;	&#339;
small tilde	&tilde;	&#732;
soft hyphen	&shy;	&#173;
square root	&radic;	&#8730;
squared	&sup2;	&#178;
subset of	&sub;	&#8834;
subset of or equal to	&sube;	&#8838;
superscript one	&sup1;	&#185;
superset of	&sup;	&#8835;
superset of or equal to	&supe;	&#8839;
there exists	&exist;	&#8707;
therefore	&there4;	&#8756;
thin space		
tilde operator	&sim;	&#8764;
trademark sign	&trade;	&#8482;
union	&cup;	&#8746;
upsilon with hook symbol	&upsih;	&#978;
upward arrow	&uarr;	&#8593;
upward double arrow	&uArr;	&#8657;
vector product	&otimes;	&#8855;
yen sign	&yen;	&#165;
zero width joiner	&zwj;	&#8205;
zero width non-joiner	&zwnj;	&#8204;

B

CSS2 Resource Guide

As cascading style sheets become more accepted and implemented, more style rules will be available for your Web pages. This appendix gives a complete list of all the CSS2 properties and values that you can use, including the aural styles, which can be used to create speaking pages for the sight-impaired.

Syntax Used in Value Definitions

<X>	Value of type X
X	A keyword that must appear literally, including punctuation
A B C	A must occur, then B, then C
[*X*]	Grouped items
A | *B*	A or B must occur
A || *B*	A or B or both must occur, in any order
X*	X is repeated zero or more times
X+	X is repeated one or more times
X?	X is optional
X{*A, B*}	X must occur at least A times and at most B times

Aural Properties

The properties in this section handle all audio style aspects of a Web site. This is typically used for sites designed for people who are visually impaired.

Azimuth

Values: azimuth: <angle> | [[left-side | far-left | left | center-left | center | center-right | right | far-right | right-side] || behind] | leftwards | rightwards | inherit

Inherited: Yes

Works with: All elements

Cue

Values: cue: ['cue-before' || 'cue-after'] | inherit

Inherited: No

Works with: All elements

Cue-After

Values: cue-after: <url> | none | inherit

Inherited: No

Works with: All elements

Cue-Before

Values: cue-before: <url> | none | inherit

Inherited: No

Works with: All elements

Elevation

Values: elevation: <angle> | below | level | above | higher | lower | inherit

Inherited: Yes

Works with: All elements

Pause

Values: pause: [[<time> | <percentage>]{1,2}] | inherit

Inherited: No

Works with: All elements

Pause-After

Values: pause-after: <time> | <percentage> | inherit

Inherited: No

Works with: All elements

Pause-Before

Values: pause-before: <time> | <percentage> | inherit

Inherited: No

Works with: All elements

Pitch

Values: pitch: <frequency> | x-low | low | medium | high | x-high | inherit

Inherited: Yes

Works with: All elements

Pitch-Range

Values: pitch-range: <number> | inherit

Inherited: Yes

Works with: All elements

Play-During

Values: play-during: <url> mix? repeat? | auto | none | inherit

Inherited: No

Works with: All elements

Richness

Values: richness: <number> | inherit

Inherited: Yes

Works with: All elements

Speak

Values: speak: normal | none | spell-out | inherit

Inherited: Yes

Works with: All elements

Speak-Header

Values: speak-header: once | always | inherit

Inherited: Yes

Works with: All elements with table-header information

Speak-Numeral

Values: speak-numeral: digits | continuous | inherit

Inherited: Yes

Works with: All elements

Speak-Punctuation

Values: speak-punctuation: code | none | inherit

Inherited: Yes

Works with: All elements

Speech-Rate

Values: speech-rate: <number> | x-slow | slow | medium | fast | x-fast | faster | slower | inherit

Inherited: Yes

Works with: All elements

Stress

Values: stress: <number> | inherit

Inherited: Yes

Works with: All elements

Voice-Family

Values: voice-family: [[<specific-voice> | <generic-voice>],]*
[<specific-voice> | <generic-voice>] | inherit

Inherited: Yes

Works with: All elements

Volume

Values: volume: <number> | <percentage> | silent | x-soft | soft | medium
| loud | x-loud | inherit

Inherited: Yes

Works with: All elements

Box Properties

The properties in this section handle all border and table styles.

Border

Values: border: [<border-width> || <border-style> || <color>] | inherit

Inherited: No

Works with: All elements

Border-Bottom

Values: border: [<border-bottom-width> || <border-style> || <color>] |
inherit

Inherited: No

Works with: All elements

Border-Left

Values: border: [<border-left-width> || <border-style> || <color>] |
inherit

Inherited: No

Works with: All elements

Border-Right

Values: border: [<border-right-width> || <border-style> || <color>] |
inherit

Inherited: No

Works with: All elements

Border-Top

Values: border: [<border-top-width> || <border-style> || <color>] | inherit
Inherited: No
Works with: All elements

Border-Collapse

Values: border-collapse: collapse | separate | inherit
Inherited: Yes
Works with: Table and inline table elements

Border-Color

Values: border-color: <color>{1,4} | transparent | inherit
Inherited: No
Works with: All elements

Border-Bottom-Color

Values: border-bottom-color: <color> | inherit
Inherited: No
Works with: All elements

Border-Left-Color

Values: border-left-color: <color> | inherit
Inherited: No
Works with: All elements

Border-Right-Color

Values: border-right-color: <color> | inherit
Inherited: No
Works with: All elements

Border-Top-Color

Values: border-top-color: <color> | inherit
Inherited: No
Works with: All elements

Border-Spacing

Values: border-spacing: <length> <length>? | inherit
Inherited: Yes
Works with: Table and inline table elements

Border-Style

Values: `border-style: [ none | dotted | dashed | solid | double | groove | ridge | inset | outset ]{1,4} | inherit`

Inherited: No

Works with: All elements

Border-Bottom-Style

Values: `border-bottom-style: [ none | dotted | dashed | solid | double | groove | ridge | inset | outset ] | inherit`

Inherited: No

Works with: All elements

Border-Left-Style

Values: `border-left-style: [ none | dotted | dashed | solid | double | groove | ridge | inset | outset ] | inherit`

Inherited: No

Works with: All elements

Border-Right-Style

Values: `border-right-style: [ none | dotted | dashed | solid | double | groove | ridge | inset | outset ] | inherit`

Inherited: No

Works with: All elements

Border-Top-Style

Values: `border-top-style: [ none | dotted | dashed | solid | double | groove | ridge | inset | outset ] | inherit`

Inherited: No

Works with: All elements

Border-Width

Values: `border-width: [ thin | medium | thick | <length> ]{1,4} | inherit`

Inherited: No

Works with: All elements

Border-Bottom-Width

Values: `border-bottom-width: [ thin | medium | thick | <length> ] | inherit`

Inherited: No

Works with: All elements

Border-Left-Width
Values: `border-left-width:` [`thin` | `medium` | `thick` | `<length>`] | `inherit`
Inherited: No
Works with: All elements

Border-Right-Width
Values: `border-right-width:` [`thin` | `medium` | `thick` | `<length>`] | `inherit`
Inherited: No
Works with: All elements

Border-Top-Width
Values: `border-top-width:` [`thin` | `medium` | `thick` | `<length>`] | `inherit`
Inherited: No
Works with: All elements

Caption-Side
Values: `caption-side:` `bottom` | `top` | `left` | `right` | `inherit`
Inherited: Yes
Works with: Table caption elements

Clear
Values: `clear:` `none` | `left` | `right` | `both` | `inherit`
Inherited: No
Works with: All elements

Empty-Cells
Values: `empty-cells:` `show` | `hide` | `inherit`
Inherited: Yes
Works with: Table cell elements

Float
Values: `float:` `left` | `right` | `none` | `inherit`
Inherited: No
Works with: All elements except generated content and positioned elements

Height

Values: `height: <length>` | `<percentage>` | `auto` | `inherit`

Inherited: No

Works with: All elements except non-replaced inline elements and table columns and column groups

Max-Height

Values: `max-height: <length>` | `<percentage>` | `none` | `inherit`

Inherited: No

Works with: All elements except non-replaced inline elements and table columns and column groups

Min-Height

Values: `min-height: <length>` | `<percentage>` | `inherit`

Inherited: No

Works with: All elements except non-replaced inline elements and table columns and column groups

Margin

Values: `margin: [ <length>` | `<percentage>` | `auto ]{1,4}` | `inherit`

Inherited: No

Works with: All elements

Margin-Bottom

Values: `margin-bottom: <length>` | `<percentage>` | `auto` | `inherit`

Inherited: No

Works with: All elements

Margin-Left

Values: `margin-left: <length>` | `<percentage>` | `auto` | `inherit`

Inherited: No

Works with: All elements

Margin-Right

Values: `margin-right: <length>` | `<percentage>` | `auto` | `inherit`

Inherited: No

Works with: All elements

Margin-Top

Values: `margin-top: <length> | <percentage> | auto | inherit`
Inherited: No
Works with: All elements

Padding

Values: `padding: [ <length> | <percentage> ]{1,4} | inherit`
Inherited: No
Works with: All elements

Padding-Bottom

Values: `padding-bottom: <length> | <percentage> | inherit`
Inherited: No
Works with: All elements

Padding-Left

Values: `padding-left: <length> | <percentage> | inherit`
Inherited: No
Works with: All elements

Padding-Right

Values: `padding-right: <length> | <percentage> | inherit`
Inherited: No
Works with: All elements

Padding-Top

Values: `padding-top: <length> | <percentage> | inherit`
Inherited: No
Works with: All elements

Table-Layout

Values: `table-layout: auto | fixed | inherit`
Inherited: No
Works with: Table and inline elements

Width

Values: `width: <length> | <percentage> | auto | inherit`
Initial Value: auto
Inherited: No
Works with: Block and replaced elements

Max-Width

Values: `max-width: <length> | <percentage> | none | inherit`

Inherited: No

Works with: All elements except non-replaced inline elements and table columns and column groups

Min-Width

Values: `min-width: <length> | <percentage> | inherit`

Inherited: No

Works with: All elements except non-replaced inline elements and table columns and column groups

Color and Background Properties

The properties in this section handle color and background styles.

Background

Values: `background: [<background-color> || <background-image> || <background-repeat> || <background-attachment> || <background-position>] | inherit`

Inherited: No

Works with: All elements

Background-Attachment

Values: `background-attachment: scroll | fixed | inherit`

Inherited: No

Works with: All elements

Background-Color

Values: `background-color: <color> | transparent | inherit`

Inherited: No

Works with: All elements

Background-Image

Values: `background-image: <url> | none | inherit`

Inherited: No

Works with: All elements

Background-Position

Values: `background-position: [<percentage> | <length> ]{1,2} | [ [top | center | bottom] || [left | center | right] ] ] | inherit`

Inherited: No

Works with: Block and replaced elements

Background-Repeat

Values: `background-repeat: repeat | repeat-x | repeat-y | no-repeat | inherit`

Inherited: No

Works with: All elements

Color

Values: `color: <color> | inherit`

Inherited: Yes

Works with: All elements

Font Properties

The properties in this section handle all font styles.

Font

Values: `[ <font-style> || <font-variant> || <font-weight> ]? <font-size> [ / <line-height> ]? <font-family> | caption | icon | menu| message-box | small-caption | inherit`

Inherited: Yes

Works with: All elements

Font-Family

Values: `font-family: [[<family-name> | [ serif | sans-serif | cursive | fantasy | monospace ],]* [<family-name> | [ serif | sans-serif | cursive | fantasy | monospace ]] | inherit`

Inherited: Yes

Works with: All elements

Font-Size

Values: `font-size: [ xx-small | x-small | small | medium | large | x-large | xx-large] | [ larger | smaller ] | <length> | <percentage> | inherit`

Inherited: Yes

Works with: All elements

Font-Size-Adjust

Values: `font-size-adjust: <number> | none | inherit`

Inherited: Yes

Works with: All elements

Font-Stretch

Values: `font-stretch: normal | wider | narrower | ultra-condensed | extra-condensed | condensed | semi-condensed | semi-expanded | expanded | extra-expanded | ultra-expanded | inherit`

Inherited: Yes

Works with: All elements

Font-Style

Values: `font-style: normal | italic | oblique | inherit`

Inherited: Yes

Works with: All elements

Font-Variant

Values: `font-variant: normal | small-caps| inherit`

Inherited: Yes

Works with: All elements

Font-Weight

Values: `font-weight: normal | bold | bolder | lighter | 100 | 200 | 300 | 400 | 500 | 600 | 700 | 800 | 900 | inherit`

Inherited: Yes

Works with: All elements

Interactive Properties

The properties in this section handle all special interactive styles and controls.

Counter-Increment

Values: counter-increment: [<identifier> <integer>?]+ | none | inherit
Inherited: No
Works with: All elements

Counter-Reset

Values: counter-reset: [<identifier> <integer>?]+ | none | inherit
Inherited: No
Works with: All elements

Cursor

Values: cursor: [[<url> ,]* [auto | crosshair | default | pointer | move | e-resize | ne-resize | nw-resize | n-resize | se-resize | sw-resize | s-resize | w-resize| text | wait | help]] | inherit
Inherited: Yes
Works with: All elements

Outline

Values: outline: ['outline-color || 'outline-style' || 'outline-width'] | inherit
Inherited: No
Works with: All elements

Outline-Color

Values: outline-color: <color> | invert | inherit
Inherited: No
Works with: All elements

Outline-Style

Values: outline-style: <border-style> | inherit
Inherited: No
Works with: All elements

Outline-Width

Values: outline-width: <border-width> | inherit
Inherited: No
Works with: All elements

Page Properties

The properties in this section handle all page layout styles.

Marks

Values: marks: [crop || cross] | none | inherit
Inherited: N/A
Works with: Page context

Orphans

Values: <integer> | inherit
Inherited: Yes
Works with: Block elements

Page

Values: <identifier> | auto | inherit
Inherited: Yes
Works with: Block elements

Page-Break-After

Values: auto | always | avoid | left | right | inherit
Inherited: No
Works with: Block elements

Page-Break-Before

Values: auto | always | avoid | left | right | inherit
Inherited: No
Works with: Block elements

Page-Break-Inside

Values: avoid | auto | inherit
Inherited: Yes
Works with: Block elements

Size

Values: <length>{1,2} | auto | portrait | landscape | inherit
Inherited: N/A
Works with: Page context

Widows

Values: <integer> | inherit
Inherited: Yes
Works with: Block elements

Text Properties

The properties in this section handle all text layout styles.

Letter-Spacing

Values: letter-spacing: normal | <length> | inherit
Inherited: Yes
Works with: All elements

Line-Height

Values: line-height: normal | <number> | <length> | <percentage> | inherit
Inherited: Yes
Works with: All elements

Text-Align

Values: text-align: left | right | center | justify | <string> | inherit
Inherited: Yes
Works with: Block elements

Text-Decoration

Values: `text-decoration: none | [ underline || overline || line-through || blink ] | inherit`

Inherited: No

Works with: All elements

Text-Indent

Values: `text-indent: <length> | <percentage> | inherit`

Inherited: Yes

Works with: Block elements

Text-Shadow

Values: `text-shadow: none | [<color> || <length> <length> <length>? ,]* [<color> || <length> <length> <length>?] | inherit`

Inherited: No

Works with: Block elements

Text-Transform

Values: `text-transform: none | capitalize | uppercase | lowercase | inherit`

Inherited: Yes

Works with: All elements

Vertical-Align

Values: `vertical-align: baseline | sub |super | top | text-top | middle | bottom | text-bottom | <percentage> | inherit`

Inherited: No

Works with: Inline elements

Word-Spacing

Values: `word-spacing: normal | <length> | inherit`

Inherited: Yes

Works with: All elements

Visual Presentation Properties

The properties in this section handle all styles dealing with element positioning.

Bottom

Values: `bottom: <length> | <percentage> | auto | inherit`
Inherited: No
Works with: Positioned elements

Clip

Values: `clip: <shape> | auto | inherit`
Inherited: No
Works with: Block and replaced elements

Direction

Values: `direction: ltr | rtl | inherit`
Inherited: Yes
Works with: All elements

Display

Values: `display: block | inline | list-item | run-in | compact | marker| table | inline-table | table-row-group | table-header-group | table-footer-group | table-row | table-column-group | table-column | table-cell | table-caption |none | inherit`
Inherited: No
Works with: All elements

Left

Values: `left: <length> | <percentage> | auto | inherit`
Inherited: No
Works with: Positioned elements

List Style

Values: `list-style: [ <list-style-type> || <list-style-position> || <url> ] | inherit`
Inherited: Yes
Works with: Elements with `display` value list-item

List-Style-Image

Values: `list-style-image: <url> | none | inherit`
Inherited: Yes
Works with: Elements with `display` value list-item

List-Style-Position

Values: `list-style-position: inside | outside | inherit`
Inherited: Yes
Works with: Elements with `display` value list-item

List-Style-Type

Values: `list-style-type: disc | circle | square | decimal | decimal-leading-zero | lower-roman | upper-roman | lower-greek | lower-alpha | lower-latin | upper-alpha | upper-latin | hebrew | armenian | georgian | cjk-ideographic | hiragana | katakana | hiragana-iroha | katakana-iroha | none | inherit`
Inherited: Yes
Works with: Elements with `display` value list-item

Marker-offset

Values: `marker-offset: <length> | auto | inherit`
Inherited: No
Works with: Elements with 'display: marker'

Overflow

Values: `overflow: visible | hidden | scroll | auto | inherit`
Inherited: No
Works with: Block-level and replaced elements

Position

Values: `position: static | relative | absolute | fixed | inherit`
Inherited: No
Works with: All elements except generated content

Quotes

Values: `quotes: [<string> <string>]+ | none | inherit`
Inherited: yes
Works with: All elements

Right

Values: right: <length> | <percentage> | auto | inherit
Inherited: No
Works with: Positioned elements

Top

Values: top: <length> | <percentage> | auto | inherit
Inherited: No
Works with: Positioned elements

Unicode-bidi

Values: unicode-bidi: normal | embed | bidi-override | inherit
Inherited: No
Works with: all elements

Visibility

Values: visibility: visible | hidden | collapse | inherit
Inherited: No
Works with: All elements

White-Space

Values: white-space: normal | pre | nowrap | inherit
Inherited: Yes
Works with: Block elements

Z-Index

Values: z-index: auto | <integer> | inherit
Inherited: No
Works with: Positioned elements

C

Differences between HTML and XHTML

Although XHTML 1.0 is now an approved standard from the World Wide Web Consortium (W3C), it bears such a striking similarity to the HTML 4.0 standard that you can start following XHTML practices now without suffering many compatibility issues with current HTML browsers.

XHTML varies from the HTML 4.0 standard in six main areas:

- Attributes

- Case

- Closure

- Document structure

- Document Type Definition

- XML namespace

This appendix explores these differences in greater detail.

Attributes

All XHTML attributes correspond to their HTML counterparts, so there are no surprises here. What is important to remember is that *all attributes must be in lowercase in an XHTML document.*

Though HTML is not case-sensitive, XHTML is, mostly due to the XML parent language from which XHTML was derived.

Another idiosyncrasy of XHTML is that all attribute values must be in quotes. In other words, an element with the following attribute and value would be okay in HTML, but not in XHTML:

```
<font size=+5>
```

The XHTML version would have to be written as the following:

```
<font size="+5">
```

Finally, no attribute values in XHTML can be minimized. Minimization occurs when an attribute can have only one value. In HTML, you can minimize such an attribute by just inserting the attribute name without any values. For example, in HTML, the following is perfectly legal:

```
<hr noshade>
```

If you wanted to insert a non-shaded horizontal rule in XHTML, however, the element would have to take this form:

```
<hr noshade="noshade">
```

Case

In XHTML, all element and attribute names must be in lowercase. This is because XML, the parent language of XHTML, is case-sensitive.

In HTML, you could write the following:

```
<A HREF="http://www.bkp.org">Link to my Web site</A>
```

You could even mix cases, because HTML browsers simply did not care. But in XHTML, this line of code would have to appear as follows:

```
<a href="http://www.bkp.org">Link to my Web site</a>
```

This is probably the most notable change from HTML, and one that is sure to bug a lot of people. In the past, HTML tags were put in uppercase to make them easier to see against the actual content of the page.

It is recommended that you use different spacing and indentation techniques as you create your Web pages so that your XHTML elements are easier to spot. Compare the following two examples:

```
<p>Although XHTML 1.0 is now an approved standard from the World Wide Web
Consortium (W3C), it bears such a striking similarity to the HTML 4.0 standard
that you can start following XHTML practices now without suffering many
compatibility issues with current HTML browsers.</p>
<p>XHTML varies from the HTML 4.0 standard in six main areas:</p>
<ul><li>Attributes</li>
<li>Case</li>
<li>Closure</li>
<li>Document structure</li>
<li>Document Type Definition</li>
<li>XML namespace</li></ul>
```

```
<p>
Although XHTML 1.0 is now an approved standard from the World Wide Web
Consortium (W3C), it bears such a striking similarity to the HTML 4.0 standard
that you can start following XHTML practices now without suffering many
compatibility issues with current HTML browsers.
</p>
<p>
XHTML varies from the HTML 4.0 standard in six main areas:
</p>
<ul>
<li>Attributes</li>
<li>Case</li>
<li>Closure</li>
<li>Document structure</li>
<li>Document Type Definition</li>
<li>XML namespace</li>
</ul>
```

Closure

Another result from this change is that all elements, be they empty or not, must be closed.

In HTML, for example, it was perfectly legal to not enter a closing `</p>` tag at the end of a paragraph. The next `<p>` was enough of a signal to end the old paragraph and begin the new one.

Even empty elements such as `<br>` and `<hr>` have to be closed. Luckily, you do not have to add another closing tag. Inserting a forward slash within the element can terminate empty elements.

In HTML, you would have the following:

```
<hr>
```

In XHTML, it would be as follows:

```
<hr />
```

Document Structure

The major change in this area is that no longer will the illegal overlapping of tags be allowed. In HTML, even though it was technically illegal, HTML parsers in browsers would let you get away with something like the following:

```
<p>I want to paint the town <font color="red">red!</p></font>
```

XML parsers reading XHTML will allow no such thing. All elements must be properly nested, like this:

```
<p>I want to paint the town <font color="red">red!</font></p>
```

A minor change in the structure of XHTML documents is that the `<title>` element must be the very first element that appears in the `<head>` element. This is an XML idiosyncrasy that XHTML has inherited.

Document Type Definition

Whenever an XHTML page is read by a browser with an XML parser, the browser needs another document to assist it in figuring out what all these tags mean. This document is called a Document Type Definition (DTD).

What the DTD does is very simple: it quickly and plainly defines how a browser will display the contents of an HTML document. This is usually done internally; most top-of-the-line browsers have the necessary DTDs built into their specifications. If a client is using a less robust or older browser, however, and the browser tries to display a current XHTML 1.0 document, the browser will have difficulty displaying some or all of the page without a DTD referenced. This is why it's a good idea to add a solid reference to the DTD—including where to find it on the Internet—within your documents. In this manner, older browsers will be able to quickly find the DTD and (ideally) apply it to the document being loaded.

When an XHTML document is created, the DTD it needs to reference is contained within the `<!DOCTYPE>` element. In XHTML 1.0, three specific DTDs can be referenced:

- Strict
- Loose (Transitional)
- Frameset

A Strict XHTML document is one that conforms exactly to the XHTML 1.0 standard. Only elements within the standard are contained within the document, which has the following DTD declaration:

```
<!DOCTYPE html PUBLIC "-//W3C//DTD XHTML 1.0 Strict//EN"
"http://www.w3.org/TR/xhtml1/DTD/strict.dtd">
```

This strict definition is typically used for documents that make use of cascading style sheets (CSS). These documents usually conform very well to the Strict XHTML definition, if only because CSS methods were introduced in this version of HTML.

Another XHTML DTD is the Loose or Transitional DTD, shown here:

```
<!DOCTYPE html PUBLIC "-//W3C//DTD XHTML 1.0 Transitional//EN"
"http://www.w3.org/TR/xhtml1/DTD/transitional.dtd">
```

The Loose DTD is used for browser-specific elements that can't be displayed in a Strict DTD document. The Loose DTD can also display older elements that have been deprecated or phased out of XHTML 1.0.

The final DTD in XHTML is the Frameset DTD. This definition is used whenever you have a document with frames in it.

```
<!DOCTYPE html PUBLIC "-//W3C//DTD XHTML 1.0 Frameset//EN"
"http://www.w3.org/TR/xhtml1/DTD/frameset.dtd">
```

If you want to know whether your document follows its declared DTD standard, you can have a validator automatically check your document. The best validator to use, of course, is W3C's. You can simply type the address of your Web page and let the validator inform you of how your document did. (The validator is located at **http://validator.w3.org/**.)

XML Namespace

For a complete discussion, please refer to page 24.

D

XHTML Resources

Here is a list of some of the best-known Internet sites that can help keep you informed about the new XHTML 1.0 recommendation and upcoming XHTML 1.1 changes.

MSDN Online for Students—XHTML
http://msdn.microsoft.com/STUDENTS/archive/xhtml020700.asp

The SGML/XML Web Page
http://www.oasis-open.org/cover/

Web Developers Virtual Library: Introduction to XHTML, with examples
http://wdvl.com/Authoring/Languages/XML/XHTML/

World Wide Web Consortium (W3C)

Building XHTML Modules
http://www.w3.org/TR/xhtml-building/

Modularization of XHTML
http://www.w3.org/TR/xhtml-modularization/

XHTML 1.0: The Extensible Hypertext Markup Language
http://www.w3.org/TR/xhtml1/

XHTML 1.1: Module-based XHTML
http://www.w3.org/TR/xhtml11/

XHTML Basic
http://www.w3.org/TR/xhtml-basic/

XHTML Document Profile Requirements
http://www.w3.org/TR/xhtml-prof-req/

XHTML Events Module
http://www.w3.org/TR/xhtml-events/

XHTML Extended Forms Requirements
http://www.w3.org/TR/xhtml-forms-req.html

XHTML.org
http://www.xhtml.org/

E

What's On
the CD-ROM

The CD that accompanies this book contains CoffeeCup HTML shareware (Windows and Linux versions), CoffeeCup Image Mapper, and sample XHTML pages as referred to in this book.

Running the CD

To make the CD more user-friendly and take up less of your disk space, we've designed the CD-ROM so that you can install only those files that you desire.

Linux

1. Open the CD-ROM tray and insert the CD.

2. As root, type the following at the command line: **mount /dev/cdrom /tmp** (replace */tmp* with wherever you want to mount the CD).

3. Start an X session (*startx* in most cases).

4. Open Netscape Navigator.

5. Choose Open from the File menu, and then click the Browse button.

6. Browse to start_here.html, located in the directory where you mounted the CD-ROM.

Windows 95/98/2000/NT

1. Insert the CD into the CD-ROM drive and close the tray.

2. Go to the Control Panel and double-click the CD-ROM.

3. Open start_here.html (works with most HTML browsers).

The Prima License

The first window you will see is the Prima License Agreement. Take a moment to read the agreement. If you accept the terms of the agreement, click the I Agree button and proceed to the user interface. If you do not accept the license agreement, click the I Disagree button, and the CD will not load.

The Prima User Interface

Prima's user interface is designed to make viewing and using the CD-ROM contents quick and easy. The opening screen contains a two-panel window. The left panel contains the structure of the programs on the disc. The right panel displays a description page for the selected entry in the left panel.

Resizing and Closing the User Interface

As with any window, you can resize the user interface. To do so, position the mouse over any edge or corner, hold down the left mouse button, and drag the edge or corner to a new position.

To close and exit the user interface, select File, Exit (your specific X setup may have a unique graphical means of resizing and closing Netscape).

Using the Left Panel

To view a sample XHTML file, click /Chapters. A drop-down menu appears containing each chapter that has sample files. Then click on the chapter you want to view. To view the programs on the CD, click /Programs and then select the desired program.

Using the Right Panel

The right panel displays a page that describes the entry you chose in the left panel. Use the information provided in the right panel for details about your selection—such as what functionality an installable program provides. To download a particular file, follow the directions that appear in the left panel.

Index

License Agreement/Notice of Limited Warranty